ROY CAPE

ROY
CAPE

A LIFE ON THE CALYPSO AND SOCA BANDSTAND

JOCELYNE GUILBAULT AND ROY CAPE

DUKE UNIVERSITY PRESS   DURHAM AND LONDON   2014

© 2014 Duke University Press
All rights reserved
Printed in the United States of America on acid-free paper ∞
Typeset in Quadraat Pro and Trade Gothic Condensed by
Tseng Information Systems, Inc.

Library of Congress Cataloging-in-Publication Data
Guilbault, Jocelyne.
Roy Cape : a life on the calypso and soca bandstand / Jocelyne Guilbault and Roy Cape.
pages cm
Includes bibliographical references and index.
ISBN 978-0-8223-5760-5 (cloth : alk. paper)
ISBN 978-0-8223-5774-2 (pbk. : alk. paper)
1. Cape, Roy, 1942– 2. Calypso musicians—Trinidad and Tobago—Biography.
3. Saxophonists—Trinidad and Tobago—Biography. 4. Band musicians—Trinidad
and Tobago—Biography. I. Cape, Roy, 1942– II. Title.
ML419.C325G85 2014
781.62′9697290092—dc23   [B]
2014000769

Cover art: Roy Cape. Photograph by Anthony Moore.

To the Children's Homes
—R. C.

To Steve
—J. G.

CONTENTS

LIST OF ILLUSTRATIONS ix
ACKNOWLEDGMENTS xi
NOTES ON THE TEXT xv

INTRODUCTION 1

1. For the Love of Music: Up from the Panyards and at the Orphanage 23
2. Working as a Bandsman 42
3. Listening to Roy Sounding 76
4. Leading the Band 99
5. Remembering with Pictures 135
6. Working with Roy: Musicians and Friends Speak 183
7. Circulation: Summarizing a Career 207

AFTERWORD Writing Voices 229

NOTES 233
SELECT DISCOGRAPHY 259
REFERENCES 261
ABOUT THE COMPANION CD 277
INDEX 279

ILLUSTRATIONS

1.1   At the Belmont orphanage   31
1.2   Marching band and band rehearsal at the Children's Home   34
1.3   Brass band of the Belmont Children's Home in concert   36
2.1   Selwyn Wheeler Orchestra's recording of "The Mocking Bird Song"   47
2.2   Frankie Francis featured as a guest star, 1972   49
2.3–2.4   Body and Soul by Clarence Curvan's band   55
2.5–2.6   The "A" Train by Ron Berridge and Orchestra   58
2.7–2.8   Bang Bang Lulu in New York with Sparrow's Troubadours   67
2.9–2.10   Behold by the Blues Busters   70
3.1   Selmer Super Action 80 saxophone and metal mouthpiece   82
3.2   Lawton mouthpiece   83
3.3   A telling 1962 record jacket   94
4.1   Juliet Robin on keyboard   109
4.2   Roy Cape All Stars at a dance club in Toronto, 2009   119
4.3   "Mr. Cape" (also dubbed "Jam Mih")   127
5.1   Clarence Curvan's band, 1963   138
5.2   Younger Roy with Ron Berridge's band, 1966   139
5.3   Sparrow with the Ron Berridge Orchestra, 1967   141
5.4   Harold De Freitas and Roy Cape in Jamaica, 1969   142
5.5   Harold De Freitas, Roy Cape, and Joseph Alexander, 1970   143
5.6   Roy Cape and Neville Oxley, around 1973   144

5.7   Fortunia Ruiz, Philip James, and Roy Cape, around 1973   144
5.8   Clive Bradley, 1981   147
5.9   Roy and Frankie Francis, 1988   147
5.10 Roy's Rasta look, 1994   149
5.11 Roy Cape playing his saxophone, late 1990s   151
5.12 Roy playing his saxophone, circa 2009   151
5.13 The whole horn section, early 1990s   153
5.14 Roy Cape All Stars full horn section, late 1990s   154
5.15 Roy and Black Stalin, around mid-1990s   155
5.16 Black Stalin and Arnold "Sly" Punette, 1987   157
5.17 Roy with Brigo, Lord Baker, and Crazy's manager, 1982   159
5.18 Chalkdust and Roy, 1989   159
5.19 Lord Kitchener and Roy Cape All Stars, 1992   161
5.20 Black Stalin, Roy Cape, and Junior Telfer, 1995   161
5.21 Superblue, Roy Cape, and Black Stalin, 1995   163
5.22 Poser, Roy, and Tunapuna Scanty, 1996   164
5.23 Gypsy, Black Stalin, Penguin, and Roy, 2001   164
5.24 Roy Cape Kaiso All Stars, 1990, *First Time*   166
5.25 Band members wearing short pants, 1995   167
5.26 Nigel and Marvin Lewis, 1996   167
5.27 Destra Garcia   169
5.28 Roy and Esther Dyer, Derrick Seales, and Blaxx, around 2003   169
5.29 Roy Cape All Stars band, 2008   171
5.30 Roy in Toronto, 1997   173
5.31 Roy and his band members, 2010   173
5.32 Roy in Toronto, around 1997   175
5.33 Roy singing at the Soca Monarch National Competition, 1998   175
5.34 Roy with Russell Latapy, 2006   177
5.35 Machel Montano, Roy, and HD and Roy Cape All Stars, Belgium, 2011   178
5.36 Roy receiving the Hummingbird Gold Medal award, 2004   179
7.1   Roy's touring destinations   216
A.1   Roy Cape and Sir George Alleyne, 2011   232

ACKNOWLEDGMENTS

ROY CAPE: Never in my wildest dream had I ever thought of writing a book. But I knew I had a story inside of me. Having been requested by Jocelyne to work together on this project, I said yes without even thinking. The idea of this book is to educate and inform, especially the younger ones, and also the elders to give a sense of where we were to where we are at this time and also to acknowledge some of the very great people that have passed through this blessed land. I want to say thanks to the University of the West Indies and Pro Vice Chancellor Professor Clement Sankat and his assistant, Mrs. Betty McComie; Mr. Dennis Ramdeen; Mr. Ainsworth Mohammed; all the musicians past and present in the band; and my special singer, Miss Destra Garcia. Much thanks to Trinidad and Tobago for giving the strength when it seemed that strength was not there.

I want to give special thanks to Mr. Jnr. Bisnath of Kaisokah Moko Jumbies for his work in developing the youth of the nation. Thanks to you, Junior, for your wonderful contribution. Thanks to my wife Cheryl, my daughter Juliana, my sons Roy and David, my baby girl Jo-Ann, my brothers and sisters and my grandkids, and my sister Elizabeth for keeping our family together. To all the promoters with whom I have worked over the years, I say thanks for keeping us working and to the people of Grenada for accepting me as a son of Grenada and also to the other Caribbean islands that have helped to sustain us through the years. And most important, to the Sisters of St. Dominic's Home, singling out Sister Paul Clarke, Sister Joseph (Marie Thérèse Rétout, OP), and Sister Arlene for their love in bringing up so many children through the years. And to all the other Homes who have developed some of the best musicians that we have seen in our land.

I would like also to thank Black Stalin's family, Mrs. Patricia Calliste, who was always there in support of me, and Ruth and Junior Telfer for being my friends—Junior, my elder brother who cushioned me through the tough times.

JOCELYNE GUILBAULT: This experiment in storytelling has involved so many conversations, it is difficult to know where to begin acknowledging all of them. But first and foremost, I want to express my gratitude to Roy for having agreed to work with me on this project. It has been inspiring to learn about his musical journey and a privilege to explore with him many of the moments that marked Trinidad's musical life over the past fifty-plus years.

In this book, you will encounter multiple voices. There is the I of me as writer, listener, and scholar. There is the I of Roy's voice. There is also the dialogic I of Roy's voice with and through mine. There is furthermore the I of other participatory voices. And there are other voices and contributors, all of whom I wish to acknowledge here.

Throughout my research in Trinidad, the following people contributed much to the development of my thinking and writing. I wish to express my heartfelt thanks to my longtime and dear friends Junior and Ruth Telfer, Leroy "Black Stalin" Calliste, Alvin Daniell, Brother Resistance, Joycelyn and Michael Germain, Hollis "Chalkdust" Liverpool, and Francesca Hawkins for their enduring intellectual and musical engagement and their generous support in helping me bring this project to completion. I thank also Jocelyn Sealy, Clifton Harris, and Winston Maynard who graciously helped reveal aspects of Roy's biography that I would have missed otherwise. To all the members of Roy's current band, and former band members Lambert Phillip, Clive Mitchell, and Curtis Lewis; to Roy's bandmates and friends Errol Ince, Selwyn Wheeler, Clarence Curvan, and Ronald Berridge: my special thanks for sharing your knowledge and insights and giving support to this project from the start. I want also to thank the Sisters of the Children's Home, Sister Francine, Sister Paul Clark, and Sister Marie Thérèse Rétout, for sharing their keen understanding of the orphanage as an institution and home for numerous budding young musicians in Trinidad.

I want to express my most sincere thanks to Joycelyn and Michael Germain, who over the years provided a home for me, lent me their living rooms to conduct interviews, and drove me countless times to distant locations to attend concerts and to interview people. I am also grateful to Cheryl Cape for her generous hospitality and help in providing a peaceful space where Roy and I could work. Many thanks also to Julie Carrington for her kindness in providing food and rooms at her hotel in Manzanilla where Roy and I were able to complete this project.

The production of this book would not have been possible without the innumerable contributions and strong support of Shawn Randoo, who brought key information to my attention, provided digital reproductions of LP covers, and supplied me with copies of recordings that are no longer available on the market. I want also to thank other mighty record collectors and researchers Fitzroy Richardson, George Maharaj, Ray Funk, Oswin Rose, and Rudolph Ottley, who, in just a few hours, helped me find rare documentation.

I am indebted to Anthony Moore, Liz Montano, Sister Marie Thérèse Rétout, Dennis Howard, Jeff Packman, and Juliet Robin and also to the *Trinidad Guardian* and *Trinidad Express* newspaper archives for giving me the copyright permissions to use their photographs in this book. I am also grateful to John Vokoun, who prepared the photographs with great expertise.

My most sincere thanks go to Christopher Ballantine, who read my manuscript and provided encouragement and perceptive comments. I thank also Richard Crawford and Percy Hintzen, who helped me refine and sharpen many of my ideas. Many thanks also go to Donald Brenneis, Beverley Diamond, Line Grenier, Keir Keightley, Sara Le Menestrel, Krister Malm, Rhoda Reddock, Patricia Mohammed, Corinne Kratz, Kay Shelemay, and Bonnie Wade, who all came to my rescue with bibliographic references with a keen critical sense of what was needed. Big thanks also to Bob Feld, on whom I called to clarify jazz musical gestures.

My research greatly benefited from the generous help of many members working at the National Library and National Archives of Trinidad and Tobago. It is also a pleasure to acknowledge the financial assistance of the University of California, Berkeley. Without its support, this book could not have been written.

The preparation of this book was greatly facilitated by my research assistants. I want to thank Kari Peterson, Sean Maddens, Annita Lucchesi, Vanessa Aldrich, Karinina Cruz, and Michael Kushell for transcribing numerous interviews. In particular, I want to thank Vanessa Aldrich for generating the computerized map accompanying this book. Special thanks go to Karinina Cruz for her keen ability in finding rare bibliographic sources and for providing the figures listing Roy's band musicians and singers over the years. I am particularly indebted to Michael Kushell for producing all the other figures included here, for sharing his computer skills, and for his invaluable web searches to find countless pieces of information. I also want to thank Elizabeth "Beezer" de Martelly for help with the final preparation of the manuscript. I am also most grateful to Sandra Nicholls for her careful editing and perceptive advice.

My most sincere thanks go to Alvin Daniell, who kindly agreed to produce the companion CD, *Roy Cape: A Calypso and Soca Anthology*. This CD features not only recordings of several Trinidadian bands no longer available on the market but also some of the latest soca songs recorded by Roy Cape All Stars. It provides a great companion to this book.

I wish to express my heartfelt gratitude to Ken Wissoker, editorial director at Duke University Press, for his strong support and good advice throughout this project, and to Elizabeth Ault, Karen M. Fisher, Liz Smith, and Natalie Smith of the editorial and production staff for their care in guiding the book through its final stages into print. I am particularly indebted to the anonymous readers of the manuscript, whose critical comments and questions greatly helped me to better shape the narrative arc of the text and refine my arguments.

Above all, I must thank my kindred soul, Steven Feld, who has been an inspiring musical and scholarly presence throughout the writing of this book, and to whom this book is dedicated.

NOTES ON THE TEXT

Terminology: Singers and composers can rightfully be regarded as musicians. However, in this book, I reserve the term "musician" exclusively for instrumentalists and bandleaders to mark the distinct work they perform.

Throughout the book, I refer exclusively to the English-speaking Caribbean. My reference to "the Caribbean" or "the islands" should thus be read with this meaning in mind.

Registers of Speaking: I have changed some instances of Trinidadian English in places where they might be confusing. Otherwise, direct quotations are transcribed as spoken.

Visual Signs: In this dialogic experiment, parentheses and brackets are useful to highlight who provides additional information. Parentheses are used when the author in question provides additional information on what he or she is saying. By contrast, brackets indicate that I am adding explanations or additional information to what another speaker is saying.

Currencies: Speaking about his tours in different parts of the world, Roy Cape refers at times to Trinidadian dollars, at other times to U.S. dollars, and at still other times to Canadian dollars. Whenever possible, the sum of money referred to in the text is translated into U.S. dollars. At other times, to avoid interrupting a dialogue, I leave the reference to foreign currencies as mentioned by the speaker. The reader should note the following conversions: 1 U.S. dollar is worth usually from 6 to 6.4 Trinidadian dollars; 1 Canadian dollar usually equals around 6 Trinidadian dollars.

INTRODUCTION

ROY CAPE: I never thought that I would be writing a book one day. Being approached by Jocelyne, I thought about it and I knew that I had a nice little story to tell about my experiences and the people I have met through these experiences who had become the pillars of my future development. I knew that I could then pay tribute to these people who had paved the way of this path that I have traveled over the past fifty-odd years. I am referring here to my teacher Sister Paul and to Frankie Francis, Art De Coteau, Sel Wheeler, Ron Berridge, Beverly Griffith, Earl Rodney, Clive Bradley, Frankie McIntosh, Pelham Goddard, and Leston Paul, who have been a great part of my training and the finest arrangers throughout the years.

It was quite challenging to work on this book in many different places—Port of Spain, Manzanilla, Toronto [Canada], Grenada—at different times over the years. There was no documentation, and we had to rely on pure memory of my living experiences. With no preparatory note, I had to dig deep inside to get back the memory and relive what has already been lived. All the things that I went through became part of living memories about the road that would eventually lead me to be maturing in the journey of my travels. I will also say that, thanks to all the people who have offered their knowledge and all the facts, we were able to put things together.

I also want to thank Jocelyne for all the time and patience. She has never once been overwhelmed by the challenges.

This is how we got here.

JOCELYNE GUILBAULT: This book is a collaborative experiment in storytelling. It joins the voice of Trinidadian saxophonist and bandleader Roy Cape and mine as a scholar of Caribbean popular music. This idea came about as we were working on compiling and evoking the complex history of Roy's labor of love as an active performer and bandleader over the past fifty-plus years. We began experimenting with voice, who takes the lead, who says what, when, to whom, and why. So at times we feature first-person narrative, at other times dialogue, and at still other times polyphony to hear bandmates' testimonies. We experimented also with different materials to elicit stories. We rely on sound recordings and photographs as well as interviews, not only because they tell their own stories, but also because they help generate additional stories about Roy's musical journey. Together and through juxtaposition, these tactics produce different ways of knowing Roy's labor of love—his sound and work through sound, his reputation and circulation as a renowned musician and bandleader in the world.

I want to thank Roy for being open to experimenting with different ways of telling stories and for caring to acknowledge not just what he did, but also the many people, sounds, and events that have marked his career. His constant emphasis that no man is an island has been inspiring and productive of a rich chapter of Trinidadian music history and its transnational connections.

For both Roy and me, this book was a challenge to write. It is the first book-length study of the journey of an instrumentalist and bandleader in the English-speaking Caribbean. So we literally started from scratch, as the following anecdote makes abundantly clear.

In one of our meetings to discuss this book, Roy remarked that we were missing some photographs. What he had in mind were images of musicians he worked with, people who were important to him and who he thought should be included. Okay, I figured, the best place to find these photographs would be at the archives of national newspapers. A few hours later, I called and made an appointment to meet the head archivist of one of these dailies. I explained that I wanted to find some photographs of musicians who were very active in the local music scene from the 1960s onward. He quickly answered, "You're not going to find that. We don't keep the photographs of musicians. What we are interested in are the stars, the singers. We cut the photographs to keep just the singers." "Why?" I asked, a perplexed look on my face. He replied, "The people here don't write about the musicians. They write about the stars. So we need photographs for them, not for the musicians." He sounded annoyed by my question, but I insisted, "Would you have any folders of photographs, say, of musical events or of the brass band festivals? Perhaps there would be some shots of musicians there, no?" Seeing my determination to find something, he reluctantly went behind the shelves and brought back some folders. I sat down at a table and began my search. Out of at least eight folders, with no less than forty photographs in each, I finally found four that would be useful for my project.

Most biographies in popular Caribbean music focus on the stars.[1] But who is a star? Who really matters in popular music? And how does star status and the category of stardom restrict who and what is known about the makers of popular music? Particularly over the past fifty years, the rather exclusive focus on Caribbean lead singers has diminished the presence of nearly everyone else involved in the production of music. As a result, no more than a mere mention of the players who headline tours and recordings remains.

This practice is not limited to popular music in the Caribbean. North American and European popular music biographies published by the most widely circulated academic presses and journals seem to suffer from the same limitations. What image of popular music is generated by this narrow focus on the individuals occupying the center stage—literally, the center of the performance stage? Who and what does it serve, and why? Is this widespread tendency a remnant of the romantic construction of the artist as the individual genius, or is it the product of marketing strategies, the commodification and fetishization of the individual? While these questions are certainly worth answering, the main query that led me to this project concerned the other side of the coin: what have (Caribbean) popular music studies been missing by focusing so heavily on lead singers?

Little is known about band musicians in the Caribbean. Yet the musicians are the ones who give the pulse, who make things happen, and who bring the songs alive. And musicians have many stories to tell, stories that are otherwise rendered only in the voice of popular press journalism.[2] Exploring the work world of a bandsman and bandleader presents new dimensions of a bandleader's reputation and offers fresh understandings of circulation histories and cosmopolitan practices. It calls attention to the tremendous importance of material resources for all musicians. Most importantly, it helps us appreciate the determination and stamina necessary for musicians of the working classes to succeed and thrive with limited access to such resources.

Examining a musician and bandleader's stories also opens a window on sound and its ephemeral qualities. It grounds sound in work, apprenticeship, and rehearsals. It links sound to a distinct local sonic environment and musical traditions. It relates sound to histories of listening and musical affinities. It also makes clear how it takes not only many different types of musicians but special instrumentalists and bandleaders to make people move, to be moved, and to share public intimacies.³

This book is about one such musician. Roy Cape is a saxophonist who has been active as a band musician for over fifty years and as a bandleader for over thirty. Roy's reputation in terms of both live performances and recordings has long been established in the islands and the Caribbean diasporas—not only in North America but also in Europe. He is highly recognized for having accompanied the most famous calypsonians of the Caribbean in both calypso tents and regional competitions and also for playing with the biggest names in the soca music industry. As a band musician, he is known to have participated in hundreds of recordings. Since 1990, his own band, Roy Cape All Stars, counts eight commercially released CDs and nearly two dozen singles in compilations. Roy's recognition in the Caribbean and in the Caribbean diasporas is unique and all the more extraordinary because in general, bandsmen's contributions have been devalued locally—not to mention academically—in favor of singers in the pop music industries. Still, for some readers, my focus on Roy Cape may beg the question, why write a book about an alto saxophone player and bandleader?

Roy Cape: A Life on the Calypso and Soca Bandstand shifts the focus away from the headliners and concentrates instead on what is happening at and in the site of live production. Writing about cinema, Howard Becker has already shown how many kinds of expertise it takes to make a movie beyond the presence of the star actors. In doing so, he has significantly expanded the very definition of who could be viewed as stars in their own right. Likewise in music, many kinds of workers and work expertise are essential to produce, promote, and perform a show or a recording. In this project, I focus on a bandsman and a bandleader to show how a musician's biography can be a powerful document, revealing how the ethics of work come together with work consciousness, work pride, and work accomplishment.

Roy Cape: A Life on the Calypso and Soca Bandstand tells the story of a labor of love. The idea of a "labor of love" in music is commonly seen as the antithesis of alienated labor described by Karl Marx. In a compelling and evocative article published more than twenty years ago, sociologist Eliot Friedson coined the expression "labors of love" (in the plural) to address work that is much more than "an unpleasant necessity, something to be merely minimized." "In contrast to alienated labor," he writes, "labors of love are voluntary." While they still refer to activities enabling one to earn a living, they can be the source of enjoyment and fulfillment.⁴ This is the kind of statement, it could be argued, that show organizers often use to underpay musicians. "They enjoy what they do, so why pay?" This book shows that even though they usually choose to play music and enjoy doing so, musicians do not necessarily enjoy everything that is integral to being a professional musician: the long hours of waiting before going onto the stage; playing the same songs over and over for months—for as long as these songs are considered the hits the audiences want to hear; sleeping on uncomfortable beds on tour; being away performing at times of important family events; the habitual little to no public recognition of the efforts they put into a show; and the relatively small salaries they earn compared to what the lead singers make. And the list could continue. In other words, playing music may be voluntary and come from the love of doing so, but the many activities that enable one to earn a living through music nonetheless constitute labor—labor that can be rewarding, but that can be the source of frustrations and alienation as well. One of the main reasons why the work of musicians is often misjudged, to use Michael Hardt and Antonio Negri's wording in relation to artistic production in general, is arguably because it is "immaterial labor." Apart from recordings released as CDs, it is "a labor that produces an immaterial good, such as a service, a cultural product, knowledge, and communication," that is, productive of sounds and affective relations (Hardt and Negri 2000: 290). So what is produced by this labor "is on the one hand *immeasurable*, because it cannot be quantified in fixed units of time, and, on the other hand, always *excessive* with respect to the value that capital can extract from it because capital can never capture all of life"—that is, all the social life that musicians create.[5] This book explores both the love and the (immaterial) labor that are involved in Roy's musical journey.

What does it take for a musician like Roy Cape to build his name? What does it take for him to circulate? And how do work ethics, reputation, and circulation work symbiotically? Reputation in the English-speaking Caribbean refers to the feats one accomplishes and the prestige and recognition one gains through such accomplishments. In much Caribbean literature, reputation is contrasted with respectability: reputation being associated with prowess while respectability is linked to discipline and virtues. Reputation and respectability are also often viewed in gender-specific terms: reputation as a male quest and respectability as a female's main pursuit. These interpretations have been contested by many feminists and do not hold true in the Caribbean music business.[6] While male musicians earn their notoriety through their feats—their numerous participations in performance or recording projects—they can also be recognized in terms of respectability through the ethical behavior they adopt vis-à-vis their peers.

This book recounts the values Roy has cultivated in order to build his reputation and acquire an aura of respectability in Trinidad and Tobago, the Caribbean region, and in the Caribbean diasporas. To point out how his name became intimately linked to the ways in which he has circulated — playing with different people in different projects, spaces, and places, becoming influential and sought after — may seem tautological: a musician who circulates is one who is renowned and who can be counted on (in terms of ethical behavior). The advantage of this tautology is that it shows how to incorporate into the notion of reputation the regimes of circulation that are conventionally left out of the analysis of a musician's acclaim. What I am referring to are the conjunctural linkages of (post)colonial legacies of race, institutions, discourses, and political economy that allow the regulation of what and who circulates, where, and why.[7] An important objective of this book, then, is to examine how Roy's recognition and circulation have reinforced each other and have been informed by particular conjunctural and historical contingencies.

Most music bands in the Caribbean, as elsewhere, do not usually last long together. The thirty-plus years since Roy Cape All Stars was formed constitutes a notable exception. Sociologists Howard Becker (2008) and Bruno Latour (2005), in their studies of art worlds in particular and the concepts of network and agency in general, argue that there cannot be any lasting group without sustained work. In their view, to account for action — such as keeping a band together — one has to trace the many things and connections that contribute to making such an action or feat possible. Put another way, one has to acknowledge that the networks to which humans are connected include not only other humans but also material worlds (material things and material cultures) of all sorts — geography, history, institutions, laws, industries, media, and globalization. As Daniel Miller insightfully remarks, material worlds have power of their own. They establish the frame for proper behavior and order life (rhythms of seasonal activities, relative access to circulation, appropriate clothing, and so on).[8] So part of the musicians' labor also includes working with, at times against, and at still other times around materiality — a materiality that is not always of their own choosing.[9]

This work with, against, and around materiality that musicians are required to do cannot be underestimated. However, I want to extend the notion of immaterial labor in relation to popular music by taking into account many other aspects that play roles in a band's longevity and success. These include the acts of reciprocity that are essential for maintaining the networks vital to musicians' circulation; the generative force of pleasure that helps sustain music making and further collaborations; the kinds of attitudes toward change that make it possible to stay current with the times and stay employed; the synergy and dynamics among band members that help create playing opportunities; the issues of race, class, and gender that articulate the bonds and boundaries of musicians' work and networks; and the formal and informal economies that inform the kind of work musicians can do, where, when, and for how long.[10]

In the particular context of the postcolonial Caribbean, how has Roy Cape been able to remain an active band member for the past fifty-plus years and to maintain his Roy Cape All Stars band for some three decades? What musical skills, personal dispositions, histories, material resources, institutions, laws, and events have been constitutive of his musical journey? Put more broadly, what has enabled him to circulate through so many musical eras, musical styles, and musical groups? How has he managed to assemble people from so many different walks of life, with different knowledges and skills, ages, attitudes, and political orientations? What relationships on and off the bandstand, in and out of the studios, in the Caribbean, the diasporas, and beyond, have created the conditions of possibility for him to play and tour? And in what ways have Trinidad's colonial legacies (for example, in relation to the particular configurations of class, race, and gender) and the material realities of the island (in terms of geography and demographics) enabled Roy Cape to reach out to certain publics and not others? This book is about a musician from the Caribbean who is widely recognized but who is not a star—as traditionally represented in the Euro-American popular music business and film industries, and music biographies. It is an attempt to learn about and from a musician's journey, out of a postcolonial context and an island's distinct material realities.[11]

ON WRITING STORIES

This book is not just about music as a labor of love. It is also an experiment in storytelling—not a biography in the conventional sense. Let me explain. Much can be learned from reading exceptionally well-documented megabiographies (five hundred pages or more) like those of Elvis Presley and Thelonious Monk, written respectively by Peter Guralnick (1999) and Robin D. G. Kelley (2009). But this book does not follow these writing models. While it recounts stories and describes places in rich detail, it does not attempt to present Roy's journey exclusively from a chronological perspective. Nor does it draw solely from day-by-day press, and personal diaries, industry, and historical data, as in the case of greatly detailed personal biographies. Neither does this book follow the "in-his-own-words" model, as with Thomas Brothers's (1999) wonderful edited book on Louis Armstrong and many other publications on great jazz or pop instrumentalists or vocalists—even though there are many pages of Roy Cape speaking in his own words here. Nor do I follow the model of biography "as told to," a form championed by David Ritz, who published collaborative biographies coauthored with the artist in question (see, for example, *Brother Ray: Ray Charles' Own Story*, Charles and Ritz 1978; *Aretha: From These Roots*, Franklin and Ritz 1999; *The Brothers Neville: An Autobiography*, Neville et al. 2000).

The writing of this book also does not draw on the classic life history, biography, and autobiography methods elaborated in *Lives: An Anthropological Approach to Biography*, by L. L. Langness and Gelya Frank (1981). It does not follow, as the authors put it, "such procedures as eliciting narratives and recording them, compiling notes and assembling a final document, and, finally, analyzing the results of these labors" (6)—even though these techniques have been refined to great sophistication in the literature of anthropology and ethnomusicology, for example, in Judith Vander's (1988) *Songprints: The Musical Experience of Five Shoshone Women*, Virginia Danielson's (1997) *The Voice of Egypt: Umm Kulthum, Arabic Song, and Egyptian Society in the Twentieth Century*, Charlotte Frisbie's (2001) *Tall Woman: The Life Story of Rose Mitchell, a Navajo Woman, c. 1874–1977*, Veit Erlmann's (1996) *Nightsong: Performance, Power, and Practice in South Africa*, Eva Tulene Watt with Keith Basso's (2004) *Don't Let the Sun Step over You: A White Mountain Apache Family Life (1869–1975)*, Suzanne Oakdale's (2005) *I Foresee My Life: The Ritual Performance of Autobiography in an Amazonian Community*, and George Lipsitz's (2010) *Midnight at the Barrelhouse: The Johnny Otis Story*.[12]

Nor does this book adopt the contemporary models featured in works such as *African Rhythms: The Autobiography of Randy Weston* (Weston and Jenkins 2010), in which pianist and distinguished jazz elder Randy Weston is presented as the composer, and Willard Jenkins, his collaborative writer, as the arranger. Or *Musical Echoes: South African Women Thinking in Jazz* (Muller and Benjamin 2011), whose cover cites Carol Ann Muller and Sathima Bea Benjamin as coauthors because, as Muller puts it in the book's introduction, "I am the book's writer," but the stories and reflections "have been shaped in conversation with Sathima" (xx). Like Muller's publication, this book is a negotiated text. In contrast, however, I am not the sole writer.

Perhaps closest to my experiment in storytelling is *Jazz Cosmopolitanism in Accra: Five Musical Years in Ghana* (Feld 2012a). The author, Steven Feld, mixes memoir, ethnography, biography, and history in ways that highlight ironic juxtapositions—disparities, conjunctures, and disjunctions. The stories are told in the voices of musicians in dialogue with his voice as well as with each other's voices, in the past and in the present, in Accra and in other places where they have found conversational space—as multilayered, interconnected, and attuned to different moods and modes of being in the world. In the same vein, my approach focuses on stories. Stories do memory work, and they transform memorable experience into a vocal (voiced) performance. Like Feld's, my approach to stories does not feature a unified or singular narrative model from start to finish. Some stories are best told in Roy's voice, others in mine. Other stories or topics are better expressed in dialogue of different types. Still others are best conveyed through images, with words in the background. At other times stories are better told with words in the foreground and images in the background. Some are best told with Roy narrating and me providing endnotes. Taken together, creative collaborations like these involve improvisation. So Roy is not simply or strictly recounting his life to and for me to write down. And I am not the sole author or reteller of the stories written here about Roy. Every detail of this book is a negotiated text, a text in which there are multiple voices that negotiate authority in and through multiple exchanges, retelling, rewriting, and rereading.

When Roy introduces me as "my biographer" to his friends, he vocally marks that I take care of certain kinds of business in this book. I assemble stories into chapters. I highlight certain themes instead of others. I develop some aspects of his career in my own voice, and I also provide historical details to help contextualize the complexity of Roy's stories. However, Roy is my editor when he tells me how to write this or reformulate that, for example, to attend to subtleties in order to avoid hurting feelings, or to avoid being misunderstood. I am also his editor when he recounts his journey. That is, I ask him at times to elaborate, to clarify, and to add details as he enunciates his narrative. I ask him to tell more in order to know how much detail is enough and how much is too much. There is a shifting ground of who is editing whom and who is presenting what. We are both trying to capture something that involves a mixture of closeness and distance, professionalism and friendship.

We are quite aware that I am a researcher, and also that while musically trained, I am not a bandsman. He, on the other hand, is a professional musician and bandleader, but not a writer or academic researcher. We respect each other's voices—our own ways of intertwining and sequencing things. Sometimes we engage in conversations; at other times, we write solo. At still other times, I invite other voices to present additional perspectives. We are both concerned with being accountable to multiple constituencies— some are overlapping, and others are quite distinct from one another.

At times, we did not agree on what should be included or excluded in the book. To give just two examples: Roy would have liked me to include a map of the numerous nightclubs that existed in the 1960s. While I liked the idea of having a visual representation of that geography, it required too much archival research that I felt was not essential to Roy's musical journey. In turn, I would have liked to know more about the migration of Trinidadian musicians overseas. But after searching his memory to find the names of musicians that migrated, where they went, and when, Roy abandoned the project.

This book is thus an experiment in storytelling that involves creative collaboration and negotiation at multiple levels. Such an experiment can be looked at as an expected outcome after the publication of *Writing Culture: The Politics and Poetics of Ethnography* more than twenty-five years ago. Following the work of many ethnographers concerned with distinctive accounts of agency, this book addresses subjectivities and voices, histories, and events in various ways—through dialogues, polyphonic interventions, and testimonies. It developed out of multiple collaborations and through what Steven Feld refers to as "dialogic editing," negotiations of what is said, how it is said, by whom, for whom, and through whom, between Roy, many interlocutors, and me.[13]

As dialogic editing implies, the goal was thus not simply to learn about Roy's musical journey through Roy and other musicians, calypsonians, promoters, and friends. As Alison Jones and Kuni Jenkins (2008) aptly point out, learning about someone may be filled with good intentions, but it does not necessarily mean that the so-called collaborators have much to say about what is written in the end. There is a difference between learning about and learning from others.

The critical issue here is how local knowledge and ways of knowing are valued. In his article "Intimate Knowledge," Hugh Raffles asserts, "Local knowledge . . . is fundamentally relational. . . . [It is] local only in relation to the supra-local of science and only as a result of their enforced emplacement." He calls for attention "to the spatialised hierarchies of knowledge production and to the entrenched inequalities in social and natural scientific research" (Raffles 2002: 332). Again, this brings us back to the delicate issue of dialogic editing. How many details in a story become too many? How many repetitions should be included? To paraphrase Raffles, among the many things I learned from both Roy's accounts and those of other commentators was how places are made. Each and every time these places were mentioned, they became invested with a new detail, a particular memory, a distinct sound. They became "formed by the movement of people and ideas and . . . constituted by traces of pasts and futures."

Similar to Raffles's and many other ethnographers' experience, I came to understand that the repetition of place names, in many of the stories included here, was not about a repeated reference to ready-made places, but rather about place making (Raffles 2002: 329). It was also about narrating time and narrating or anchoring experience. Many other examples could be given to show how, "distilled to a question of method, the issue becomes not what is known, but in what language that knowledge is expressed."[14] In this sense, writing a biography through storytelling and dialogic editing draws attention to the hierarchies of social practice, ways of knowing, and ways of saying, in relations of power.[15]

This point has been highlighted in many ethnographies since 1986, after the issue of ethnographic authority was brought under intense scrutiny by publications like *Writing Culture: The Poetics and Politics of Ethnography*, edited by James Clifford and George E. Marcus (1986), and *Anthropology as Cultural Critique: An Experimental Moment in the Human Sciences*, by George E. Marcus and Michael M. J. Fischer (1986).[16] Many monographs, manuals, courses, and guides, such as *The Chicago Guide to Collaborative Ethnography* by Luke Eric Lassiter (2005), and even a journal called *Collaborative Anthropologies* (created in 2008) have since promoted different forms of reflexive writing to render explicit and legible what is involved in dialogic and collaborative practice—the poetics and politics that come into play in every aspect of the construction, conception, and articulation of a text based on dialogue and collaboration. It was from this perspective that this book was conceived.

Biographies, written in any form, never tell the whole story. They depend not only on access to knowledge—to archives or the people concerned—but also the filtering of memory, the political sensitivity of certain topics, and one's wish—or the family's wish—for privacy. They also greatly depend on who speaks, to whom, for whom, about what, why, and when. The stories biographies can tell are also greatly informed by whether the subject is dead or alive and the stage of the artist's career. It should be clear that there are things about an artist one can learn only in conversation with the artist himself. There are also things about an artist one would not address out of respect or care in conversation, or following a conversation, with the artist in question.[17] Hence the use of dialogic writing in biographies provides no guarantee of completeness, any more than other styles of writing in this genre. What it makes clear, however, is how knowledge about oneself and others is deeply relational and constantly negotiated.[18]

MEETING ROY

I met Roy Cape some twenty years ago during carnival season. The name of his band was on just about every poster announcing the "fetes" (a local term for parties of all sorts) in and outside Trinidad's capital, Port of Spain, for the entire season.[19] One night, with some friends, I went to hear his band at a fete held in Pier One in Williams Bay, Chaguaramas, just twenty minutes away from Port of Spain. To hear twelve band members perform live was a treat. Apart perhaps from Latin bands that continue to perform in such a formation, few other bands in the islands can afford to include as many musicians. The live sound of "the brass section"—which in the English-speaking Caribbean refers to both wind and brass instruments and includes, in the case of Roy's band, two saxophones (alto and tenor), one trumpet, and one trombone—combined with that of a keyboard, a guitar, a bass, a drum set, and a music sampler accompanying three frontline singers was "massive," to use a Trinidadian expression. That sound had a powerful effect on the crowd, including me. The band's tight coordination and punchy arrangements mobilized not only my ears and eyes but my entire body. The bass's low-frequency notes, amplified by the kick bass drum, grounded my body while the brilliant, forceful sounds of the brass section energized me. The sweet melodic lines played on the guitar, the rhythmic chord accompaniment of the keyboard, and the wide range of sampled sounds punctuating the energetic singing all reached me. Roy's band impressed me and left me with lingering memories.

I had heard about Roy's feats and his accomplishments through two of his closest friends (also my good friends), Junior Telfer, affectionately called simply "Jay," who worked for many years as the unofficial manager of Black Stalin, and also from Black Stalin himself, one of the most highly respected and renowned calypsonians of the Caribbean. One night at Jay's place, on the small porch that was protected from uninvited onlookers by a wall of green and clouds of incense, I met Roy on his way to play at a fete. If the tales I'd heard about his stature as a musician and bandleader were truly impressive, his physical appearance was no less striking. About five foot two, Roy's very small frame and light-skinned complexion, combined with his smiling brown eyes, remarkably soft voice, and calm presence in and of itself, were arresting. His abundant gray dreadlocks, tied in the back and falling all the way down to his ankles, added another dimension to his otherwise slender body, an imposing trace of his spiritual and philosophical orientation. His demeanor bore no pretense, only warmth and care. I knew then that I would like to learn and write about his remarkable career, but it was not the right time for him or for me. I was in the midst of another research project, and he was making strides with emerging young artists, performing soca — a musical style that had been around but was just then taking off in new directions. Studying the cultural politics of Trinidad's carnival music since 1993 undoubtedly prepared me to focus on Roy Cape's journey. I heard his band play regularly in calypso tents and fetes during carnival, heard Roy accompany top vocalists as well as beginners at concerts and at competitions, and heard him rehearse the latest songs of the season in the band's room in Trinidad. Traveling for my other research project to various Caribbean and Canadian cities where carnival is celebrated, I also heard Roy Cape All Stars on tour, at times playing in large stadiums for more than twenty thousand people, at other times performing at chic hotels for a few thousand aficionados, and on a few occasions at school gymnasiums for no more than a hundred people in the most horrible acoustic conditions. Attending these many live performances over the years proved invaluable and set the stage for me to hear and appreciate better what Roy later shared with me in our numerous conversations.

ON ASSEMBLING SOCIAL AND PERSONAL HISTORIES

Roy's stories about his active musical life all have been about tracing connections: conjuring up the spaces and places that made him grow up with a particular sensibility, identifying the musics and musicians that led him to play in certain ways, casting the sounds and scenes that made him move from one band to another, and describing the people at the heart of his decision to leave and then return to Trinidad. His stories were all about how his many connections with different people, things, and events, at different times and places, have been central to who he is and what he has been able to accomplish. In contrast to the widespread notion that people are the products of their time, it was revealing to hear that Roy never spoke of himself as a product of these different connections, events, times, and places, but rather as being part of them as much as they have been part of him. The difference is significant. Roy described how he had been part of a configuration or, more accurately, of several configurations that both influenced him and that he helped influence. As he made abundantly clear in the many hours of conversation with me, his journey has never been just musical but social, living by and through many different circuits and connections at various moments of his life. Given this perspective, this book is an attempt to reassemble, in written form, the storied texture of how individuals, working relationships, institutions, sonic environments, economic and sociopolitical conditions, skills, beliefs, and passions have been part of the making of Roy Cape.

As Roy Cape's musical journey clearly shows, to speak about personal experience is never just to speak about individual intimacies. It is to speak about history, place, and time. It is to speak of events and the assemblage of people who were there. It is to reveal those who were absent, and the material worlds that contributed in so many ways to what he has become. It is a musical journey that establishes connections that have not been written about and yet that had a major impact on that journey.[20] It is a journey that reveals belonging or, better put, multiple senses of belonging—to a nation-state, a brotherhood, a family, a musical scene, a community of affinities, a diasporic network within and across borders of all sorts (race, language, age, nation-states, and so on). Speaking about one's individual journey this way reveals the creative value and agency of the I and addresses the world—in its material, political, economic, and cultural senses. It is thus a story that is at once intensely personal and overwhelmingly social.

ON WORKING TOGETHER

Celebrating his fifty-year anniversary in the music business in 2008 incited Roy to make more time to speak about his journey. In that year our work together began slowly. Roy was acutely aware that we needed several hours uninterrupted to be able to have an in-depth conversation about his life as a Trinidadian musician, bandleader, manager, family man, and so on. We met twice in Toronto at the end of July a few days before he and his band began to perform for many Caribana-related events. We also met twice in Trinidad just before Christmas and before he began in earnest to play nonstop every night during the carnival season. On one other occasion, we had a series of exchanges just before his departure with his band to go on tour.

It is a challenge to conduct interviews with musicians who are regularly rehearsing and performing all year, either locally or on the road. At home in Trinidad, a musician and bandleader like Roy is busy not only with musical life, but also with family obligations and friends, and with the chores of daily life. He has little time for interviews. On the road, planning ahead for the next show or resting from the previous night's show, dealing with the unanticipated breakdown of equipment or problems with transportation—these also reduce the time when musicians are disposed to have a conversation about their musical careers. After the first two years, we decided to meet in Grenada, away from his daily preoccupations, to be able to concentrate on our work.

After a long flight from San Francisco to Miami, with a two-hour wait, and then another flight from Miami to Grenada, I arrived around 10 p.m. at the hotel where I was going to meet Roy for a four-day work session on the book. It was only two weeks after carnival, and Roy's band had played every night, often with two bookings a night. Yet Roy looked relaxed and refreshed and ready to work on the manuscript.

It was not long after the greetings and the thoughtful welcome, which featured local fruit juice, that Roy declared with a smile he was ready to go over the chapters and transcriptions I had sent him ahead of time. So I opened the many folders I had brought with me and began to show Roy the plan for the book, and the ways I imagined mapping his musical journey. This was simply a warm-up for the four intensive days of work that were to follow before I boarded the plane back to San Francisco.

Roy's habits as a bandleader overflow into many aspects of his life. His attention to detail, his high standards of achievement, his quest to update himself constantly—whether on new sound technology or computer software—and his insatiable appetite for reading everything he can on local and international news by devouring daily newspapers from cover to cover make him a very engaged and engaging interlocutor and collaborator.

The next morning, our work began in earnest. Roy's markings on the first chapter struck me immediately. They were not simply notes addressing misinformation or the need to expand on certain sections, but full editorial comments. This revealed to me his professional work ethic and the passion with which he dedicates himself to everything he does. His emphasis on working toward the highest musical standards, on improving his knowledge constantly, and on multiplying his efforts to stay competitive in the highly cutthroat music market marked him, one could say, as a modern subject—as someone who shares many of the aspirations that are aligned with the Enlightenment and its notions of progress, teleological development, and unitary and coherent subject. Yet Roy's agency in the music world does not follow a simple, single, and teleological trajectory. His associations, at different times in his career, are with not only Trinidadian calypsonians but also American jazz musicians and Jamaican singers, and with different music scenes—including Trinidad's carnival, European festivals in France, Germany, Sweden, and England, and multisited Caribbean diasporic show circuits both in the Caribbean and in numerous cities in the United States and Canada. These multiple associations led him not only to live as a cosmopolitan but also to think, as contemporary lingo would have it, as a postmodern subject. His memory of events, musics, influences, and associations often fuses times and places, people and things in ways that proceed by leaps and bounds, moving across and amid things according to multiple logics, knowledges, and interests.²¹

After going over the first chapter, we turned to the transcriptions of our conversations, as drafted by my students. The transcriptions were filled with misspellings and the narratives they transcribed appeared fragmented. We both agreed that we needed to proceed differently. Instead of recording, I proposed to write on my computer as Roy would speak. As the teller of his story, I knew that Roy would speak slowly, deeply engaged in the act of remembering. At the same time, I thought, by looking at the computer screen he would now be able to ensure that the recording of his words would be accurate and that his story would unfold smoothly.

WRITING AS AN ETHICAL PROJECT

For Roy, recalling the past was hard work. It required time and concentration to go back to the years of his childhood, at home and then at the orphanage, to describe his life as an up-and-coming saxophone player and his activities in recording studios, to recall his time in bands playing in dance halls, to detail life on the road (such as walking in the streets while performing with a band during carnival Monday and Tuesday), and to recast his tours. And this storytelling demanded concentration, as well as eliciting strong emotions. At times, he paused and smiled reflectively before resuming his story. At other times, he requested a break to smoke and rest his mind. On some occasions, he continued to speak, but more slowly, weighing every word, measuring the possible impact of his narrative on Trinidadian readers, particularly on his fellow musicians.

I was struck by how Roy was constantly monitoring how he should tell his story and the care he took to pay tribute to his fellow musicians. I was equally impressed by how he weighed the ways in which he phrased things to ensure that his narrative would not dismiss anyone. In Grenada, typing his script into the computer as he spoke led us to deal with ethical issues of voice. It helped me to understand the details that mattered to him, and to use what he saw as the proper speech register (the language appropriate to the people he would like to reach—poor, with basic formal education). So, for example, I learned that he did not want me to use a contraction like "don't," because it would make the reading of the book much harder for many people he knows. In that sense, Roy's conception of telling his story mattered to him insofar as it did not read as simply the journey of a sovereign subject—that is, decided by and acted upon by him alone. His interest was to recount how his life had unfolded socially: with people in a narrative that could be understood by people. It mattered to him that his claims be fair, not only from his perspective but also from the perspective of others. It mattered to him to offend no one, and to pay respect to specific people. It also mattered to him that the book would pay homage to significant others, not only musicians, but also to people with whom he grew up.

In this sense, for Roy to tell his story is not only a personal project to further his fame—although it is that too—but also an ethical project, one that is concerned with acknowledging the work and help of others, and the friendships that sustain band musicians away from home during their many months of touring. It is also an ethical project in the sense that Roy hopes teaching youths about the past may enable them to have a better future. For Roy, speaking about his musical life over the past fifty years is thus about writing a social history, paying tribute to those who helped him along the way, and producing a pedagogical document that could be used in schools. It is also about sharing his passion for music and his love of people.

In telling his story, Roy cites the voices of many people. He quotes musicians, friends, promoters, and fans. He narrates their deeds and explains how his life has been entwined with theirs. In the same vein, I integrate into my story of Roy's journey the voices of several people whose lives have been enmeshed with his. To do this I interviewed heads of organizations and institutions, calypsonians, musicians, promoters, and friends. I also quote some of the journalists from Trinidad and elsewhere who wrote about Roy as a musician, bandleader, Rastaman, and veteran figure in the Trinidadian and Caribbean music business.

MAPPING ROY CAPE'S MUSICAL JOURNEY

I use the term "journey" to refer to Roy's fifty years in the music business because it underscores the notions of regimes of circulation and reputation that are central to this book. Journey conveys the idea of "traveling from one place to another" and "the experience of changing from one state of mind to another."[22] Journey signals that there will be stops along the way, fast and slow lanes, and unanticipated detours. It also makes it clear that similar to the ways in which reputation is publicly acknowledged, there will be vivid snapshots of specific events, places, and people and only vague recollections of other occasions, sites, and encounters. It thus indicates that Roy's story will be recounted at times by leaps and bounds and at other times in minute detail. And while the notion of journey summons particular spaces, it simultaneously recalls specific times. I like the notion of journey also because while it specifies the beginning point of the travel, the focus is on motion, the process of living, with all its unpredictability, disappointments, hopes, and pleasures—never a completed circle or simple linear expanse. Through this notion of journey, this book ties together the time and space of a life's work, revealed through stories.[23]

Accordingly, chapter 1 begins with the first sixteen years of Roy's journey. From the start it shows how Roy's multicultural and multiracial family ancestry and the multiple locales where he spent his early life are both unique and at the same time typically complex, as is the case for most West Indians. Most important, it shows Roy's curiosity and determination to learn music against all odds. In addition to acknowledging the profound influence of pan (the instrument and the music of steelbands) on a youth like Roy, someone addicted to music, for the first time in academic writing, it addresses the profoundly influential role that Christian orphanages have had on the musical life of Trinidad and Tobago, and, perhaps, on the English-speaking Caribbean as a whole.

The different aspects of Roy's journey that are highlighted in this book require different ways of telling. In the first chapter, to recount the specific conditions—economic, social, political, cultural, gender, racial, religious, to name only a few—in which Roy emerges as a musician, I use several voices to offer different perspectives on Roy's childhood: my own voice, at times as a historian, at other times as part of an exchange to elicit history in the making; Roy's voice as the leading part in our dialogue when we reflect on some moments of this early part of his life; and the voice of Sister Francine, the director of the orphanage (today renamed the Children's Home), to provide her own recollection and views of the institution.

Two things strike me in chapter 1. First, for both Roy and Sister Francine, narrating time and narrating experience is done through the mention of places. Particular place names—which abound in the text—do temporal work as well as providing geographic orientation. So when asked about what happens, the answer often points to where it happens.[24] In other words, time, space, and memory work together through place in chapter 1, as in the entire book. Second, for Roy, the idea of growing up as a child at the orphanage is related to body skills, what he learned to do with his hands—like tailoring clothes or playing the clarinet. In this chapter, Roy powerfully relates body memory and place memory to the sensuousness of knowledge and agency.

Chapter 2 maps Roy's journey as a saxophonist and band musician between 1959 and 1977. It reveals the consciousness of a working musician and foregrounds the immaterial labor that goes on in the production of music. It addresses pride of craft and acknowledges those musicians who have been Roy's models of mentorship. It shows how name is forged through work consciousness and the materiality of sound production and circulation.

In chapter 2, Roy takes a solo. Apart from our brief exchanges in the text where I help him clarify certain aspects of his collection of memories, I use endnotes to map my listening: to provide details beneath the descriptions, to establish connections, and to put in perspective what I am learning from Roy's stories.

Chapter 3 addresses Roy's history of listening as his history of sounding.²⁵ It thus describes Roy's voice on the saxophone not in the singular but in the plural. It details how at different times and also for different reasons—musical, material, social, economic, political—Roy has sounded and played differently. It shows how a player's sound or musical aesthetic is thus never merely a technical musical issue. As a corollary, it emphasizes how musical flexibility is key for a musician to survive and, indeed, to thrive.

In chapter 3, I take the lead. I write about my interest in Roy's unique sound and playing as both a musician and an academic ethnomusicologist. I seek to learn technical details about Roy's playing, to help performers and music aficionados better appreciate Roy's sound production and predilection for certain approaches to improvisation. I also aim to situate historically the genealogy of the aesthetic values that inform his playing, as both a soloist and a band member in a brass section.

Chapter 4 addresses what being a bandleader has entailed in postcolonial Trinidad and Tobago since the early 1980s. It shows how economics has been Roy's constant preoccupation as a laborer paid on a performance basis. It also shows how Roy's ability to manage and nurture multiple relations—his affective labor—has contributed highly to his success as a bandleader.²⁶

In chapter 4, Roy recounts not only some of the events that marked his career as a bandleader but also a unique moment in his life when he performed on stage as a singer during one carnival season. The stories recounted here are thus about a series of transformative moments in Roy's musical career and the consolidation of his notoriety through his performance in an increasingly wide range of circuits.

Chapter 4 takes the form of a conversation. It exhibits the dialogic relationship that Roy and I established in writing this book. It is punctuated by questions, anecdotes, and the reconstruction of important moments. Roy's desire to document certain aspects of his life combines with my interest in learning about the conditions of possibility that permit a band like Roy Cape All Stars to emerge, to thrive, and to last as long as it has. In our second year working on this project, we were both more relaxed. Roy saw what I was writing by looking at the computer screen, and he knew that he could intervene at any time and go back on what he said, delete, add, abridge, reword, be more specific, and even come back later, insert a new track, backtrack, and over track—for hours, days, or months afterward until the manuscript was complete and to our satisfaction. He also knew that he could rely on me to fill in the details if and where the need arises. I also felt more comfortable because I knew Roy better—his personality, speech pattern, and attention to details. I also felt more comfortable because I knew more about Trinidad from the late 1970s on than I did about the former periods. This is partly because many publications on Trinidad focus on sociopolitical conditions and cultural productions in the aftermath of independence, and partly because I have been deeply involved in research on Trinidad's carnival music scene from this period on.[27] I thus feel that I can be a better interlocutor in many guises—annotator, researcher, translator, friend, provocateur, editor, commentator, questioner, and amplifier.

Chapter 5 looks at photographs illustrating different moments of Roy's journey. Here the visual is in the foreground and the words in the background. In this chapter, my goal is to explore how Roy's acclaim and his circulation have been visually mapped through photographs—in local newspaper archives and in Roy's press book and personal collection. Roy's efforts, in turn, focus on the memory work that these photographs generate.

In chapter 5, Roy first introduces the people, the moments, and the sites indexed in the photographs. His introduction often serves as a point of departure to emphasize the social relations and the particular political or social moments that the documents make visible. At other times, his description uses the images to pay homage to his musical mentors, peers, and friends, and to the local heroes that have inspired him. Sometimes, the photographs themselves ask questions that compel Roy to address how the images of past incidents or moments relate to the present. In turn, I use the introduction of this chapter to engage in a critique about the relationship of the popular music concept of stardom to our visual culture or, more specifically, to what Deborah Poole calls "visual economies."[28] While I address, to use Corinne Kratz's expression, "the various potentials of photographs" to boost the recognition, map the circulation, and archive the musical feats of musicians (Kratz 2012: 242), I also explore how photographs are deeply enmeshed in cultural practices and (re)produce specific artistic hierarchies and conventions in the popular music industries.[29]

Chapter 6 is based on testimonies. Here I call on a well-informed group of calypsonians, soca artists, friends, band members, and other musicians to comment on Roy's career as a bandleader and saxophone player. I use their testimonies to examine how Roy's fame is constructed in the local musical milieus, and to learn about Roy's practice on a daily basis, his habits as a bandleader, and the dynamics that he creates with his own musicians. I also include excerpts from articles written by local and foreign journalists to acknowledge how Roy's accomplishments, in tandem with his circulation in different music milieus and among different people at home and abroad, have been (re)presented in the public media.

The inclusion of these many voices and many perspectives, drawn from interviews I recorded with numerous musicians, calypsonians, and friends, makes this chapter highly polyphonic. To produce this montage of voices, this chapter is laid out as if I had filmed the musicians' and artists' interviews on video and constructed an editing plan for a documentary. Based on this idea, I resort to opening shots to first establish the multiple musical experiences of these colleagues and to medium shots to understand the vantage point from which they speak about their relations with Roy. At times, I use jump cuts to condense the time of the interview exchange, in order to focus on particular themes. At other times, I resort to other documentary techniques such as fade and dissolve, to allow some of the voices to resonate, emphasize, or overlap with one another.

Chapter 7 traces Roy's circulation throughout his musical journey. It describes Roy's touring schedule and critically addresses the many other factors that have informed his access to certain sites and not others. While touring constitutes a crucial aspect of Roy's musical career, this chapter does not simply chronicle or focus on Roy's physical travels from point A to point B. Circulation here is conceived also in terms of the different spaces in which he has played; the social relations he has been able to establish in different milieus, as well as the role he has played in helping others make connections; and also the transmission of musical knowledge and experience to other musicians and singers. These different ways of conceiving circulation help show how a musician's fame is constructed across a variety of sites.

In this chapter, I take the leading voice for the most part, but I mix up different ways of telling a story. At times I include ethnographic snapshots—the story of my experience of particular events and performances. At other times, I quote the words of people I interviewed to add important details on the particular practices I am exploring and also to benefit from the insights of local observers. At still other times, I present excerpts of dialogues I have had with Roy and several other musicians in order to theorize what circulation has entailed over a long and active career.

This experiment in telling stories comes from my ethnographic commitment to learn not just about, but also from Roy's musical journey. Different ways of telling say different things. My attention to voice in this text has thus been to learn as much about the poetics as the politics of speaking selves. It has been about respecting how Roy and the many other contributors to this book organize, sequence, juxtapose, intertwine, and highlight their stories. But as Mikhail Bakhtin once said, speaking always entails entering an ongoing conversation, whether it is from the past, in the present, or in an imagined future.[30] So I have reproduced a number of dialogues to show how many of the ideas, notions, and stories in this book were prompted and came into being through conversations and negotiations. I have also reproduced many of the dialogues to show how, as is typical of most conversations, dialogic editing—to know what to include in, or exclude from, the stories, how to address some particular events—was an ongoing decision-making process as much for Roy as for me. While I was the first ear at the moment of record, the stories told were ultimately meant to be heard as widely as possible.

Band musicians in the Caribbean have been listened to, but not seriously heard. They have been seen, but not deeply known. This book begins to acknowledge what is involved in a working musician's journey in the Caribbean, both as a postcolonial subject and as an islander. It begins to show what it takes to earn an enduring reputation like Roy's, with the conditions he has worked in. It begins to call attention to the regimes of circulation that so deeply inform what such a reputation for a Caribbean musician entails, how it is built in the media, where and by whom it is appreciated, what kind of money it generates, and some of the other ways—sometimes in lieu of money, and sometimes not—by which it is rewarded. This book is a first step toward more deeply hearing, knowing, and engaging what Caribbean musicians' stories say about the pleasures and pains of their lives at work.

1 • FOR THE LOVE OF MUSIC
Up from the Panyards and at the Orphanage

There were a number of questions on my mind when I first met Roy Cape. As a young boy, he had grown up in poverty, yet he had gone on to become a musician and bandleader of broad reputation. How had this come about? What conditions enabled him to break out of the cycle of poverty? How did his early apprenticeship deepen his love for music? What instruments were available to him and where did he learn to play? In order to fully appreciate how far Roy had come, I needed to know where he began. So I started with his childhood.

Many sociologists would be quick to point out that knowing the socioeconomic conditions and class status that marked Roy's childhood would help explain his personhood, his habitus, both then and now.[1] Yes, to some extent, but not entirely. More than economics figure into the genesis of a labor of love. Roy's love for music demanded time and effort to listen and learn, and not without some sacrifices along the way. The point here is that simply living in an environment where steelbands are ubiquitous does not lead one to have music in the blood. Against any essentializing narrative, I wish to detail the considerable personal efforts and punishments Roy endured to pursue his love affair with music.

The second section of this chapter focuses on Roy's life in the Belmont orphanage, from 1954 to 1958. It clearly shows that human agency cannot be exercised outside of the socioeconomic forces and physical conditions that inform one's life. It reveals how, while Roy was developing his musical skills by playing the pan, the severity of family hardships led him first to the streets and from there to the orphanage. I address the important role that orphanages played in the musical education of brass band musicians in Trinidad, beginning with a brief history of the emergence of the Belmont orphanage. This story links the Catholic Church's efforts to provide humanitarian aid while engaging in its missionary mandate and colonizing process. I also describe its educational programs, including academic instruction, teaching a trade, and finally, music lessons—who taught music and what instruments were taught, and the playing opportunities provided by the institution.

In addition to drawing from historical documents, this chapter provides different perspectives on life in the orphanage by including not only my voice as an ethnographer but also excerpts of an interview with the current director. It also features a conversation with Roy, who describes his experience at the orphanage in his own words.

GROWING UP AMID POVERTY

Roy Cape's family ancestry is unique, and typically complex, as is the case for most West Indians. It is both multicultural and multiracial, and it involves a family narrative of migration and separation. Roy's maternal grandparents were both from Grenada. His grandmother, whose last name was Nancoo, was of Indian descent; his grandfather, whose family name (Cape) was given to Roy, looked Creole—that is, of African and European descent. After the couple married, they migrated to Trinidad, "just like everyone else in those days, looking to make a better life," as Roy put it. By the time his future mother was fifteen, Roy's grandparents had separated. His mother, the eldest of the family, stayed with her father, while her sister, Cordelia, returned with her mother to Grenada. Three years after the separation of her parents, Roy's mother became pregnant. She gave birth to Roy in 1942. Roy never met his father nor saw a photograph of him. All he knew was that his father was a white American in Trinidad on business, who had returned to the United States without leaving a trace.

Poverty marked the first few years of Roy's life. The support that both he and his mother received led him to live a life deeply entangled with the Catholic Church and with women of all ages. Roy was only a few months old, living with his young mother and his grandfather, when the latter fell ill and died. His neighbors, whom Roy refers to as "churchly people," took Roy and his mother into their house and treated them like their own children. Roy grew up with these neighbors almost from the time he was born until the age of five or six. They turned out to be the great-grandparents of Mark John, better known in the calypso world as Contender. Roy fondly recalls Mama Z, whom he used to call Granny, wearing a "big, flowing dress with a serious head tie" and looking very "Martinican."

As soon as Roy was old enough, Mama Z sent him to the Sacred Heart Girls School on Park Street. Perhaps they wanted him to live in a safe environment because of his small size; and since he had long hair, Roy could pass for a girl. Or perhaps it was simply the closest school where they could send him. In any case, from the beginning, Roy grew up in a Catholic environment with many women around—a granny, his mother, and many nuns and girls—with a touch of French Creole color and most certainly Creole cuisine.

Even though from early on Roy's life was enmeshed in multiple networks, Roy's telling of his childhood centers on his mother and his emerging love for music. Roy was the only child for a few years, but his life changed after his mother married and had two more children, Isabella (Bella) and Hollis.[2] But the union soon went sour. Roy was old enough to remember the violence, the crying, and the blood flying when his mother found her husband with his girlfriend. The girlfriend got jealous and hit his mother's head with a bottle. After that incident and the eventual separation, his mother moved them both to Roy's godmother's place in Sea Lots.

Sea Lots was a shantytown that even today, as Trinidadians would say, "has a stigma." They lived at Labasse, a place filled with junk and garbage, next door to the abattoir where they used to slaughter the cows, goats, and other animals for market. Roy and his mother lived there only briefly, until his mother took her family back to live with her husband. Although she returned for the sake of her children, it wasn't long before the relationship broke down once more.

Roy's mother went back to the tannery to live with Roy's godmother. She became engaged to Andrew Rivas, who then became the father of Roy's sisters and brother, Patricia, Kay, and Brian. For a while, even though they were poor, the family was able to make ends meet. His mother was the economist of the family and ran a mutual aid society like a "sousou."[3] The family moved to Picton Road, in John John, reputed to be a poor and tough area. They lived near his mother's friends, Jean and Jap.

The family rented a two-bedroom place in St. Barb's in Laventille— a bedroom, a kitchen, and one other room where the children slept.[4] With no beds or mattresses, the children slept on piles of clothes laid out each night. They all went to the Laventille RC (Roman Catholic) School until Roy missed classes so often that his mother, with the help of a priest, took Roy to Rosary Boys Roman Catholic School on Park Street with the hope that he might do better there. To this day, although the school is not seen as a rich man's school, it is recognized nonetheless as a prestigious one. Even after the family moved from St. Barb's to 16 La Resource Street, and his brothers and sisters went to nearby Rose Hill School, Roy stayed on at Rosary Boys. But he continued to miss class to pitch marbles and, more often than not, to hear music play.

Roy's memories of his childhood are filled with images that, despite his poverty, included simple things that brought pleasure. On the one hand, he recalls that his mother "never knew about automation" and had to wash the clothes for everyone in the family by hand, and that the oven they had was "an oil tin from CGA" (Coconut Growers Association). On the other hand, he also recalls that the little oil tin enabled his mother to make cakes and bread; and that even though they were poor, his parents would try to make the house look like Christmas for the kids. He recalls that he had fun back then. But these memories of family life were soon to come to an end, after his mother fell ill with tuberculosis. From that moment on, Roy's life dramatically changed.

His mother was first sent to the Masson Hospital on Long Circular Road. However, her close proximity hardly diminished the hardships her illness imposed on her children. Roy and his siblings were not allowed to go inside the hospital and could only speak to their mother across the mesh wires. As her health slightly improved, she was sent to the Caura Sanatorium in the eastern part of the country. Separated from his mother and living in dire poverty, Roy, then only eleven years old, ran away from home with Hollis, one of his younger brothers. They lived in the streets, eating fruits and cane growing by the river in Cascade while they hid in the bush. They begged for money and would slip inside cinemas to "make up time" away from the public and the police. They slept under trucks until morning, when they would resume their struggles to survive. After a month, Roy's stepfather caught them entering the Royal Theatre and took them home. They were told that they had to go either to Grenada to live with their grandmother or to the orphanage in Trinidad. Roy already knew some children at the orphanage and chose to go there. His stepfather took Roy and his brother to court, the only way that the children could be sent to the orphanage. The court determined that they both would stay at the orphanage until the age of sixteen. Little did Roy know that this turn of events would help him further his involvement with music.

IN SPITE OF IT ALL: LEARNING MUSIC THROUGH LISTENING IN PANYARDS

Before he was sent to the orphanage, Roy's love for music had already begun to dominate his life. The move to John John, in particular, proved to be profoundly influential on his career as a musician. He often stayed out long after everyone else in his family went back home, listening to rehearsals, such as those at Stanislaus Street, led by one of Jean's sisters, a member of the Girl Pat Steel Orchestra, the first female steelband orchestra in Trinidad.

Roy's attraction to music led him to seek out the company of musicians. Perhaps it was also the community that musicians formed around themselves that attracted him. At any rate, Roy's musical connections began to grow by leaps and bounds. His location, Laventille, made it easy for him to meet some of the most well-known pan musicians in the country. His musical journey began with one of Jean's sisters, who let him listen to the Girl Pat Steel Orchestra. A few steps from his home, he could hang around the famous steel pan inventor Fillmore "Boots" Davidson, who was among the pioneers of the steel bass pan. It was Fillmore who, after accompanying the Trinidad All Stars Steel Pan Orchestra on its first tour to England in 1951, decided to migrate to the former colonial country.[5]

ROY CAPE: I would pass and Boots would be tuning the pan, grooving the pan, and I would run and get wood for him, for him to burn, to tune the pan. And I would forget about school and everything, then! And I got a little *cuttail* [a beating when he returned home] for that. I was so turned on [by the pan]. Like I said, right in my backyard: Desperados on the Hill, City Syncopators, right here, Renegades one way, Casablanca, Trinidad All Stars originally on Charlotte Street (and today on Duke Street), Fascinators, Hill Sixty, City Symphony, Tokyo, all of the steelbands [and] there I was.[6]

JOCELYNE GUILBAULT: You were surrounded by them.

RC: When I went by any one of the panyards, the elders "run me" by telling me to go away and go home to study my books. And this actually happened to me [*laughs*]. I was in Synco[pators], and among the players there was a tailor named Mr. Harold who liked me as a young person, and who took me under his wing. So I used to go up to the back of the club and listen to the band practice. And there was this man named Tuddi. One day, he took off his belt, and he gave me a few strokes and he would say to me, "Leave the panyard and go home and study your books."

Roy would go by the Renegades' panyard in the quarry on Basilon Street, and then hang out at the home of their captain, famous for his herculean strength and known by his sobriquet, Gold Teeth. After being encouraged by him and many other musicians in the band, Roy was given a tenor pan by Pancho Benjamin who, at the time, was the tuner of the Renegades' band. However, the day he brought the pan home, his mother squarely refused to have the instrument around. The negative connotations associated with pan men back then—as violent, drunkards, and so on—were sufficient for her not to want her son to become one of them. She gave the pan away to Mano Porter, a man working at the docks.

"So, I was still going to school, but school didn't talk to me and didn't get into me." Roy continued to miss school and to hang out in the streets, flying kites, pitching marbles, and listening to music. After his mother fell ill and he ran away, the court order that sent him to the orphanage changed the course of his life in more than one way, but most importantly also musically.

UNEXPECTED TURN OF EVENTS: LEARNING TO PLAY IN THE ORPHANAGE
Musical Education in the Country in the 1950s

The pivotal role that orphanages have played in the musical life of Trinidad is a story that has never been fully told. While most musicians, especially those over forty years old, know that the great majority of reputed wind players come from either the orphanages or the Police Band, most Trinidadians are not aware of the significant role these institutions have played in their country.

In 1953, when Roy entered the orphanage, there were no schools of music in Trinidad. As Jocelyn Sealy—a respected Trinidadian music teacher and seasoned music competition judge, long recognized for her numerous contributions over the past forty-some years—recalled in an interview with me, music instruction was offered privately at the home of music teachers to those who could afford weekly music lessons.[7] Music teachers—mainly women—taught exclusively classical music repertoire on piano and violin, and sometimes guitar. They prepared their students to take music theory exams administered by the Royal School or the Trinity College of London—the two main institutions and the main location of the governing bodies for most British colonial subjects at the time. These teachers further helped the few students who were able to reach grade eight to obtain the sought-after degree, the Licentiate of the Royal School of Music. As Jocelyn Sealy remembers, in Woodbrook alone, a well-to-do section of Port of Spain, "there were a lot of families that had a piano and they went for music lessons. So there were usually one or two people in the house who could play. [A resident in Woodbrook], I used to walk as a young girl. I would walk around at six o'clock, and I would hear all the piano, people practicing as you go up and down the streets. I would come down the street and at each street, I would hear at least three practicing pianos." In the 1950s, music teachers could be found all over the country and in the more affluent areas, in just about every neighborhood. And some of them, like the famous Melissa Roberts on Carlos Street in Woodbrook, once had over one hundred students.

In addition to private lessons, students could learn music theory and take music appreciation classes, as well as participating in a choir or learning to play the recorder at some of the most prestigious high schools, convents, and colleges in the country, such as Bishop Anstey High School, Bishop Centenary College, and St. Joseph Convent in Port of Spain, and Naparima Girls' High School, Fatima College, and Presentation College in San Fernando. Students there learned to sight read and took singing lessons. However, these institutions were accessible to only a few—mainly students from middle and upper classes or those with exceptionally high academic scores. And, as was the case for private music lessons, music instruction at these institutions did not include any woodwind or brass instruments. Following the British military brass band model, brass instruments in Trinidad, as in most British colonies, were taught mainly, if not exclusively, in the Police Band and in orphanages.[8]

The Orphanage's Mission in Trinidad

Over the years, many musicians I spoke with would mention in passing that they came from an orphanage. In one of my interviews with Enrique Moore, the current director of the Trinidad and Tobago Police Band, I learned that as many as five of the six Police Band directors since Trinidad's independence came from an orphanage.[9] So I was not too surprised to hear that, as one of the most prominent musicians in Trinidad and the Caribbean region, Roy Cape also came from one.

The relationship between music and the orphanage comes from a long tradition. In Italy, it dates as far back as the fourteenth century. In eighteenth-century Venice, the Pietà Ospedale (the Pietà Orphanage) became forever associated with the Italian priest-composer Antonio Vivaldi (1675–1741), along with his progressive approach to music education and his highly acclaimed works for chorus and various combinations of instruments for disadvantaged girls (see Tiedge 1993; Cross 2012). This tradition, found not only in Italy but in most other European countries, linked together orphanages, humanitarian aid, music education, and Christianity and was exported to the New World as part of the colonizing process. By the late eighteenth and nineteenth centuries, orphanages were beginning to emerge in most Latin American countries and Caribbean islands, as well as in the United States.[10]

The emergence of orphanages in Trinidad and Tobago followed this typical colonial pattern. To explain the role of French missionaries in the Belmont orphanage where Roy went, however, I want to recall briefly Trinidad and Tobago's intricate colonial history.[11] From the time of its colonization by Spain in 1498, the main and perhaps most powerful religious denomination in Trinidad until recently was Roman Catholic—even after the country was taken over by the Church of England when Trinidad became officially British in 1802.[12]

To encourage immigration to Trinidad, the Spanish King Charles III issued a royal proclamation, or Cedula, in 1783, offering free lots of land to citizens friendly to Spain, provided they were Roman Catholics. Following this invitation, numerous French planters and free colored people from Martinique, Guadeloupe, St. Lucia, Dominica, St. Vincent, and Grenada came to settle in Trinidad, and in the aftermath of the Haitian Revolution a number of Saint Domingue Royalists followed suit in the 1790s. Since the French migrants quickly outnumbered the Spanish colonial settlers, it followed that even though Spain reigned, France ruled, particularly in matters of religion. During the nineteenth and the first half of the twentieth century, French missionaries administered a large number of schools and provided Roman Catholic instruction. As a way not only to rescue souls but also to provide humanitarian aid, they were also responsible for instituting St. Dominic's Orphanage, the second orphanage on the island.[13] Roy went to this orphanage in Belmont, a parish in Port of Spain. It was founded in 1871 by a French priest named Mariano Forestier, OP (Roman Catholic Order of Preachers, Dominican) and managed first by a devoted parishioner of the Rosary Church, Miss Stephanie Blanc, until the arrival of the Dominican Sisters from France in 1876, who then took charge of the institution. It continues to be run by the Dominican Sisters to this day.

Having scheduled a meeting with Sister Francine, the director of the Belmont orphanage at the time of the interview (2009), I headed to Belmont with a Trinidadian friend who was as intrigued as I was to learn about the history of the institution. Sitting at the top of a hill, with a magnificent view and a permanent light breeze, the orphanage today still occupies a very large area, encompassing several terraces. We were received at the administration building, situated next to the chapel, at the top of the hill. On our way there, a large empty space which is now a car park reminded us where two wings of the boys' quarters stood before they were destroyed by the Great Fire of 1996. Further up, we could see large buildings constructed in

1.1 At the Belmont orphanage: Two family units in two interconnected wings named St. Martin's and St. Dominic Savio's Homes, 1958. Courtesy Marie Thérèse Rétout, OP.

the style of the missions in California, serving as the main dormitories or "family houses" for boys and girls.[14] Arriving at the top of the hill, both my friend and I were impressed by how close to downtown Port of Spain the orphanage was located and, simultaneously, how far from everything it felt by being isolated at the top of this hill.

My meeting with Sister Francine began with a telling mistake. I started the recorded interview as I usually do, by identifying the speaker and where the interview is taking place.

JG: I am now with Sister Francine at the St. Dominic's Orphanage in Belmont.

SISTER FRANCINE: The St. Dominic's Children's Home. Really and truly, the children, they don't like to hear the word "orphanage" at all.

JG: Because it . . .

SF: It has a stigma. When you're talking to them, particularly the present ones, [it's the] Children's Home. That's fine. And many of our children are not orphans. Some children are orphans. Some children became orphans while they were in here. Some children we don't know if they were orphans because if they were abandoned, we don't know. The children we take care of are children from various, challenging situations in our national community. And we receive them and take care of them. It might be a case of drug addiction or substance abuse. . . . Um . . . incest is a problem. Sometimes poverty, well, poverty, I don't think we have a real, real, real poverty here. But sometimes people cannot cope with all the expenses, right? So those are the children we care for. Sometimes children are in unsafe environments, and they are taken away and put in a place of safety. So those are the children. It's not an orphanage because they are not all orphans.

JG: And Roy Cape is a good case in point because Roy had his mother, but she was sick.

SF: Yes.

Two months after opening, the Children's Home received eighteen children. The numbers increased rapidly. By 1876, there were sixty-six children; by 1913, there were two hundred; and by the time Roy left the institution in 1958, the number of children had reached its peak of 668, including 393 boys and 275 girls.[15]

The orphanage was granted government recognition as a public institution in 1871, and from that time on, the children were sent to the Children's Home with a court order. Until recently, the court committed the children up to the age of sixteen years.[16] The Home, in Sister Francine's words, was by then "a total institution." It provided both lodging and schooling in the same compound. At the time of Roy's arrival in 1954, even though primary school was compulsory, secondary school was not. So when children reached a certain age, they learned a trade as part of their school training during the day. Girls learned to paint and do embroidery, sewing, handicrafts, and printing work for the Catholic newspapers, as well as housekeeping and laundry. Boys learned other trades such as cabinetmaking, tailoring, and shoemaking, and they also learned printing.

Since its inception, the school has been under the supervision of the Ministry of Education. However, over the years, it has also been under the aegis of the Social Legal Government Ministry and the Ministry of Social Development. At one time, the orphanage even fell under the national security umbrella because the children were considered wards of the state.

Roy puts himself in the picture like this:

RC: I had to go to the court. Since my brother was younger, I think the court did not want to separate us. And they sent both of us off to St. Dominic's Home. And . . . going in there . . . I had to go through all the normal disciplines of life that . . . I still had to go to school and finish my schooling. That institution was run by French nuns of the Dominican order. French nuns. You had to learn all the prayers, and all of the worship that the Catholics

... it was part of the education. In Catechism, you have to make your First Communion and make Confirmation, and ... I fitted in well—except that I had some venom in me. I wanted to blame others for the predicament ...

JG: In which you were.

RC: Which I was in, yeah. And I was old enough to know that I created that for myself. But, as it turned out, further down the road, I have to say, I really appreciated being in there. And I finished my schooling. I went up to the highest class in school—meaning up to the end of high school. So I studied for a British examination to get a school-leaving certificate. And when you get a school-leaving certificate, in those days, you could get work with government, or a decent job. With a school-leaving certificate, the next thing was college and university and degrees and anything like that, then. I sat the school-leaving examination because I was going through the routine. I want to tell you I failed it because I wasn't really interested in school anymore. At that time, I had already gone to the pan. I was playing pan in the orphanage steelband. We had four pans: a tenor pan, a single second, a single guitar, and what we called a duddup (a lower two-note pitched pan).[17] It doesn't have as many notes as a bass pan. And for the first carnival they ever had there, I played the tenor pan to carry the parade around because the tenor pan was the pan that played the melody. And then I went to the conventional music band (e.g., brasses, woodwinds, and standard percussion), and the demands of the band ... [it was] so demanding that I forgot everything else then. But apart from the band, I still had my chores that I had to do there. So I was a tailor by trade. It was very good. ... The more you could do at the institution, it made life a little easier for you because you are somebody who is producing then. I even acted in "The Way of the Cross," which was the Stations of the Cross where they crucify Jesus then. And I was the Jesus!

JG: Really?

RC: Yeah. And I did a little acting. They put a crown of thorns on my hair.

Music as an Instrument for Discipline, Play, and Prestige

In the small pamphlet published to celebrate the 125th anniversary of St. Dominic's Home, it was reported that "it was ... in 1910 that Father Sutherland, O.P., much interested in the boys' welfare, thought it would be a good thing to create a 'Musical Society.' Commander Combs collected the necessary funds to buy the instruments. Mr. Turner devoted himself entirely to the training of the boys. Since then, the St. Dominic's Home Band has

1.2 Marching band and band rehearsal at the Children's Home. Courtesy Marie Thérèse Rétout, OP.

produced fine men for whom music was the springboard that led them to great achievements in life."[18]

While sports was (and continues to be) considered crucial to the development of children's physical and social skills, and a great source of pride in competitions between schools, music was judged equally important. This was not only because of the crucial role it played in the celebration of carnival and other special occasions, such as Christmas parties, but also because it helped instill discipline, both for those who were learning music and the other children as well.

As Sister Francine explains:

SF: So music was always forefront. The children used to play a march every morning, early in the morning, and the children marched down to school. It was just a discipline because it set everybody in a tune for the day. So the musicians had to be up early and ready.

JG: So some of the children would play the march on brass instruments?

SF: Yes, well, on wind and brass instruments, they used to play marches. They used to play a tune to march them to school every morning. So, they played simple tunes and they played marches. And as you developed, you got more difficult tunes.

JG: And apart from the marches, what other types of music would they learn, let's say, when Roy was there in the fifties?

SF: Well, first of all, it was orchestra music. And they played the music that was popular at the time. Like for instance, in Trinidad, every year, we have different calypso tunes. Now we have soca and those things, but in those days we didn't have soca and soca artists and so on. But, yes, we had calypso march. They have sports coming up, so they play for the sports. They practice a calypso march. They would learn to play the national anthem because at every function they would have to play that. And the children would take part in music festivals. Music festivals always had a test piece. So they learn those kinds of things.

JG: I see. So they would play at sports events and participate in the music festivals?

SF: Oh yes, and they used to win music festivals too. The children played trumpet solo, flute solo, trombone . . . and they would learn their pieces and they would practice and practice.

JG: Apart from the festivals, would they play sometimes in public, say, on special occasions?

SF: As I said to you, it's only now that nothing much is happening. The number [of children] has dwindled. But I remember being here with them [the children] at Christmas time. Every Christmas, there is a party at the prime minister's residence, and they would have the children's band playing. That means that the children could have played four, five tunes, you know? And maybe played a serenade. In the eighties, I used to say to Mr. Edward Alfonso [the music instructor], "prepare the children to do a little concert once a term—a concert here." The family comes to visit them, and they have a concert and the adults are here and let music come alive. And things got set up. Sometimes you just have to plan something. You have to keep the creativity juices flowing. And you had to keep them busy because if you have four hundred, three hundred children, and you don't keep them busy, right?

JG: So who provided the financing for the purchase of the instruments? Who supplied them? Wind and brass instruments are quite costly.

SF: Well, the Home always had the instruments. It's the tradition to pass things on and sometimes people would give a gift. They would say, "This is toward the music in the Home." Sometimes you had people who used to be musicians, and they have good, new instruments still. They no longer use them, so they gave them to us. Or somebody passed on. The family then would come and donate an instrument. The Police Band [members] used to repair our instruments, so we tried to keep them in a state of good repair. They [the Police Band members] would just be very good to us. We had instruments to repair? The Police Band repaired them.

1.3 Brass band of the Belmont Children's Home in concert. Courtesy Marie Thérèse Rétout, OP.

JG: So it would be mainly brass instruments and wind instruments. You wouldn't have string instruments like cello or violin or bass?

SF: Well, yes. We have . . . but right now we don't have anybody playing them. But we have a few.

JG: So you also had these instruments in the past.

SF: Yes . . . a few years ago, about three or four years ago [in 2005 or 2006], the ministry wanted to revive music. They were trying to form an orchestra, a national orchestra from children of schools and institutions, and they started, you know. Some children were playing cello and violin. . . . So you see, there are so many different opportunities now [that project with the schoolchildren was soon abandoned for reasons that I have not been able to assess].

I was intrigued by the fact that after more than half an hour in conversation with Sister Francine, there was no mention of girls in connection with music at the Children's Home. I soon learned that there were clear boundaries between boys and girls. While boys may have had access to music, girls would do sewing and cooking and dressmaking. This segregation of tasks was reinforced by a segregation of space. The band room, I was told, "was in the middle of the boys' dormitory, in the basement of the boys' dorm, and there was no entry area for the girls. So the boys alone were in music." Boys learned music not at school, but in their dormitories. And the dormitories for boys and girls were separate. So what were the conditions in which the boys learned to play a musical instrument? I turned to Roy to explain the musical instruction he received at the Children's Home.

JG: When you began to do some acting at the Children's Home, you were not playing saxophone yet, right?

RC: No, no, no. Saxophone came a long time after. At the Children's Home, the instruments were not accessible to the number of people who needed them. So you probably would have had a year, two years, observing and looking and learning theory before you can touch an instrument.

JG: There were not enough instruments?

RC: There weren't enough. There were two saxophones, an old Boosey and Hawkes from England, which was very popular, and then we had some horns from Czechoslovakia, and some of those instruments weren't so hot. The instrument was assigned to the senior guy. You couldn't touch that alto, because he was responsible for it. So I first sat and learned the E-flat clarinet, which is a very small, tiny clarinet. Because of my size, it was just right for me. And they didn't have much E-flat clarinets; they had one. And there was a brother named Cecil Joachim, who was the senior man, and he would give me a little blow on the instrument now and then, but . . . I didn't stay there too long because that clarinet was assigned to that senior. There weren't instruments for everybody. So you found yourself maybe two years, sitting around . . . learning theory, observing what the other guys are doing and when someone reached the age of sixteen, they would leave. It was up, then, to the bandmaster to say who, among the best players, would go on the instrument. So [eventually] I moved from there to the B-flat clarinet, which was at that time the simple system.[19] And . . . I had problems . . . in trying to absorb literature [to do sight reading]. But the manner of teaching I can't criticize, no. But it was terrible. I understand a little bit about psychology now . . . and if you're teaching a young child and you paranoid him, it freezes up the mental capacity, and you're not going to get nothing out of him.

JG: Nothing at all.

RC: Because they're blocked up. And, at that time, I don't want to blame them because maybe these were things that were handed to them, but the teachers were tolerant-less, especially with children. And, at the end of the day, I would be sitting by myself and I would see him [the music teacher] coming up the road through the big gate. I used to find myself standing behind the music stand playing just over the fear of him then. Um . . . so . . . I had been in the band for some time. People leave, you know, people leave. People progress a little further. In the clarinet section, there's a solo clarinet, first clarinet, repiano, the second clarinet, and the third and fourth clarinet.

So, after playing the fourth and then the third clarinet part, I ended up on what they called the repiano stand.[20] The repiano part is recognized as performing solo, simply to a lesser extent than the solo and first clarinet. . . . But I still had a problem with the reading, because I never really got the true tutoring. . . . Most of the guys that grew up with me at my time, those around my age, didn't have that opportunity as the guys who were a little older. They got a better teaching.

JG: Older guys like Frankie Francis?[21]

RC: Yes.

JG: He would've had much better training?

RC: Yes, very much so. Having just four years to do so many things—finishing my schooling, learning a professional trade, and also dealing with the music—that did not give me the opportunity to concentrate on one thing. Um . . . but I liked to play by ear the music of some of the great musicians that I had heard. While doing this, myself and a couple guys, we would say that we were playing jazz. The reason for that is that we were trying to improvise ad lib solos.

JG: So already then you started learning how to improvise.

RC: One day I was in the band room with some of the guys. We went to the instrument room and we decided to have a jazz session. One of the other musicians who was not part of this experience took the padlock and locked us in the band room. This caused great panic around us. I was unmounting the clarinet, and I had it in two parts. I swished the clarinet to take out the saliva accumulated in it, and the mouth piece flew and broke. I was kind of frightened because discipline was the order of the day.

JG: You were in trouble then.

RC: I was in trouble. So they put me to make concrete bricks, and I was getting a penny for one brick.

JG: To pay for the repair of the instrument?

RC: Yes. But I was not wearing any shoes or slippers, so after a couple of weeks of that, the cement started to eat my hands and my feet. I could not walk properly without pain! A decision was then taken to take me out of this punishment, which taught me a serious lesson.

Reflecting on the period he spent at the orphanage, Roy adds:

RC: So I spent those four years there. I can say that I am the first person who ever made a mattress inside of Belmont orphanage, the first boy that made a mattress. There was a French nun named Sister Reginald who was in charge of the tailor shop. So they would have this thing that was called a *casier* (a small locker), which is like a hole and they had your number in it (mine was 106), and all my clothes went in there, then. And I ended up when I was about fourteen or fifteen years old to be the top tailor in the institution. So I had a special dialogue with Sister Reginald, as the sister was directly responsible for us then. I used to make the priests' and the nuns' clothes.

JG: Really?

RC: And there was also a lovely French nun named Mother Joseph. She had a gold tooth. She was a pretty lady. And Mother Joseph taught me how to beat the fiber up in the attic. We called that a garret. So we used to beat all the fiber in there. You had to have a fiber mask and things like that. Um . . . these were rough times. And I would say, not to degrade the lovely jobs of the sisters . . . and what the system has done . . . because a lot of delinquent people came through, and a lot of positiveness came through, you know, with no mother and father, and . . . the sisters couldn't give us individual love because there was so many children. Yet though, there were little special people that needed that softness according to how delicate the situation of these people might be, then. Um . . . it was tough.

Training Ground for Future Professional Musicians

The learning of a trade was part of the school curriculum, and so it was taught during class time. By contrast, music was considered an extracurricular activity and was taught early in the morning or after school hours. After the initial few years of the orphanage, during which private citizens provided musical training to the boys, the instructors who took over music instruction were usually musicians who grew up in the Children's Home and who were now part of the Police Band. The musical instrumentation was based on the British marching band, and accordingly, the children learned marching band repertoire, including classical music from Beethoven, Bach, or even Strauss. It was because, as Roy explained, this was the music that the

Police Band played. Through this connection with the Police Band, the children were provided with copies of music scores. And through this training, those who qualified were recruited to fill vacant posts in the Police Band. This was the case, for instance, during Roy's stay, of Sergeant Thomas, who grew up in the Children's Home. While he assumed his duties as a corporal and then as sergeant, he would go to the Children's Home two or three times a week to supervise the music instruction provided by his assistant.

The Children's Home thus became a training ground for the Police Band and at times its replacement. When the Police Band was too busy to perform, the Belmont orphanage band or the other orphan home in Trinidad at the time, based in Tacarigua (now renamed the St. Mary's Home for Children), would often be sent to play in their place. For example, they might play at the botanical gardens, at the governor's house, or at the president's residence. This was thought to be an excellent preparation for the music students, allowing them to acquire professional training for their future careers.

Some of the biggest names in the history of Trinidadian music came from children's homes.

RC: Roderick Borde distinguished himself by being among the "early people" in documenting calypso and the musical form. Frankie Francis, who had perfect pitch, and who could write an entire score without any instruments around him, became one of the most respected arrangers and saxophone players in the region. Errol Ince is probably one of our best trumpet players ever. On attaining independence from England, which I will call "the changing of the guards," the last British bandmaster, Superintendent Taylor, returned to England. The late Mr. Anthony Prospect, who came from the Home, joined the Police Band and after going through the ranks—corporal, sergeant, inspector—went to England to study at the Royal School of Music, qualifying for the licentiate of the Royal Schools of Music. He then rose to the highest rank of superintendent of the Trinidad and Tobago Police Band. Mr. Prospect was the first local musician to attain such a rank and the first bandmaster to play marches in calypso at the most official moment of the year, the Independence Day parade.[22]

As Roy explained, his initiative to rework marches in the local musical style was significant in the nation-building process and brought him the support of the nation. His desire to fuse military music with local calypso, while maintaining military discipline with a party atmosphere, was not only a feat but a great inspiration for generations to come. It drew massive crowds to participate in this parade yearly.

Roy's experience at the Children's Home was formative and had long-lasting impact in his musical life. As Sherry Ann De Leon indicates, "Growing up in the orphanage between 1954 and 1958, Cape met some of his best friends, who all evolved into great, great, great . . . musicians. . . . Among them were Ron Berridge, Major Eddie Wade, Norbert Pesson, Fortunia Ruiz, Roderick Borde, and Frankie Francis. Together they all made music in the institution's religious musical productions staged on the orphanage lawn, like 'The Way of the Cross' and at Christmas time, 'The Nativity'" (1996: 12).

ON LEAVING THE INSTITUTION: A MIXTURE OF JOY AND ANXIETY

RC: Yeah, yeah. In that period of time, when you had one year again to go, you count every day, you know—364 days, 363, 362, and down the road, you know. And you'd be looking to go! But when it get closer, you start to get a little scared because, although we were living in a kind of collectiveness, and you couldn't have individualism in that sense, there was a form of security. We were looked after, supervised. So after four years, one didn't know after going out what you was going back to. Because that amount of time [I spent at the orphanage] didn't make no difference for Mommy and Pappy. They was still seeing hell. All the time in my mind I'd be hearing, "Go to school, boy, go to school, go to school. Later on in life, you're going to regret it." I won't say that I regret it. But what I can say to a young person is education is important. And if you have the spirit to be able to take an education, then an education is the means of getting out of poverty and squalor and living that is unfit to a human being. Because God has made human beings all dignified . . . and because of man's system, there are people that have so much and people that don't have any. One of my beliefs is that all the tumult we have in the world is because of all of this: some people have so much and some people have none. Some people don't even have a hope. This wonderful human species that God has created just goes up just like that . . . [Roy pauses]. So, when the time came, I had to leave on April 1958, at the age of sixteen.

2 • WORKING AS A BANDSMAN

Bandsmen have a specific relationship to the music they play. Unlike producers, composers, arrangers, or individual stars, they do not usually own copyrights. They are wage laborers. In the narrative that follows, Roy speaks as a bandsman, with the consciousness of a working musician. He sets the stage for the work that goes into the production of music. It is important for him to explain what goes into preparing for a show, and doing a master tape at a recording studio. It is equally vital for him to specify the socioeconomic conditions in which he performed as a band member on the island or on tour, and to describe the sound technologies that enhanced or constrained the ability of the bands in the 1960s to be heard at their best. In the same vein, it is also critical for him to mention which bands he played with, and where they could perform. In this chapter, Roy addresses what can be called the materiality of sound production. By "materiality of sound," I do not simply refer to acoustics, to sound as a physical manifestation of energy. Rather, I mean to connect acoustics to the things—for example, the musical instruments, recording equipment, and sound amplification devices—that led the bands Roy played with to acquire their distinctive sound. Moreover, I wish to connect acoustics and things to material culture more broadly. This is crucial because the habits that Roy and his bandmates have formed, and the aesthetic values they have privileged, are connected through the use of sounding and sound-making materials. These materials, these things, have been constitutive, even if not at all times determinant, of Roy's musical sensibility and his work ethic.¹ In what follows, Roy shows how both the material worlds and the social relations that have informed his life as well as his own efforts must all be taken into account to explain what enabled his circulation and reputation as a musician.

As a working musician, Roy's narrative also demonstrates pride of craft, what it means to care about the work of playing music and doing it well. This pride, it should be stressed, is different from ego. It concerns the meticulousness of an arranger or the flawless technique of a musician—the deliberateness of playing to surpass oneself. It is intimately linked to working consciousness. In his story, Roy pays tribute to the musicians he has played with, and those who have demonstrated this kind of work pride.

Roy's narrative constantly makes reference to the synergy of musicians working together, its crucial importance in music making and learning, and its role in one's personal journey and development. Throughout this chapter, Roy recognizes those musicians who have been both models and mentors—those who have been generous toward him and helped him go forward.

Roy provides more than simply lists of facts or names. He is producing a memoryscape, one that reveals the consciousness of a working musician at particular times and in particular places.² As a bandsman who cares about his work, he reveals what he finds important to remember. His recollection of the past covers nearly two decades of self-transformation. His view of the past changes as it travels from the consciousness, frustrations, and desires of an adolescent to a young, aspiring, and struggling musician; to a thriving and recognized saxophonist; to a nostalgic adult; and to a tireless, forward-looking, experienced working musician performing with some of the best musicians from the Caribbean, the United States, and Canada.³ So, in the following pages, the themes that Roy addresses vary greatly, yet they are all intimately connected to what the life of a working musician in a postcolonial country like Trinidad, for more than fifty years, has been all about.

In this chapter, Roy takes the lead. I am sitting next to him, writing on the computer as he tells his stories. Roy concentrates hard, and I try not to interrupt his flow of memories, even though at times I have to ask him to spell the names of people or places. My exploration of Trinidadian daily newspapers of the late 1950s and 1960s confirmed that there was hardly any documentation or even mention of the musicians he speaks about during that period. Typically, only the names of bandleaders, if that much, were mentioned to promote a dance or concert. So I wanted Roy to tell the stories as best—and as much—as he can recall. My interjections in the text only reveal myself as an avid listener. Sometimes, during one of Roy's stories about a particular band, I would ask him to speak about certain aspects he had not addressed yet. These aspects became the headings of the different sections of Roy's band stories.

Roy's stories can be seen as the A side of the record. I wanted to offer a B side, my take on some of the themes that Roy focuses on. I also wanted to explore the connections Roy's stories helped me establish in terms of local, regional, and international music industries, academic concerns, and personal interests. I decided to do this in a parallel text, both to avoid interrupting Roy's voice and also to be able to engage Roy dialogically. My side of the record came after rereading and reflecting on the stories Roy told. It shows the spiraling effect of learning new knowledge, more specifically, of my learning from Roy, and from conversations with friends and colleagues in and outside the Caribbean—conversations generated by Roy's stories. It shows how Roy's stories prompted the rereading of academic and journalistic publications and sparked much new thinking. My side of the record is set in endnotes, to elaborate, amplify, connect, revisit, discuss, and engage with Roy's richly detailed account of his musical journey, and that of many other musicians in this significant moment of Trinidad's history—on the eve and the aftermath of its gaining independence.

"Okay, Roy, I am ready. Right after the orphanage, you were saying . . ."

TIME OF RETURN
Work by Day, Music at Night

RC: So, in those days, they would say that a musician was a "sweet" man—referring to a man who dressed nicely and was taken care of by a lady. My mother, she didn't want the children to mess with music and become musicians with the kind of environment such as the nightclubs. She was concerned that music was not at the time a meaningful profession—as the history had shown up to that time that a musician's life is very hard and financially unpredictable. And this why she wanted me to have an education because she thought it would give me a form of security in life to come.

After leaving the orphanage, I began working as a tailor with Mr. Mackie Boyce, who also came from the orphanage. (Mackie Boyce was also one of my music teachers in the orphanage. He later became a member of the Police Band.) After two weeks, I was not happy doing tailoring as it had no financial advancement. I spoke to my mom and I showed her how frustrated

I was in that job, and she understood what I was saying to her. The owner of the tailoring establishment paid us a visit and asked why I had not come back to work. My mom told him that I was not happy with what I was doing, and that it was my decision to leave this job since I was the one who was involved and she could not make a decision for me.

JG: Two weeks?

RC: She tells me, "I cannot force you, but I would hope that you don't do the same thing you did before you went to the orphanage: you have come back home to continue and just sit on the side of the road." So, one morning, I put on a white shirt and tie, and I went to town to the Alston Hardware, a big British company. They had all sorts of shipping and glassworks and travel agency. (Today, most of these things are owned by McEnearney, which is a big, reputable company in Trinidad.) The boss was a man named Mr. Roy Veira, a kind of Portuguese-looking man, a white guy, kind of short, stocky; he was a neat, neat man. Mr. Veira was all right. I went to him, and he gave me a job for twelve dollars a week. I was so glad. This is around the end of 1958, 1959, around there. Even though I had to go to work to the hardware store at eight o'clock in the morning, I was still going to the clubs at night. When I got home from work, I went to the clubs. Playing in nightclubs looked like a nice life, working in the night and sleeping all day. And well, I liked clothes. So older musicians keep telling the guys in my band, "When this guy was young, he was one of the sharpest guys in town."

I wanted to be in things. I would get an instrument borrowed here or there, and sometimes the guy can't find me for months!

JG: Because you had his instrument and you didn't want to give it back?

RC: It might be a big, bad guy, and I didn't care! [laughs]. It took me from 1958 to 1963 before I could buy my own horn. . . . It cost $600-plus in those days, and Pappy was working for $12 a week, so it was a lot of borrowing instruments going on.[4]

Jamming with the Brothers from the Orphanage

RC: In 1959, I began jamming with musicians. This is when I began to play with John Alexander (trombone) who ended up as a corporal in the Police Band. I met John Alexander at the Miramar nightclub where he was playing. John had taken a liking to me since I was also from the orphanage. He was from Tacarigua [now called St. Mary's Home] and I was from Belmont [St. Dominic's Children's Home]. I had first met him at the orphanage in Belmont where he sometimes came and jammed with us. He would play every part individually and teach us songs.

I used to go to meet John at night and hang out with him. He was then staying at the St. Mary's After-Care Home. Most times we would leave the club at morning time. So I would go to the After-Care Home and sometimes I would sleep there.[5] My mom knew that I was with John and thus knew that I was safe. John was a guy of good size—someone you wouldn't mess around with.

I used to go to the clubs every night—one night it was Miramar or Reno or Stork or Casbah or Pepper Pot. On Park Street, there were many nightclubs: Waldorf Astoria, Club 48. You just had to go to get the vibe. It was something you had to do. Sometimes you could not even get to play, but if you were promising, the elders would give you a little push and find songs that you could play so you could get a chance to gig with them.[6]

All these nightclubs had little quartets, four people plus maybe two horn players. There would be bass, guitar, keyboard, drums. And you might have two horns with it, so, you make it a sextet.

I started to draw a little closer with the Catholic Youth Organization, the C.Y.O. Band. Claude Martineau was playing in the C.Y.O. Band. He was the secretary in the C.Y.O. Band. Some of my friends who grew up in the institution had also come out and we were associating there together. However, even though we were jamming, we still needed to get a job.

In the meantime with the help of John Boodoosingh, I was hired as a tally clerk at the Camacho Brothers Dry Goods Outlet.[7] I used to check all the groceries that would come in from the Port of Spain wharf, and I would have to check all items that went out to delivery.

SELWYN WHEELER ORCHESTRA, 1960–1961
The Highs and Lows of the First Tour Experience

RC: When I left the orphanage, I began to play the alto saxophone. From that time on, anything I got to play was alto. There was a brother whose name was Selwyn Wheeler who plays trombone. He presently lives in New York. He was great to us. We were learning, and he was teaching us. We were in a band with him because we were from the same institution and brotherhood.[8] His mom had a big house in Trinidad, but she was now living in the United States. So we as young fellas had some place to hang out.

After I left the Camacho brothers, I went on a tour in 1961 with Sel[wyn]'s band to Grenada, Antigua, via Martinique to go to St. Lucia to meet the band. From there we went to Barbados. I went there with Lord Superior and

2.1 Selwyn Wheeler Orchestra's recording of "The Mocking Bird Song" on 45.

Lord Brynner [sobriquet for Kade Simon, who won the crown for the best calypso in the first Calypso King competition for independence in 1962].

We first went to Grenada, then, Antigua. We were kicked out of the hotel after the promoters could not pay the bill. As I was the youngest one, Superior and Brynner kept me with them. As the owners of the hotel wanted to evict us, we went through the window with a bedsheet tied as a rope to get out. There was this guy from Antigua named Bill Abbott who had a nightclub, but I would call it a "garden nightclub," because he had rooms and he had ladies doing their trade there. He took us in. Being an entertainer, he could have.

Clarence Wears (the guitarist) met a girlfriend whose father had a bakery. They also had a lime tree, so it was bread and lime juice. But, by that time, all the guys said, "We got to get a girlfriend!" So a lady named Daisy who used to work at the club had seen me and she had liked me, but she didn't like me, say, for a lover. She had liked me because I was small and cute and looked so delicate. And she took me up by her house! And I was eating and living and drinking—nice!⁹ So when the time came for us to leave, they couldn't find me, and the band left for St. Lucia. But my bandleader Sel[wyn] stayed back with my passport. So when I did come from the hills in Antigua, he was still waiting on me. By then, the band had gone straight to St. Lucia.

Sel[wyn] and I could not take a plane from Antigua to St. Lucia at the time we wanted, so we left and went to Martinique to get to St. Lucia. In Martinique, there were a lot of bars extending to the sidewalk with a canopy over that otherwise open space. We sat on the sidewalk with our BWIA [British West Indian Airways] ticket exposed. When some guys passing saw the BWIA ticket, they asked us whether we were from Trinidad. As we answered yes, they said, "No problem. We're Trinidadians." They were dredging the port [in other words, since these guys were working and earning money in Martinique, they could help Roy and Selwyn]. So they took us out, fed us, and took us to their home. In the morning, we got up and ate French bread—the very first time I had seen French bread, the long bread! [Roy laughs heartily.] They gave us money and took us to the airport for us to go to St. Lucia.

The show we did in St. Lucia was the best attended show we had in terms of economics, but a St. Lucian lady working at the door ran away with all the money. And Lord Brynner and Superior ran her down what we call a dry river (which has water in it only when heavy rains fall).

We ended up in Barbados and we met a man named Mr. Johnson who had a company named Johnson and Redman. He and his partner had a bakery and they had also a club named Cloud 9. Both of them liked the band and gave us some gigs at the club.

While we were staying there, we met some girls and their brothers who happened to be named also Johnson, but with no relationship with Johnson and Redman. And we made friends. When they found out that we were musicians, they invited us to their home and we met their mom and dad. I could have done barbering, so I trimmed the dad's hair. I cut his hair! I ended up the favorite in the house. So here I was with the mother and father and the sisters, and I liked one of them. She was older than me, but I was too young to understand these things then. I was madly in love with her! They had two houses, one on either side of the street facing each other. One of these houses was very close to the beach. And it was in this house in which I lived. When the guys were leaving for Trinidad, Sel Wheeler, Clarence Wears, and myself decided to stay back in Barbados.

After everybody went back home, my mom wrote to me and told me, "Time to come back home." So I went back to Trinidad. And when I went back to Trinidad, Mr. Frankie Francis came to me. I had known about him,

2.2 Frankie Francis featured as a guest star, 1972.

because he had also come from the orphanage. Listening to the elders, you would hear them talk about the good musicians, you know. And Frankie Francis was reputed as one of the best ones in the country.

FRANKIE FRANCIS'S STUDIO BAND AND CALYPSO TENT BAND, 1961–1962
Recording at TELCO Studio

RC: After my tour with Selwyn Wheeler, Frankie Francis came to me and asked me to join him at the studio. I don't know whether it was because I played alto saxophone and he also played alto saxophone, for which he was very famous, or whether he saw me as family, like his son, since he too came from the orphanage. He asked me to come with him, and I said, "Frank, we have a whole band, and there are many guys that I have grown up with. I just can't leave them there." So he answered, "I will take the whole band." We were based at TELCO Recording at Champ Fleurs. And Frankie was the musical director-producer of TELCO recording studio.[10]

Whenever Frankie said, "Record," we recorded. The recordings at TELCO were done with an Ampex machine, which was used by all the radio stations in those days. The radio station people used to go to the calypso tents and record the live shows, and do radio broadcasting.

Recordings in those days were done with two microphones. One microphone was directed toward the whole band, and another one aimed at the singer. And everything would be recorded all at once [Roy claps his hands].

JG: In one take.

RC: Yeah. The difficulty was, if you're doing a calypso, and you do it fifty times, and on the fifty-first time, on the last band chorus, one of the horns made an error, it was all over again.[11] It is not like today where you have individual tracks that you can delete individually and record individually.

One day, Frankie had done an arrangement for one guy in England, and he wanted to send a copy to another guy somewhere in Europe. Well, I did not know anything about transposing, but he gave me the music to transcribe. One reason was for me to make some money and another reason was that he wanted me to develop my skills. (In those times, there were no Xerox machines.) But I would make mistakes. However, slowly I learned.[12]

Playing On the Road on Carnival Tuesday

RC: I played mas' [a local expression for masquerade] when I was in the orphanage. And then after coming out, I played mas' in 1958 and 1959 with Trinidad All Stars. And by 1960 the music started to happen a little and I lost those inclinations to play as a masquerader.

I began to play on the road on carnival day with Francis in 1962.[13] And as young musicians, it was an opportunity to play with the elders. So Frankie took us on the road and we had four saxophones, three trombones, four trumpets and bass drum, snare drum, and percussion. We had no vocals. You had the bass drums strapped on like a marching band, the snare drums on like a marching band, and you would have some pieces of irons and other percussion—many instruments because of the inaccessibility of amplification and also because it was hard work to play on the road all day long, and you needed support.[14]

JG: So you did not have any bass or guitar?

RC: No, you wouldn't have these instruments because we were on the road. There was no amplification yet. It was all acoustic. The instrumentation I just described to you was a fantastic band.

JG: So you had to have a great number of musicians.

RC: Yeah. Since in those days there was no electronics and we were walking, we had to have numbers [many players]. So the saxophones would play the verse (which was always the longer part of the melody in calypso), and the chorus would always be the part that you jam on. So the brass would always be jamming with a full chorus (the full band together). There were never arrangements for these things. Sometimes you would walk two blocks, and the elders would say: saxophone you're playing the verse, trumpets and trombones, the chorus. In a very quick time, we would have the verse, they would have the chorus, and by the time we walk about two blocks, that song would be cooked [done]. So we would go to another song. So you had to be able to retain quickly. It was lovely.

As we were walking with the people, we had a technique of how to walk and play on the streets. We had to drag our feet to avoid stumbl[ing] over canal holes and bust our mouth.

That was around 1962. By the end of the 1960s, you would have a guitarist who had an amplifier with an electrical device (battery or something) with the help of somebody pushing the battery and amplifier in a box cart—a box cart was a cart with some wheels that we would just push like those used by the stevedores [the dockworkers] to deliver goods from the port to the merchants around the city. And you know, the people like Dutchy Brothers and Mano Marcelin [the leaders of the groups by the same name] probably were the people, the innovators with mobility.

JG: What do you mean by that?

RC: Well, when we were pushing a box cart, Dutchies and Mano had already gone on a pickup truck.[15] With a truck, it was, "Okay, let's go!" But until then, we actually used to walk—all of us walking!

JG: And playing!

RC: But in those days, the noise decibel wasn't as large as today. Today the world has modernized. All these machines and factories running in the morning: that is a form of noise pollution. That's pollution. And that type of pollution creates a hum, which means that we have to talk louder and we have to play louder in that party. Before it was more quiet.[16]

Playing on the road during carnival was a fantastic experience. But at the TELCO recording studio the pressure was on with me because Frankie Francis was a super alto saxophone player. He could read on sight. So, when I replaced him, I felt a lot of pressure, and I was still very young. So there used to be a lot of tension. The studio is a contagious something: if there was mistakes and you lost your nerves, sometimes you can't recover it. So I found out about Clarence Curvan's band, and I went to see them. Their arranger was Beverly Griffith. He was a very famous arranger for music bands and eventually for the Desperadoes steelband. I saw Beverly teaching the guys how to play the way you learn in a panyard, and I said, "This is what I want to do! I want to learn to play." They were killing me in the studio with music, music, music! And I was impressed by the method that Beverly Griffith was using to motivate all the young guys. I decided to go and hang out there. So one night we were recording at TELCO, and Clarence Curvan was playing at Couva. At that time, Clarence's band was the youngest band in Trinidad, and he was the youngest bandleader. Well, all of us was young, so there was young girls of our ages, and it was exciting and challenging. So there I was in the studio. I was making mistakes because my mind was in Couva and all the excitement I was missing.

So, that night, Frankie said to me, "Young boy, before we fall out, look, the sax is there, take it and go. And when you get one, bring it back in one piece for me." I joined Clarence Curvan's band and that groomed me into the musician that I am today.

However, before I moved on to play with this other band, I played in the calypso tent in 1962 with Frankie Francis. The first time I played in a calypso tent was at the Original Young Brigade, which was headed by Lord Melody and Sparrow. They had singers like Nap Hepburn, Conqueror, Zebra, Commander, Spider, Caruso, and so on.

Coming up from the struggle, working in jobs from $6 to $12, my first time in a calypso tent, I got $100 a week. And Pa, who was the man of the house, was working for only $12 in a Chinese laundry. So my sisters used to say, "Oh, look at all the money Roy's making!" But in those days, we were young, and we were spending the money.

JG: But when you left Frankie for Clarence Curvan, you left the tent, you left that scene?

RC: Yeah.

Performing Local and International Musical Styles

JG: Before we move to the next band you played with, could you tell me what type of repertoire you mainly performed with Frankie Francis? Did you play calypso exclusively at the recording studio?

RC: Not only. We played boleros; we played foxtrot; we would've played jive, Latin. Because in those days, for dances—before my time—there were big bands. So it was all like the Tommy Dorsey and uh . . . swing used to happen in the nightclubs. We were having American tourists. So you had to be able to play swing. We were always ambitious to play jazz because we were aware of jazz in America.

There was an American radio station named WVDI in Trinidad while the Americans had the naval base in Trinidad. So we were able to hear American music. Plus, since the war had just finished, there were a lot of ships and sailors coming to Trinidad. So you would see and hear the sailors' Navy Band and things like this.

In those days, the music that was played was not like today—playing only one type of music, like we do now with soca. We played an all-round session [meaning many different musical styles]. And in those days, a party would have started at 8:00 p.m. or 8:30 p.m., and finish at 4:00 a.m. with only one band, no microphones. You couldn't take much of a rest. And in those days those people used to drink. A man look at another man and yell, and a fight break out, then. And if a fight break out, we have to play music, because the only thing then is to distract them from the fight.[17]

JG: So you would continue to play? Mmm . . . would you have, say, three bolero tunes and after that three other tunes in another style, and so on?

RC: We played foxtrot, bolero, samba, bossa nova, Latin music (Tito Puente, etc.), calypso, R&B (Temptations, the Spinners, Aretha Franklin, Ray Charles). We would have a session of one hour followed by a fifteen-minute break and then you come back on again and then you would play until 4 a.m. in the morning. We would make up a program where we begin the program cool and then we go up and up to close the night off at the faster tempo. Making a program is trying to anticipate the thinking and the pleasure of your audience and what you would think, by market trends, people would like.[18] We have always been playing a wide repertoire of music. But I guess as the country evolved and we got independence, there was an effort to compose and write our own local music and to have our own Hit Parade.

There was a program called 610 Hit Parade on the radio station named 610 Radio Guardian. We had a [local] song called "610 Saga," which stayed on the Hit Parade longer than any other song. And then we had songs like "Crying in the Rain," "Rhapsody in Blue."

JG: So you would play everything.

RC: Everything. And we used to take the American songs and British songs and play them in calypso.[19]

JG: And this is the repertoire that you were playing in the early 1960s with Frankie?

RC: Well, we played the same kind of repertoire with both Frankie and Clarence Curvan.

CLARENCE CURVAN'S BAND, 1962–1964
New Start as a Professional Musician

RC: I left Frankie Francis's band, and I went to Clarence Curvan's in 1962. It is with Clarence Curvan's band that my career really began. Ron Berridge had gone to Fitz Vaughn Bryan's band, but he didn't stay there long. He heard us play at a dance, which was then a nonstop, with Fitz Vaughn Bryan and Clarence Curvan at the Maple Leaf Club on St. Vincent Street.[20] Although Fitz Vaughn Bryan had musicians who were older than us and with more experience than we had, Clarence Curvan's band had a very good showing against the might of Fitz Vaughn Bryan (then called Sir Fitz Vaughn Bryan, knighted by the people because of his greatness). We were all young and full of energy. Berridge was impressed by our performance against Fitz Vaughn Bryan, and made up his mind to join the band.[21] He said, Scrape (he used to call me Scrape), I think I will come now." And he sat right down and talked to Clarence, and Berridge joined the band.

When I went with Clarence, Clarence's band had three altos: Lloyd Benjamin, Carlton "Choylin" Aman (who is now living here in Toronto), and me.[22] I said to Bev [the arranger Beverly Griffith] that I had heard from the elders that the combination for the woodwind instruments is the alto sax and the tenor sax, not three altos. The tenor has a full sound, whereas the alto has its distinct melodic sound. He said to me, "Who will play the tenor?" I answered, "Me." But I had never played a tenor. We borrowed one, and I did maybe two albums with Clarence playing tenor saxophone.

Berridge and myself grew up together, so we had a friendship. I encouraged him to come to the band room to sit with the arranger, Beverly Griffith, and do the alto parts. I would then use it as my master score. When Berridge would leave, Beverly would sit with me. I didn't know anything about transposing, but he used to call the tenor notes to me and I would watch the alto part and write the tenor part.

Competing with the Elders

RC: It was a wonderful experience because we were all young and we had our own audience. The others like Fitz Vaughn Bryan or Sel Duncan or Watty

2.3 and 2.4
Body and Soul
by Clarence
Curvan's band.

Watkins, the bigger bands had their own audience. When Fitz Vaughn Bryan or Sel Duncan were playing in San Fernando, we could not play in San Fernando proper as we had to keep out of the way of those two bands.

But as the years went on, we realized that these musicians and their fans were getting older and the greater part of the population was young. So after a while, the young bands took over. These included Clarence Curvan, Dutchy Brothers, and Joey Lewis. During this period we had people like Fitz Vaughn Bryan or Sel Duncan or Watty Watkins and some like that. [These were the] bigger bands [that existed] before the combo days.[23]

JG: When you were playing with Clarence Curvan, was it mainly instrumental or did you have also some singers in the band?

RC: It was all instrumental. We played at a lot of fetes and we probably did in two years or something over six albums, and we did maybe thirty small 45s. We used to record a new 45 maybe every month. We used to have a record company in Trinidad called Cook Recording, which was founded by an American man named Mr. Emory Cook.[24] And Mr. Cook had mastering and stamping in Trinidad. In those days, the tape had to be mastered. Cook had that facility, so we could have done a song today, and in two days' time, the song could be ready to be released.[25] TELCO and RCA had to send it to Barbados or the United States to be mastered. And then, after receiving the master, Dr. Roy Sampath and Mr. Whiteman (who were the owners of TELCO) and Mr. Leslie Samaroo (who had an RCA franchise in Trinidad and Tobago and owned also the local label Tropico) used to press their records in Trinidad and Tobago.[26]

Playing Days and Performing Venues

JG: In the early 1960s, would you perform usually on the weekends?

RC: Friday, Saturday, and Sunday, but more often Saturday and Sunday.

JG: And would there be other occasions to play, for example, at weddings?

RC: You would have had weddings, yeah. We would play on tours and in hotels. The calypsonians were doing their thing, and the dance bands were doing their own thing. As a dance band, we would play a mixture of music; for example, songs like "April Love," Minuet in G, most of the top forties, including the Beatles, Marvin Gaye, Gladys Knight, Aretha Franklin, Elvis Presley, Duke Ellington, Count Basie, and Glenn Miller.[27] And of course, we would play a fair share of our calypso music, but all in instrumental versions since there were no singers in this era of dance bands in Trinidad and

Tobago. Each band did its own arrangement of the popular songs of the season so that each band would have its unique sound.

JG: Did these dance bands go in the calypso tents or competitions?

RC: No, no.

JG: You were not a part of that scene?

RC: No, that was a whole scene by itself.

By the end of 1964, I made a move. Ron Berridge was offered to work at the Original Revue Calypso tent, which was based at the Strand Theatre on Tragerete Road. While Leslie Samaroo was into the music, his other brother Dennis was into the cinema. Dennis, who was in the cinema, gave Leslie a concession to have the cinema, and Leslie turned the cinema into a calypso tent. And he made the stage with a catwalk. Up to that point, all stages were flat. So for the first time, we had different levels of ramps, so visually the musicians playing in the lower ramp would not interfere with the musicians in the higher ramps. This was new to Trinidad as we would normally have performed on one flat stage. But Mr. Samaroo belonged to a family into cinemas and the film industry. He was thus aware and very conscious of the movies' aesthetics. He was thus giving the calypso tent audience the visuals of what you would see in the movies at that time. He was a visionary who was way ahead of the times in Trinidad and Tobago.

And so in 1964 I left Clarence Curvan with Conrad Little (the bass player) to go with Ron Berridge to be part of Ron Berridge's Orchestra to play at that calypso tent named the Original Revue.

RON BERRIDGE'S BAND, 1964–1967; SONGS INCORPORATED, 1967; RON BERRIDGE'S BAND, 1967–1968

RC: Ron Berridge accepted to work at the Original Revue because it was the easiest platform to launch the band and to have exposure with top-class material and artists. As one of his band members, I was playing in the Revue in 1965 when Sniper won the Calypso King title with the song "The Portrait of Trinidad." The recording of this song with Ron Berridge's band in 1964 is a classic that is often played up to today.

Ron Berridge Orchestra didn't stay at the Revue, however, because we had our eyes set out somewhere else. After the carnival, an impresario, a guy from Guyana named Clifton Frasier, took people outside to other countries, and at that time it happened to be Barbados. After hearing the band

2.5 and 2.6
The "A" Train by Ron Berridge and Orchestra.

at the Strand Theatre, Clifton said, "I never pick a wrong horse. This band is better than any other band I've ever heard." He took us to Barbados. But the promotion wasn't good. The band was playing beautiful music, but nobody knew us. So we went through hard times, sleeping on mattresses on the floor. That's how bad it was then. By the time we returned to Trinidad, the songs that we had recorded by the Tropico label had been released. Michael Tobas and myself went to the Dutchy Brothers and asked them to do what we call a nonstop.

Playing Opportunities

JG: A nonstop refers to two bands competing?

RC: Yes. As soon as one band finishes playing, the other band gets on and plays. We called it a nonstop because it was continuous music. In an ordinary dance, there was one band performing for the whole night. The band would be advertised to start at 8:30 p.m. and finish at 4 a.m. The evening would always end with "God Save the Queen," and typically the audience would ask for an encore on the F jam. [An F jam is based on a standard chord progression—I–VI–II–V–I—and at times, in an extended version, playing off the repeated bass sequence F–A–B-flat–B-natural–C–D–G–C–F—while the other instruments would play typical riffs in a call-and-response over this harmonic progression.]

After this nonstop with the Dutchy Brothers, we headed for the dance hall, and we were instantly successful.

In Berridge's band, we had Ron Berridge on first trumpet, Peter Bonnelle on second and solo trumpet, who was called by the elders "Diz," in reference to Dizzy Gillespie. This gives you an idea of the high-quality musicians we had in the band. Another band member, Neville Oxley, is known as one of the best trombone players in the history of Trinidad. Neville Aird, who used to play with Fitz Vaughn Bryan, played tenor sax, and I played alto. Our band also included Scipio Sargeant, a fantastic guitarist who could have played jazz. Sargeant and I played together in Clarence Curvan Band, and then we continued with Ron Berridge band. But when Berridge, Little, and I left Clarence, Sargeant didn't leave immediately and only later joined us when the band became more popular. Together we did 1965, 1966, and 1967 in Berridge's band. Kitchener came back sometime late in 1963. Mr. Leslie Samaroo had hired Lord Kitchener as the star of the Revue when he opened the tent in 1964. And in 1965 the Ron Berridge Orchestra found itself accompanying many new singers at the Revue.[28] Kitchener came back to Trinidad to live permanently in Trinidad in 1965 or something like that, and Ron

Berridge Orchestra did Kitchener's LP albums in 1966, 1967, and 1968 and also Sparrow's 1968 album.

After the Ron Berridge Orchestra left the Revue after the carnival season 1965, the Dutchy Brothers band gave us a nonstop. Toby and myself didn't have a paint brush to stick up the posters to advertise it. So we stuck up the posters with starch with our hands on the lamp poles all around town [Port of Spain].[29] The dance was at Naparima Club in San Fernando. It had a nice audience. After that night, we got every Saturday booked for the next six months.

By then, we were well known. We had played for the calypso semifinals in 1965 and we had also played for the finals. It was the first time that one band was playing for the whole competition. Before 1965 each calypso tent would have brought the tent band to perform for the artist performing at the competition. But in 1965, the Ron Berridge band was hired to play for the whole competition. We had the confidence of all the artists, so it wasn't a problem.

We had lots of nonstops with the large bands of Joey Lewis, Clarence Curvan, the Bonaparte Brothers, and Fitz Vaughn Bryan, and also with smaller bands like Casanovas Combo, Esquires Combo, Ansel Wyatt Combo because by the mid-1960s, the young people began to gravitate toward music. However, young musicians did not like saxophone and trumpet. They were very influenced by musicians like Chet Atkins (an American guitar player who played country and western) and a couple of guitar players known internationally. So all the young people were buying guitars. In addition, it was easier to get a guitar than a saxophone.[30] There were many combos from the mid-1960s onward. They usually included two guitars, an organ like the Hammond B-3 that Jimmy Smith used to play [Smith's performances are credited for having popularized the instrument], and a drum set.

On Boosting Pride and Reputation through a Band's Distinct Sound

RC: In the 1960s, you immediately recognized a band by its sound. Ron Berridge's band had its distinct sound. Clarence Curvan had his distinct sound. From an arranger's perspective, you would know immediately that's Clarence playing there. Joey Lewis has his own sound up to today because he arranged his own music, and his songs always reflected his vision. Fitz Vaughn Bryan, the same thing. Dutchy Brothers, the same thing. Cito Fermin Orchestra, the same thing. Norman Tex Williams, the same thing.

JG: So these bands always played new arrangements?

RC: Yes. When you played a nonstop, you compared the arrangements. When Dave Brubeck came with "Take Five," we all played it! I and Beverly were a little open minded: although we liked our own version, we recognized that Dutchies had the edge on us. We played our own version of "Take Five" in calypso, whereas they played their version in calypso and also a part of the song in 5/4, as Dave Brubeck and Paul Desmond had originally done it. You know, we had the opportunity to see Dave Brubeck with Paul Desmond in Trinidad in those days. So to play on the original memory of that song was nice.

So the band went along with Ron Berridge from 1965 to 1967. There was some problems, desires, and feelings, and five of us left Ron Berridge.

In 1967, Scipio Sargeant and Beverly Griffith went to America, and Clive Bradley replaced Beverly as the arranger of Clarence Curvan's band.[31] Bradley was then upcoming as a musician. He could absorb any kind of music: he was a mathematician! Bradley used to teach nuns mathematics! He was able to apply his knowledge of mathematics to music, because music is really maths. Bradley and I had a good thing going. It was an easy relationship. I had known Clive maybe since 1959 because he used to hang out in different nightclubs.[32] Shortly after five of us left Berridge, five musicians, including Clive Bradley, also left Clarence Curvan.

Experimenting with Other Bands: Songs Incorporated and Felix Roach's Band

RC: In 1967, around March or April that year, Clive Bradley, Lennox Church, Jerome Francique, of Clarence Curvan [band] and Michael Tobas, Neville Oxley, and myself, together with Thomas Patton in our everyday free time would hang out and obviously talk about music and what we would like to see in the music scene in Trinidad. And in that conversing, we decided to merge this group of musicians to form the band Songs Incorporated, led by Clive Bradley, bandleader and musical arranger. At the end of three months we had rehearsed thirteen songs. We then sought to have a nonstop with Ron Berridge. We did that nonstop. We played and sounded good, but we were no competition for Ron Berridge's big repertoire. Although Ron was going through changes as a result of us leaving the band, he was able to still maintain the strength of Ron Berridge's band. This nonstop did demoralize the members of Songs Incorporated and mostly us, the former members of the Ron Berridge Orchestra. So that band, Songs Incorporated with Clive Bradley, lasted about three months.

Some members had actually come into Songs Incorporated with an arrangement to join one of our premiere piano players, Felix Roach, at the Trinidad Hilton if things did not work out. At this time, the decision was made by some of the guys to join Felix Roach at the Trinidad Hilton. We immediately started working on a weekly salary. This was great because it was the first time that we were experiencing having a salary every week. Even though the work was good at the Hilton, after six months, complacency and lackadaisical [lazy] behavior led us to be fired by Mr. Florin, who was the food and beverage manager.

Returning to Ron Berridge's Band

RC: Neville Oxley and myself were good friends, and he was my senior with a vast experience of the music business. At this time, Ron Berridge requested for Neville to rejoin his band. Neville said to him that he would come back on the condition that he includes me back in the band also. Ron Berridge readily agreed.

When you had a name as Ron Berridge's band, most of the time you would work on Saturdays and Sundays. As the follow-up of Kitchener's 1966 and 1967 annual recordings, we also did the Kitchener 1968 album. Ron Berridge was the first person who recorded with Kitchener when he returned to Trinidad. In addition, we would always do instrumental versions of Kitchener's songs and other calypso hits of the carnival season. In 1968 we also did Sparrow's album with "Mr. Walker," "Jane," and "Too Much Wood in the Fire"—a big album of Sparrow also that year. This was the first time that the same arranger had arranged for both Sparrow and Kitchener. That had never happened before.

Ron Berridge was preparing the band for the 1968 carnival. Having recorded Kitch's album and Sparrow's album, all of their music had become like originals to us, having been the first people to hear and record these two albums. We had a very successful carnival season and after the season we had a long rest. Some Trinidadians who were employed as security personnel at the United Nations in New York City held a dance commemorating Trinidad and Tobago independence. We were contracted to do this job. After completing this job, we learned that Ron was disgusted with the whole musical situation in Trinidad. He then decided that he would be staying in the United States to try to make a new life for himself and his family. The majority of the members returned home.

Catering for All Musical Tastes in the Mid-1960s

JG: Before we move on to speaking about your experience in Sparrow's band, could you describe the repertoire you played with Ron Berridge's orchestra between 1965 and 1967? Did it change much from what you were playing with Clarence Curvan's band?

RC: No. There was a new consciousness in the country heading for internal self-government and independence. The whole movement went patriotic to embrace more local compositions.³³ This, for example, happened with Joey Lewis as the leader of a music band at that time who composed many hits as a musician and not within the normal trend of the calypsonian. Joey in that era had his music on the airwaves as prominent as the top calypsos of that era. He had a song called "Joey Saga"—with a distinct sound on the guitar where the guitar played a bass line that ran right through. And that song "Joey Saga" ended up with the public making a particular dance to that song—a dance that was then called Saga Ting.

At that time, we were committed to be ourselves, that is, to play calypso. We always played calypso at the end of every session, the local hits. But since we are playing popular music, not playing just for ourselves, but also for the people, we had to play the songs that the people know. We were playing the hits, including foreign hits—for example, songs by well-known Cuban artists such as Mongo Santamaria or by Perez Prado. We had a band from Cuba that came to Trinidad at some point.

JG: In addition to the music from Cuban musicians, what other foreign hits did you play during the 1960s?

RC: The Beatles: "She loves me, yeah, yeah, yeah," "Hey Jude," and all them. Remember we are a member of the British Commonwealth. Being in the music business, it is our business to pay attention to the things that light up the whole musical environment. This would have meant playing Elvis Presley's songs such as "Love Me Tender." I remember, I went and saw the movie *Jailhouse Rock* many times.³⁴ Whether it is the Beatles or Michael Jackson, or Frank Sinatra, it is our duty to know these artists so that we know where we stand then.³⁵

JG: And you were playing that not in the calypso style but in the original style?

RC: There were songs that could have taken the calypso arrangement and the type of tempo, and there were songs that may have stayed the same way, but you would have had a little change in the rhythm. Well, Ron Berridge did almost all the songs from *The Sound of Music* in calypso with serious arrangements. In those days, when a band played a calypso, each arranger of the respective bands would make that particular calypso as if it were the composition of the individual arranger. This means that the person who is responsible for the sound [the arrangement] is the most influential member of that band. There is the confidence that this arranger can take the band and the musicians to higher heights.

In the 1960s we were doing cover versions, that is, the reproduction of the original works by another individual band. Our population in those days, I would have to say, was more musically literate and appreciative because they came through the good old days of big bands. Today cover versions are the exact replica of the originals. And this is not specific to Trinidad, but to the whole world. But in the past, if you took a song, your band would arrange it in its own distinct way, completely different![36]

Learning from Bertram Inniss and Ron Berridge

RC: Until his untimely death in 1968, Bertram Inniss, the personal arranger and bandleader for the Mighty Sparrow, was very much involved with us in the Ron Berridge band. Since Bertram Inniss was nearly blind, Ron Berridge would transcribe all the music he was doing for Sparrow and whoever. Bert could make three horns sound like five, ten!

Since 1964 Bertram Innis and Ron Berridge had been working together. Bertram would sit at the piano and he would play over and over the song that they were going to work on. Bertram would demonstrate to Ron what he wanted him to write, and give him the whole arrangement. Ron would score the arrangement and write down the master score. He would take it and transcribe it at home and bring it back to Bertram for whoever the artist was. Bertram was a serious contributor to calypso. He was a lovely man. In doing this book, I could never leave out people like him, and other great musicians like Frankie Francis and the late great Art de Coteau. I could never really leave out these guys of anything that I speak about, because it is through them that I have learned what little I have learned.

When we rehearsed with Ron Berridge's, Bert[ram] would rehearse the band and deal with the maps of expression.[37]

JG: By "maps of expression," you mean staccato, legato, and so on?

RC: Yeah, all this. He would give us the maps of expression and the feeling of the music. His arrangements were very, very musical. Sometimes, he would specify that a certain phrase had to be played with detached notes, "dah dah dah" instead of "dah-dah-dah" [legato notes]. He would speak about the punctuation. He took that responsibility to give the band color and shading, and to make it produce different kinds of sounds out of the band. I still regard Ron Berridge as the best brass band in the history of Trinidad and Tobago. Even though people have said a lot of nice things to me, I still consider Ron's band as the premier band in the last fifty years.

SPARROW'S BAND, 1968–1970

RC: After playing with Ron Berridge in New York until August 1968, I returned to Trinidad. Michael Tobas then informed me that Sparrow had an advertisement in the papers for musicians. Conrad Little and myself visited Sparrow and learned that he needed several players, not only to play the bass and the alto saxophone, but also the keyboards and the drums. We insisted that we were intent on keeping the whole band going and on replacing only those who had stayed in New York. Following the tradition then, Sparrow used to travel with a few calypsonians on his tours to the Caribbean. He decided to adjust this to have the whole band, and to cut on the number of calypsonians who used to be on tour with him. He went to his bedroom and came out with a dictionary and chose the word "Troubadours" — "Sparrow's Troubadours" — to refer to a band of roving entertainers. The musicians from Ron Berridge's band had now become the core of Sparrow's Troubadours. To complement the band, Sparrow hired a few other musicians, including, among others, Earl Rodney, a reputed bass player and pan arranger. [As a pan player, Rodney distinguished himself by playing with four mallets as opposed to the usual two.] Sparrow and Byron Lee became the only two people who could take a fifteen-piece organization on the road.[38]

Touring with the Mighty Sparrow

RC: We immediately started rehearsals on Sparrow's repertoire. By the end of September, early October of that year, we went on a tour in the Caribbean with stops in St. Martin, St. Croix, St. Thomas, and Tortola. On that same tour, we flew to New York to play at the Madison Square Garden. A few weeks after, we went to Canada at the site of Man and His World, one year after the Expo in 1967. After performing in Montreal, we continued our tour and went to Nassau, Freeport in the Bahamas, Belize, Curaçao, and Aruba. Just before returning home, I remember when we were in Tortola [British Virgin Islands] and Sparrow told me, "Roy, come here!" He wanted me to hear something. He started to sing, "Sa Sa Yea."[39] I was the first person he called to sing it for. We were very close and I was mesmerized by the talent that he had. And he told me, "Hear this."[40] He picked up his guitar and started to sing the song. He was a confident person, but I think the feeling we had between each other led him to want to know how I felt about it. And this song ended up as the Road March for that year.[41]

When we returned to Trinidad in December 1968, we recorded Sparrow's recording *More Sparrow More*, including "Sa Sa Yea," for his 1969 carnival album. [Artists typically record their albums a few weeks before the New

Year, and the carnival season begins soon after.] In *More Sparrow More*, Sparrow hired Ed Watson to write the arrangements for a few songs.⁴² However, he wanted different songs to have different kinds of sound. So I brought Clive Bradley and Bradley did a few songs for Sparrow and then he disappeared. Recommended by Ricardo Brewster, who was the drummer of the Troubadours, Earl Rodney also arranged a few of [the] songs, including "The Lizard" and "Sell the Pussy," for that album.

After completing this 1969 album, we went back to the Virgin Islands and the Bahamas in December. We returned to Trinidad about the thirtieth of December 1968 and went straight into rehearsals for Sparrow's Calypso Tent [known as "The Original Young Brigade," or simply as the "OYB"]. We had one-day rehearsal to rehearse all the calypsonians (around thirty) in the tent. The tent opened on the first of January 1969.

Playing through Sparrow's Band Fallout and Sparrow's Band Reconstituted

RC: When we came back home [*long pause*] . . . Sparrow had a problem with Conrad [Little]. Conrad was the bandleader and also the first bass player in Sparrow's Troubadours. Sparrow found that Conrad was working more on behalf of the musicians than for his own benefits. Sparrow got rid of Conrad. At the time, Fortunia Ruiz was the first trumpet and solo trumpeter of the Troubadours. He was recommended by Sparrow to be the next bandleader. And we all agreed with that recommendation of Señor (nickname for Fortunia) to be the bandleader.

We worked the whole of the carnival season with the calypso tent. Based at the tent, we would make appearances at the cinemas at Point Fortin, San Fernando, Tunapuna, San Juan, in Port of Spain on Besson Street next to the old Besson Street police station. On Ash Wednesday we started touring again, first to Guyana for seventeen days, and then in the English-speaking Caribbean, including the U.S. Virgin Islands and the British Virgin Islands. We then flew to Montreal and performed for two weeks at the Edgewater Country Club. At the end of these performances, we drove straight to Rochdale Center in Jamaica, Queens, to perform one show on that night on the night of our arrival. And then we did three shows at Madison Square Garden, and we also performed at the jazz club Blue Coronet in Brooklyn.⁴³

Sparrow booked a studio in New Jersey for us to do an album entitled *Bang Bang Lulu in New York* with Sparrow's Troubadours. This was our first time experiencing recording in a professional recording studio. We were accustomed [to] recording in much smaller rooms. In this studio, we were separated by baffles [space separators made of sound-absorbing material], and this posed some problems for us and slowed us down. But we perse-

2.7 and 2.8
Bang Bang Lulu in New York with Sparrow's Troubadours.

vered, and after a few hours we did two songs and after that we did ten more songs. This album, I believe, is still in the record stores to this day. This was the first album of the Sparrow's Troubadours band [Sparrow's musicians]. Sparrow was not the normal feature as was usually the case in Sparrow's career. But he did sing to enhance the album and assisted us wherever we needed assistance. And "Bang Bang Lulu" was vocalized by Sparrow as this song was one of his spicy little things that he would have done on his nightclub shows. As we know, Sparrow is a consummate performing artist. However, he hired Tony Ricardo from Guyana as the main vocalist for the Sparrow's Troubadours band, and he also hired the Blues Busters of Jamaica to do the background vocals on that album. After this recording we went home to prepare for the 1970 season.

Between September and October 1969, we recorded Sparrow's 1970 album entitled *Sparrow Power* with all music arranged by Earl Rodney. And we also did immediately after a second album entitled *Sparrow's Troubadours: Hot and Sweet* [Sparrow's band musicians without the Mighty Sparrow]. Following what was becoming our normal routine, we then left again for the most part of November and December on tours and returned home for the 1970 carnival season. Sparrow had made a decision to employ Ed Watson to do the accompaniment in the calypso tent OYB and he contracted us out to play in dances. We preferred to play in the calypso tent as the earnings with the calypso tent were more reliable than in the parties. So there were some grumblings of dissatisfaction. Some of us began to think about our futures as the music was still not a secure profession in the Caribbean. Neville Oxley, Harold De Freitas, and myself resigned from the band and decided to go to New York after carnival.

On the Experience of Playing for the Mighty Sparrow

RC: Doing the whole of 1969 with Sparrow had brought me to the greatest part of my career at that point in time.

JG: In what ways?

RC: Although, musically, we had enjoyed Ron Berridge, a premiere band in the country, and the discipline, uniform, and everything, with Sparrow, we went into new frontiers of music. Let me explain. Sparrow had a voice with limitless range. That afforded him to do songs from many different singers like Brook Benton, Frank Sinatra, Sammy Davis Jr., Johnny Mathis, and so on. Although he is known as a calypsonian, Sparrow sang songs from many musical styles and in different languages. He did not only calypso, but also ballads and rhythm and blues, to name only a few; he did songs in French

Creole and he did some songs on Dutch topics with Dutch words. He is very versatile and also a very charismatic person. He brought stagemanship and camaraderie with the audience. He was also a lover of Redd Foxx (the comedian), and in the same vein joked about everything between songs. So he would do two forty-five-minute sets. Sparrow learned to speak eloquently. He schooled himself. And he loved to work and sing. In the history of world entertainment, Sparrow has worked nonstop, until very recently, every weekend. I was very close to him. I loved what he was doing. I was proud. He is the highlight in my career. When I would see the kind of respect he would receive, I was impressed. Jocelyne, working with him was an educational experience for me. The whole of '69 was a beautiful year.

I never wanted to go to New York because I saw it was going to change my way of life. But it was the only escape after leaving Sparrow and going through so many bands and making it to the top and having to start over and over.... We were a little disillusioned at our age.

NEW YORK, 1970–1975, AND 1975–1977: PLAYING WITH TRINIDADIAN AND JAMAICAN BANDS
Moving to New York

RC: Although I was never happy to leave my country, I was always fascinated with America and the development of America. I had never really thought of America as a place where I wanted to live. But came a time when I had to make a change: I had seen everything I could do musically in Trinidad, and there were no more goals to achieve. Most of my friends had left because they had figured out that they could not earn a good living playing music in Trinidad. And there was no form of security when they would reach the time to retire.[44]

I had played in Madison Square Garden in '69 with Sparrow's Troubadours. Ron Berridge was at the Mother's Day show at Madison Square Garden—which was the groundbreaker for our music in New York City. Ron had visited us at the Penn Garden Hotel on Seventh Avenue in the city. He had told us that he was interested in forming a new Ron Berridge orchestra. At the Garden show, myself and Neville Oxley spoke to Granville Straker and told him that we were interested in coming up to New York after the 1970 carnival season. Granville Straker was (and continues to be) one of the calypso recording pioneers in Brooklyn and also the owner of Straker's Calypso Record Store on Utica Avenue, Brooklyn. Little did we know that Granville was already speaking to Ron Berridge about reassembling the band in New York. We agreed to return to New York to organize the band,

2.9 and 2.10
Behold by the Blues Busters.

and Granville became our producer. Shortly after arriving in New York, we had to find all the personnel and that took some time.

When I went to New York to live there in 1970, my partner Cheryl was still in Trinidad. I did not like having to leave her there but I knew that I had to spend time in New York to find myself. Cheryl's sister, Angela, was living in New York, so I went to live at Angela's house. Shortly after, I advised Cheryl to go to Toronto, Canada, as her brother was a resident there since at least she would be closer to me. Even though I visited her in Toronto, I finally said to Cheryl to come over to New York because I told her, "Come on up here, because if we stay so far from one another, it won't ever work out." After some time, Cheryl came to live with me in New York.

Performing with Ron Berridge's Band and Hugh Hendricks's Jamaican Band

RC: One day we went to the Manhattan Center for a party. On my tour with Sparrow in 1969, I had met the Jamaican musician Hugh Hendricks, who had a band called Hugh Hendricks and the Buccaneers patterned after Byron Lee and the Dragonaires.[45] When Hugh Hendricks saw me at the Garden, he asked me, "What are you doing here?" I answered, "I will be here for a while." He immediately replied, "You are the right man that I would have wanted to see." He explained that his alto sax player had just enlisted in the army, and he asked me if I would join his band. I answered yes. I started working with him playing in Jamaican parties.

Everything was going fine with me playing with Hugh's band, but after three months I needed to make a choice. I spoke to Hugh and informed him that my original plan in coming to New York was to be part of Ron Berridge's new orchestra. All the musicians in Ron Berridge's band had been the people with whom I had been around my whole life, so I had to go. He did understand my position.

In New York, the new Ron Berridge orchestra did an album called *Revolution*. We were playing fetes on the weekends. But as things went along, Ron became dissatisfied with the progress of the band and the conditions in which he had to work. This made him very unhappy, and he decided to call it a day.

With Ron resigning, I was requested by Granville Straker, Neville Oxley, and Harold "Vasso" De Freitas to be the leader of the band. I decided to make the effort to do that on behalf of the band. Straker suggested that we call the band the Caribbean Strikers, and we decided to go along with the name. We performed a little while but with Berridge gone, the band was not the same. Around the same time, Michael Tobas was offered a job with Harry Belafonte. He accepted and left.[46] With his departure, one of the strengths of the band had gone. We tried to replace Tobas with a drummer named Wayne from St. Vincent, but after some time we all got fed up. I then spoke to Hugh Hendricks and rejoined the Hugh Hendricks band.

Joining Hugh Hendricks's Jamaican Band and the Blues Busters' Band

RC: After two years I was pretty settled in the band. I had the opportunity to spend some time with Hugh and to get to know him well, because I used to travel with him to and from the gigs in his truck. I remember in 1972, just at the time Hugh was going to do a record, I learned that Earl Rodney was in New York. Earl had just done the arrangement for Sparrow's "Drunk and Disorderly," and "Rope" for carnival. Hugh used to focus on Jamaican music, but he was also playing the calypso. I said to Hugh that the Jamaican musicians are not that versed in playing calypso music, so I recommended to him to use Earl Rodney to do the arrangement for Sparrow's two songs. I then encouraged Hugh to use Fortunia Ruiz and Oxley and myself and some other Trinidadian musicians who were living in New York at that time to do these songs with him.[47]

Hugh Hendricks's band had fantastic singers. While I was playing in Hugh's band, I met Rugs, who became the lead singer of Third World [a famous Jamaican band], and also the Blues Busters duo of Phillip James and Lloyd Campbell [also from Jamaica], who were also doing gigs with our band. I had known about the Blues Busters since the early 1960s as they had worked with Byron Lee. They had had a couple hits, "Wide Awake in a Dream," "If I Had Wings of a Dove," and "Behold." In New York, myself and Philip James became real tight. While he was working with Hugh Hendricks, Philip also had his band and I would do gigs at times with the Blues Busters. I was having lots of happiness with the Blues Busters. So I decided to quit Hugh's band. Again, I spoke to Hugh about what I was contemplating, and he said to me, "Roy, what's wrong with you? I have all the jobs and you want to go with Philip. What's wrong?" I said to him, not wanting to hurt his feelings, that I enjoyed very much working with the Blues Busters and that Philip James's voice turns me on. He had the raspy voice whereas the other brother, Lloyd Campbell, had the sweet voice. I left Hugh's band to work with the Blues Busters. Myself and Hugh have remained friends up to this day.

I would start performing by one o'clock in the morning just to play calypsos, and Philip used to advertise me around the Jamaican people for them to hear my contribution. After a while, Jamaicans knew me because they had seen me playing with a top Jamaican band. As they associated me with that band, I got the same kind of respect as the other band members received. I played with the Blues Busters until 1974.[48]

On the Hardships of Living in New York

RC: I stayed in New York from 1970 to 1974. West Indian music in New York only happened on the weekends, as most of our people have Monday to Friday jobs. So I had to find some work and ended up taking on the 8 a.m. to 4 p.m. gigs, during which I was doing very menial jobs. I was most unhappy with this situation. I had already anticipated before I went to New York that this was going to happen. In 1972, my last child, Jo-Ann, was born and by 1974, I decided to go back to Trinidad. Cheryl, Jo-Ann, and myself went back home. My mother had died in 1971, and my son Roy had been until then with my mom. After her passing, Roy had been living under the care of my younger sisters and brothers and Pa. In returning to Trinidad I got a little house in River Estate, Diego Martin, and I fixed it up to the best I could of with the little amount of money I had.

After five months, however, I went back to New York by myself. I spent three more years in New York, working as a maintenance man at a housing development in Brooklyn where I spent those three years. At that time, I still tried to continue playing music. Edgar Fitzgerald, Neville Oxley, Scipio Sargeant, and myself formed a new band, the Jambalassie, in 1977, but it just lasted about four or five months. Living in New York, our music could not afford to pay the bills, so one had to do some sort of day job. So there were not much room for music after you finish working from 8 to 4 p.m. and taking three trains to get home. There was not much energy to practice one's instrument then. Nevertheless, we formed this band Jambalassie, and most of the music was original compositions by Scipio Sargeant and the Top 40. This was a different experience from all the other bands I had played with before. After five months, we lost much [of] our tolerance. It seemed that we were going no place, as it is not easy to have a band in the big city. Our people being working people, they work from Mondays to Fridays. So the only time they have for entertainment is really Saturday night. And Saturday night alone could not have taken care of business then.

At this time, I had spent nearly three years in New York and was very disgusted. My woman was in Trinidad and so were my kids, and I was alone in New York. One morning, I received a letter from Trinidad asking me what I was doing and what were my plans. If our plans had changed, I could let her know so that she could move on with her life with the kids. The next morning, I landed in Trinidad with $125 U.S.[49]

BAND MUSICIANS ROY PLAYED WITH BETWEEN 1959 AND 1970

The Cathedral CYO Band, 1959–60: Roy Cape (alto sax), Carlton "Choylin" Aman (alto sax), Ronald Berridge (trumpet), John Alexander (trombone), Stratford Ahee (piano), Claude Martineau (guitar), Noble Williams (bass), Anthony Roosevelt (drums), John Rodriguez (percussion)

Selwyn Wheeler Orchestra, 1960–61: Roy Cape (alto sax), Ronald Berridge (trumpet), Selwyn Wheeler (trombone), Robbie Ifill (piano), Clarence Wears (guitar), Noble Williams (bass), Anthony Roosevelt (drums), Michael Tobas (percussion), Andre (congas)

Frankie Francis Studio Band, 1961–62: Roy Cape (alto sax), Ronald Berridge (trumpet), Frankie Francis (tenor sax), Robbie Ifill (piano), Clarence Wears (guitar), Carlyle Eversley (guitar), Art de Coteau (bass), Anthony Roosevelt (drums), Michael Tobas (percussion), Russell Gale (bongos)

Frankie Francis Calypso Tent Orchestra, 1961–62: Roy Cape (alto sax), Harold "Vasso" De Freitas (alto sax), Ronald Berridge (trumpet), Frankie Francis (tenor sax), Roderick Borde (tenor sax), Robbie Ifill (piano), Clarence Wears (guitar), Carlyle Eversley (guitar), Fitzroy Coleman (guitar), Cyril Mitchell (piano), Desmond Harper (bass), Hendron Bocaud (tenor sax), Forde (drums), Anthony Roosevelt (drums), Michael Tobas (percussion), Russell Gale (bongos)

Clarence Curvan, 1962–64: Roy Cape (tenor sax), Carlton "Choylin" Aman (alto sax), Lloyd Benjamin (alto sax), Colin Dennis (tenor sax), Oswald James (tenor sax), Ronald Berridge (trumpet), Lloyd Irish (trombone), Beverly Griffith (piano), Scipio Sargeant (guitar), Darlington Brown (guitar), Freddie Harris (guitar), Noble Williams (bass), Luther Cuffy (bass), Conrad Little (bass), Happy Williams (bass), Clarence Curvan (drums), Michael Tobas (percussion), Mervyn Callender (congas), Selwyn Frederick (bongos), Sonny Etienne (cowbells)

Ronald Berridge Orchestra, 1964–67: Roy Cape (alto sax), Neville Aird (tenor sax), Joseph Alexander (tenor sax), Colin Dennis (tenor sax), Errol Ince (trumpet), Ronald Berridge (trumpet), Clement Berridge (trumpet), Peter Bonnel (trumpet), Neville Oxley (trombone), Kelvin Hospedales (trombone), Ulric Sobian (organ, piano), Scipio Sargeant (guitar), Earl Lezama (guitar), Gary Salandy (guitar), Conrad Little (bass), Michael Tobas (percussion), Ricardo Brewster (drums), Terry Moe (congas), Learie Faria (congas), Edgard Fitzgerald (congas, percussion), Kenwyn Hunte (percussion), Kenneth Sylvester (percussion)

Sounds Incorporated (Clive Bradley), 1967: Roy Cape (alto sax), Lionel "Tex" George (tenor sax), Thomas Patton (trumpet), Neville Oxley (trombone), Jerome Francique (trombone), Clive Bradley (piano, arranger), Lennox Church (bass), Michael Tobas (drums), Terry Moe (congas), Kenwyn Hunte (percussion)

Felix Roach, 1967: Roy Cape (alto sax), Thomas Patton (trumpet), Jerome Francique (trombone), Felix Roach (piano), Clive Bradley (piano), Gary Salandy (guitar), Larry Atwell (guitar), Gordon Collins (bass), Kenrick George (bass), Michael Tobas (percussion), Terry Moe (congas), Kenwyn Hunte (percussion)

Ronald Berridge, 1967–68: Roy Cape (alto sax), Colin Dennis (tenor sax), Ronald Berridge (trumpet), Neville Oxley (trombone), Fortunia Ruiz (trumpet), Ulric Sobian (piano, organ), Gary Salandy (guitar), Conrad Little (bass), Ricardo Brewster (drums), Terry Moe (congas), Kenwyn Hunte (percussion), Edgard Fitzgerald (percussion)

Sparrow's Troubadours, 1968–70: Roy Cape (alto sax), Harold "Vasso" De Freitas (alto sax), Joseph Alexander (tenor sax), Neville Oxley (trombone), Fortunia Ruiz (trumpet), Benedict Gomez (trumpet), Johnson Sanchez (trumpet), Ulric Sobian (organ, piano), Mervyn Messiah (guitar), Johnny Cayenne (guitar), Earl Rodney (bass, arranger), Conrad Little (bass), Ricardo Brewster (drums), Tony Ricardo (vocalist, percussion), Ann Marie Innis (vocalist)

3 • LISTENING TO ROY SOUNDING

> Roy was playing with Sparrow, as the opening act for Duke Ellington's show in Trinidad in 1969. After the show, Russell Procope—an American clarinetist and saxophonist who played with Duke Ellington's Orchestra from 1946 until Duke Ellington's death in 1974—told Roy that in New York he could count on his assistance anytime. **PERSONAL CONVERSATION WITH ROY CAPE, JULY 2008**

> Roy has a phenomenal sound as a saxophonist. When Roy plays, he talks to you just as how he would speak to you without his saxophone. So, whenever he plays, it's just an extension of him talking to you but with another medium. **TENOR SAXOPHONIST GARVIN MARCELLE, DECEMBER 2010**

> Roy is a fella that always believes in grooving your music, groove it. Because when you watch Roy dance—and Roy don't dance fast—Roy has a certain swing when he moves. He grooves, he loves to groove his music. **TRUMPETIST CLYDE MITCHELL, OCTOBER 2011**

In October 2011, Roy received an honorary doctorate from the University of the West Indies at the St. Augustine campus in Trinidad, for his exceptional contributions to the musical life of Trinidad and Tobago and the Caribbean region, and its diasporas in North America and Europe. The doctorate honored his career as a saxophonist for over fifty years, and as a bandleader from 1980 on. On such occasions, most honorees would draw a piece of paper from their pockets and recite their words of thanks. Not Roy. The crowd of over five hundred people packed inside the large stadium hosting the event, including graduates, families, and friends, all watched silently as Roy went down the steps from the stage to pick up his saxophone.

Joined by his musical director, Carlysle "Juiceman" Roberts, who was now sitting at an electronic keyboard placed on the main floor at the left corner of the stage, Roy, without a word, began to play. He could have chosen to play anything, given his long experience performing in many different musical styles. But he chose to play a calypso called "Stay Giving Praises," a song composed by his close friend Black Stalin. Many young people in the audience had never heard Roy play solo. From where I stood, I could see people in extreme listening mode, concentrating on Roy's sound, their eyes fixed on him, with smiles of delight. Roy had not even finished playing when a thunderous round of applause buried his last few notes. For many people, including me, it was a memorable moment. Hearing him play solo on his saxophone, after having read or heard about his sound from so many musicians, calypsonians, journalists, and old friends, was a once-in-a-lifetime experience. Some audience members clearly wanted to share this special moment. Only a few minutes after Roy's performance, it appeared on YouTube.

As the epigraphs at the beginning of this chapter clearly attest, Roy's sound is often described as unique and compelling. While some of the comments hint at what makes Roy's sound special, the question remains only partly answered. What is Roy's sound? What makes it so unique? I want to explore these questions by conceiving sound as part of a world of interactions or, put another way, as part of a circulatory history. Sound is not only acoustic, never just material. It is also profoundly social, and related to broad socioeconomic conditions. Sound is not about the size or height of a player, but about the player's selective tone production. And this selectivity of sound comes out of the relationships between sound, the body, personality, and listening to various musics.[1] In the first section of this chapter, I focus on these various interrelationships and their synergies, not as a detour, but as a way to account for what comes into play in Roy's distinct sound.

A player's sound is often described using metaphors. Many listeners speak of sound as reflecting a musician's personality or as being a musician's voice—being de facto unique and different. But for musicians, making music operates on at least two levels. On the one hand, musicians are listeners; they learn from each other and refer to each other in their playing. On the other hand, musicians listen to themselves. Put another way, musicians associate themselves with other musicians and also dissociate themselves in a very short amount of time. After playing a riff or swoon associated with, say, this one saxophonist, musicians often move on to interpret a phrase in ways that display their unique technical or melodic skills.

If this was not complex enough to demonstrate a player's voice, the factors of musical trends linked with distinct historical eras make it even more difficult to speak about a player's sound in the singular. So in what follows, I address Roy's voice not in the singular but in the plural. I show how at different times and for different reasons, Roy has been called upon to play and sound differently. In the second section, I focus on Roy's history of listening as his history of sound production.

In the third section, I address Roy's consciousness of sound as a musical worker. Roy's playing is not only an act of love but also an act of labor. It is through music that he earns a living. As an act of labor, music making becomes interwoven with the socioeconomic and material conditions in which it takes place. Put another way, while music making helps generate particular economic markets, it is also highly conditioned by the material realities in which it is produced and circulates. Music making is also greatly influenced by dominant musical trends throughout the world. Even though music making itself helps constitute the sounds of the time, it is also informed by the dominant soundscapes. And in the (post)colonial context, it is furthermore bound in one way or another with state politics and, particularly around independence time, with nationalistic musical expectations. State politics do not determine what musicians play. However, musicians who want to play and earn a living must be attentive to the political climate of the time and the political convictions of their listeners. In the second section of this chapter, I show how a player's sound or musical aesthetics are thus never merely a musical issue.[2] As a corollary, I emphasize how musical flexibility constitutes a major asset for a musician like Roy.

ROY'S SOUND AND MUSICAL PHILOSOPHY

> The amount of people that today would tell you . . . "Well look, I met my wife when Roy was playing 'Kisses' in a dance in Port [Services]. I mean, we married three months after we met in that dance, but Roy was playing, you know?" The band was playing, and Roy used to be in the middle of the whole band, and then come off the stage blowin'. . . . *People used to fall in love!* I mean *seriously.* They'll tell you, it's one of the most beautiful horns that they would hear in the dance hall. That tone and everything that comes out of that saxophone is Roy Cape. Roy's a lover.
>
> **BLACK STALIN, JUNE 9, 2009**

This laudatory comment by Black Stalin, one of the most respected calypsonians in the Caribbean and Caribbean diasporas, echoes what I have heard repeatedly from so many of the musicians, calypsonians, and fans I interviewed. How does Roy produce such powerful and moving music? As a non-wind player (I am a pianist), I asked Roy to tell me what helps him produce his distinct sound. Roy's answer came in the form of a story, one designed to show me how someone's sound cannot be dissociated from his personality. The story went like this: "One day, an elder bass player from Choy Aming's band, Mr. Jules, asked me, 'Young boy, what do you play?'[3] I answered, 'I play alto sax.' He said to me, 'You are going to be a very sweet alto player.' He [Mr. Jules] said this to me because of my coolness and the way I was dressed." For Roy, the look and personality of a musician influence not only his approach to his sound, but also how his sound is going to be perceived. Roy has a soft tone of voice and calm demeanor, and he dresses in fashionable clothes, which, remarkably, always look as though they came straight from the dry cleaners. Roy's attack on the saxophone is similarly never brusque and, as many musicians to whom I spoke admiringly put it, "Roy has a clean sound." While there might not always be a correspondence between a musician's personality, look, and sound, in Roy's case, there is.

When acousticians talk about an individual's sound signature, they talk about the envelope of the sound—which refers to the balance between the attack, the body, and the decay of the musician's sound, its amplitude (volume or force), and the duration of the sounds produced. Based on this vocabulary, I want to try to describe Roy's sound.[4] To do so, I focus on four different musical moments in Roy's career, to demonstrate how his sound embodies different voices at different times in relation to his ongoing musical experience, personal choices, and different musical trends, both locally and globally.

In the early 1960s, Clarence Curvan's orchestra recorded "Moulin Rouge," the theme song of the film by the same name, in a bolero style.[5] In this recording, Roy played a solo lead part on saxophone after only a few years on the instrument. Typical of musicians who first learn on the clarinet, Roy plays with hardly any vibrato, with an attack dead on pitch, and very few overtones. Already known for his ability to project the lyricism of the song, he adds grace notes and light reedy trills, then bends and swells a few notes with crescendo before accentuating significant notes in the melody in a style reminiscent of Johnny Hodges—Duke Ellington's lead saxophonist, who was very influential during this period. Roy's legato phrasing, combined with the sustained body of his sound, produces an arresting vocal quality to his playing.

In the mid-1960s, Roy took a solo in "Lollipops and Roses"—a song associated with the singer Jack Jones—recorded by Ron Berridge's orchestra.[6] Here he adopts a swing approach for the medium-tempo arrangement of this song. Roy's relaxed improvisation, closely based on the song's chord progression, emphasizes offbeats that give a lilting swing effect to his solo. In contrast to the more raspy and edgy sound of American bebop and post-bebop saxophonists, Roy's clean sound is typical of that era's dance bands and recording studio sound, both in the United States and in Trinidad.

In the late 1960s, Roy played in the horn section of the Mighty Sparrow's band, the Troubadours, and recorded the famous calypso song "Sa Sa Yea." In this recording, he does not take a solo (Harold "Vasso" De Freitas does), but he demonstrates his deep understanding of the aesthetics of togetherness typical to the calypso horn section. The light tonguing of the three saxophonists, Roy, De Freitas, and John Alexander, is identical. The rhythmic, syncopated articulation of the three players is tight. Their centering of the notes blends perfectly and produces a "fat" sound—larger than what a single player could produce.

Skipping the period from 1970 to 1977, when Roy lived in New York and played more live than recorded sessions, I focus next on Roy's 1979 solo—not a solo lead part, but his improvisation—featured in the song titled "Name the Game," with Roy Cape All Stars on the Black Stalin Live album released in 2006. Here Roy's sound is bright and mellow. His attack, as was the case early on in his career, is dead on pitch. He does not use a staccato bite to produce his sound, and his attack is fast and leads to a sustained body. By sustaining the body of the sound, Roy lets the timbral richness of the sound, the overtones, come out. His sound decay is perfectly balanced with his attack in both duration and amplitude. The way Roy plays emphasizes a round, full-bodied sound. This is what leads many people to refer to Roy's sound as fat. He produces a sound that balances well with the trumpet, the electronic instruments, and the percussion used in the band. His sound cuts through the ensemble without him huffing and puffing during his performance.

These kinds of overtones, along with the roundness and bigness of sound Roy produces, have a lot to do with his breath control, as well as his choice of instrument, reed, and mouthpiece. This choice arguably stems as much from his personal taste as from the fact that he plays in an ensemble. It is also deeply embedded in what I called earlier a world of interactions or a circulatory history. From a scholarly perspective, the interface between a musician's body and his instrument is a concrete site to investigate the materiality of sound. With this in mind, I asked Roy to explain how he chose his instrument, his reed, and his mouthpiece since, apart from his distinct approach to playing the saxophone, these choices greatly influence the sound he is known for.

RC: I started to play on clarinet with an ebonite (hard rubber) mouthpiece for small ensemble and large orchestras. When I began to play saxophone, I used the Berg Larsen metal mouthpiece that was used in Trinidad in the 1950s or 1960s.

When I could buy my own saxophone, I bought a Selmer Mark VI. The first one I bought was a tenor sax from National Music Supply by Claude and Franck Martineau, who used to be the agents for Selmer Paris saxophones in Trinidad during that time. Since then, I have had five Selmer Mark VI and now two Super 80. I came up with that preference of Selmer by looking at some of the top saxophonists of those eras [the 1950s and 1960s] and my good friend Harold "Vasso" De Freitas. . . . I like Selmer because the sound is smooth. The keys are very close, and it is not a complicated setup. I have short fingers. I like it for the mechanism of it. And all Selmers guarantee a particular sound. . . . I go for this instrument that touches me when I play.

I liked Paul Desmond's sound; he probably used a rubber mouthpiece. But I prefer to use a five-star Selmer metal mouthpiece [the number of stars represents the strength of the mouthpiece]. Even though I would get a mouthpiece when I bought the instrument, I would use my metal piece. Particularly in an electronic environment, I prefer a metal piece because it projects better and it makes the sound brighter.

As this narrative makes clear, Roy's choice of instrument and mouthpiece is influenced by social relations (the music suppliers he knows well, and his friend Harold "Vasso" De Freitas), material relations (the interaction of Roy's own body with his instrument in the production of sound), and performing conditions (Roy playing in dance bands with a full horn section and needing to project in order to be heard). As the next story reveals, Roy's choice of saxophone pieces in particular is also linked to touring and his exposure to different brands while he was playing with fellow musicians in various parts of the world.

In 1986, Roy accompanied calypsonian Chalkdust (Dr. Hollis Liverpool) for a tour in Sweden that included fifty-six shows in forty-two days. During that tour, he met Leslie Coard, in Roy's words, a "fantastic tenor saxophonist from Grenada who also lived in Trinidad in the 1950s."[7] Roy and Coard became friends, playing together ten times in the band that accompanied Chalkdust. On one of these gigs, Coard gave Roy a metal mouthpiece—a Lawton five star. Since then, Roy has been using a Lawton mouthpiece. When he asked a musician who lives in England in 2010 to locate one for him, he learned that the maker had died. Roy currently has two Lawtons; the one he uses is a five-star B.

3.1 Selmer Super Action 80 saxophone and metal mouthpiece.

For musicians, these details about a mouthpiece matter greatly. The mouthpiece literally connects the body, the mouth, the lips, the throat, and the air; it connects the agency of the musician's body to the instrument. The mouthpiece is the shaping site of the musician's voice. It is where the musician uses his body to make a voice. The choice of a reed and of the mouthpiece is critical to the labor of love.

There are many different reeds for saxophone, and musicians choose the reed according to how it responds when they are performing. When Roy was still young, he used a number 3 reed. As he put it, "I was young and full of energy to waste." Today, he uses a 2½ reed because it is much softer to play. As he grew older, Roy learned from the elder saxophonists how to prepare his reed before playing. Roy used to take his reed from the box, warm it up in his mouth, and just play. With the warmth of the saliva, Roy explained, "we're breaking the reed then." However, an older tenor sax player

3.2 Lawton mouthpiece.

named Kenneth Layne from Trinidad taught Roy to put the reed in a glass of water before going to a gig. Today, Roy puts two reeds in a glass of water before playing. He even carries a box with at least ten reeds, as reeds can easily break, split, or warp. Moreover, as Roy explained, "a new reed does not guarantee the sound that you expect." Roy learned by example from the people around him, and particularly the musicians from the Police Band, as well as saxophonists like Cyril Diaz, who would always bring back boxes of reeds when he went on tour.

I would now like to return to another telling moment about Roy's voice. In October 2011, when Roy picked up his saxophone and played to express his gratitude to the University of the West Indies for his honorary doctorate, as well as to thank the audience for their continued support throughout the years, hardly anyone there knew what to expect. At sixty-nine years old, his interpretation of the calypso "Stay Giving Praises" demonstrated many aspects of the styles that were part of his repertoire over his long career. In fact, that interpretation foregrounded—or more accurately, "foresounded"—a unique sensibility that came from his multiple sense of belonging to and his deep knowledge of many different musical expressions. After introducing the melody of the song, Roy began to improvise as though he was composing a new melody over various segments of the song. But each time, he quickly stopped to come back to the original tune. He explained to me afterward that he did not want to stray too far away from the melody for fear of losing his audience—a telling remark that revealed he is always thinking with the consciousness of a musical worker.

Even though "Stay Giving Praises" is written in the minor mode, at times Roy used a whole-tone scale. At other times, he played blue notes. At still other times, he played triplets before landing on a given note or played a run so fast as to produce a blurring effect—two gestures typically associated with bebop and, in particular, with Charlie Parker. His solo was steeped in a pan-African American language, including the language of blues and soul in his choice of ornaments and rhythmic delivery. Long part of his musical expression, his use of offbeats in some passages injected a swing feel to the melody. This assemblage of distinct and yet interrelated playing styles could lead North American listeners hearing the YouTube recording of Roy's performance of "Stay Giving Praises" to hear Paul Desmond here and Julian "Cannonball" Adderley there, Phil Woods here and Johnny Hodges there, Paquito D'Rivera here and Sonny Stitt there. They could easily hear the full range of blues, soul, bebop, swing, Latin, and jazz encompassed in this broad range of players.

However, this is not the way Roy hears himself, nor is it the way he narrates the history of his influences. Roy's quest is for a sound of his own, even knowing full well that he is the product of the extraordinary range of styles he has played and listened to. He is not self-consciously trying to sound like or go against certain layers in the history of contemporary music, but he is, like all musicians, the product of place, time, and experiences.

To me, Roy is more than simply a solid band member in a horn section. He is a saxophonist who has mastered the vocality of a singer. After having listened to and accompanied singers for decades, he plays with light tonguing, diminuendo and crescendo, bright staccato and legato sounds the way a singer would, and he performs rhythmic phrasing like a sung melody. And, like a singer, he is able to dance the melody and to suggest that he knows the dance moves. As Black Stalin remarks in the epigraph at the beginning of this section, Roy is a romantic. He has a commanding, vocal-like ability to solo on a ballad, with a sustained legato emphasis on the melody.

As a melodist, Roy's ability as an improviser is both to embellish phrases or riffs and also to play countermelodies or new melodies over the given ones. As a section player, Roy uses his sax as the bridge between the horn section and the vocal. He takes his cues as much from the way the singer lays down the phrases as he does from the punchy horn sections. He works to push, to pull, to enunciate, and to frame the vocal phrases. This is one place where listening to the brass sections in the big bands of Duke Ellington, Count Basie, the Dorseys, and all the ensemble jazz material must have contributed to his sense of style.

While Roy's style of improvisation can be associated with some of the great saxophonists of the post–Charlie Parker, bebop era—in particular, to my ear, that of Julian "Cannonball" Adderley when he played bossa nova[8]— it simultaneously distinguishes itself in one important way. It does not feature the technical prowess associated with Charlie Parker's disciples. This, I believe, is not because of Roy's lack of potential to do so. Rather, I connect Roy's avoidance of fast scalar runs, quick arpeggios, and flights of chromatic lines to the local calypso aesthetics he grew up with and his musical philosophy concerning the audiences for whom he plays.

Calypso melodies are, for the most part, diatonic. Written to highlight the craftsmanship of the calypsonians' lyrics, they promote the syllabic delivery of the artists. The melodic contours of calypso are usually within a relatively modest vocal range (rarely more than an octave and a half). The rhythmic phrasing is usually highly syncopated, but moderate in tempo, to allow the listeners to understand the sociopolitical commentaries and the play on words or double entendres which calypsonians are internationally known for. To improvise in a calypso style, local horn players usually work with the musical elements of diatonic scale, moderate tempo, and economy of melodic material with maximum effect.[9] Particularly for a musician like Roy, who performed from the late 1950s to the late 1970s in dance bands and in calypso orchestras, playing instrumentals or accompanying calypsonians, borrowing a virtuosic, postbebop style of playing would have been (and would continue to be) viewed as either diluting the traditional style of calypso or at odds with it.

This may be why I associate Roy's style of improvisation not only with some American jazz players but also with musicians from Guadeloupe, in particular with alto saxophonist Emile Antile. Emile (son of the famous Emilien Antile, better known as Mr. Sax in the French Antilles and France) is today viewed as the king of the biguine (Vidal and Delacroix 2011). Antile's explicit and public choice to feature biguine's aesthetics, which in the 1940s and 1950s highly resembled calypso in terms of melody and chordal progression, might help explain why Antile's solos, like Roy's, do not feature the virtuosic style of playing associated with the postbebop saxophonists.

Undoubtedly, Roy's musical philosophy also greatly influences his playing style. For Roy, audiences matter. As a musician in dance bands, he realized from the outset of his career that bands must cater to their audience's tastes. In one of our conversations, Roy made the distinction between the Berklee and Juilliard schools of music. He linked the Berklee school with musicians such as Quincy Jones and Grover Washington, whereas he associated Juilliard with the likes of John Coltrane. His association of musicians with certain schools has little to do with whether the musicians actually went there. In the same vein, Roy's distinction between Berklee and Juilliard has little to do with a particular sound aesthetics but rather with his association of musicians who play more popular music and who are more involved with the business aspect of music with Berklee. For Roy, jazz musicians like John Coltrane are the equivalent of those classically trained at a school like

Juilliard, in that they are interested in performing, in Roy's words, "more 'eccentric,' nonmainstream, exploratory sounds—whether an audience likes it or not." This is what I think Roy means when he distinguishes these two schools—which for many people mark a class distinction between a populist school and an elitist conservatory. This is why Roy connects Quincy Jones and Grover Washington—two musicians who have been massively successful commercially and popular among a variety of audiences—with Berklee. Roy's preference for a Berklee approach makes sense in relation to his own musical journey as a dance band member and bandleader who has in mind not only to sound good but also to cater to his audience's musical tastes.

HISTORY OF SOUND AS HISTORY OF LISTENING (aka Cover aesthetics)

To cater to his audience's musical tastes, Roy had to listen to the music aired on radio and presented live in Trinidad. As he explained to me, a musician has to know what is going on musically in the world in order to situate himself in relation to that world, and also to be part of the aesthetics of the present. From this perspective, I try here to map the soundscapes that Roy has been exposed to, and the musical culture of calypso he grew up in. This helps to situate Roy's musical thinking (the kind of saxophone sound he has) and practice (his solo performances and playing in wind sections). Addressing Roy's sound and performance this way helps to highlight what is so profoundly social about music. Instead of analyzing sound simply according to its musical parameters, I aim to show how Roy's sound is at once unique to him and at the same time part of a complex web of human interactions, pedagogical instruction, media exposure, specific historical moments, and political movements.

In the 1960s, Roy would listen to the two local radio stations—Radio Trinidad and 610 Radio (Radio Guardian)—and the American radio station WVDI to hear foreign songs, jazz, and a few calypsos.[10] This is how Roy heard Perez Prado, Chubby Checker, old hits like "Over the Rainbow" by Judy Garland (from the movie *The Wizard of Oz*) and "Stella by Starlight," recorded in 1947 by Frank Sinatra (based on the instrumental version featured in the 1944 film *The Uninvited*). This is how he heard Elvis Presley's "Love Me Tender" and "Jailhouse Rock," the Beatles, James Brown, and all the songs from *The Sound of Music*. It was also by listening to the local radio stations that he discovered Glen Miller, Count Basie, Duke Ellington, Charlie Parker, Miles Davis, Clifford Brown, and John Coltrane. In addition to being an avid radio listener, Roy would also read about music. As he recounts, "I would go to the U.S. Embassy library and there I was able to get the *Down Beat*, because at that time the *Down Beat* magazine was the authority of who is who! So in those days, I would read about Gerry Mulligan, Cannonball Adderley, J. J. Johnson, Yusef Lateef, Tommy Dorsey, Duke Ellington, Count Basie, Oscar Peterson—the greatest names that have ever lived then. Through WVDI (the American radio in Trinidad), we were hearing a lot of American things, and this made us aware."

During his formative years as a musician, Roy knew well the music of the older reputed tenor sax players such as King Curtis, Earl Bostic, Frank Foster, Dexter Gordon, John Coltrane, Sonny Stitt, Sonny Rollins, and Coleman Hawkins from the United States, but he did not try to emulate them. Their sounds have a much bigger and harder tone than Roy's. As Roy stressed to me, such tones did not correspond to his personality. Similarly, while Roy admires the alto saxophonists of his own generation, for example, Maceo Parker—most connected with the history of funk and for his exceptional contributions to James Brown's and George Clinton's bands—he does not attempt to reproduce Maceo's growling, forceful tone. Roy conceives sound as personality, as voice, as being a discourse of self. When Roy speaks, he uses a soft, warm tone. Hearing his voice on his answering machine, I am always struck by the caring and compelling sound of his voice. It is important for him that his personality be heard in sound. Put another way, it matters for him, in his own words, "to be yourself."

Along these lines, Roy mentioned to me that he was impressed by the alto saxophonist Paul Desmond—the composer of "Take Five," who played with Dave Brubeck for many years (1951–67 and for several reunion tours in the 1970s) and whom he heard play live in a concert in Trinidad. However, even though he likes Desmond's tone, Roy prefers and produces a sound that is richer in overtones.[11] The rich timbral quality of Roy's tones could result from the combination of the pressure Roy applies to the mouthpiece and the density of the reed. As Roy confirmed, he uses a harder mouthpiece than Paul Desmond. Could it be that Roy's preference for a harder reed—which enables him to produce mid- to low-range frequencies—comes from his desire to blend better with the lower frequencies of the bass, whose sound and register is considered central to, and the grounding of, the musical aesthetics of popular music not only in Trinidad, but also in the English-speaking Caribbean as a whole?

To be well informed musically, Roy also reads the daily newspapers. This is how he got to know about the tunes favored by the public at particular times. He would have learned, for example, on March 15, 1963, in the *Trinidad Guardian* evening news, about the next show coming "all the way from Rio de Janeiro" featuring Gallo, "considered the King of the Bossa Nova in Latin America, who comprise[d] 15 of the best variety artists in South America, including bossa nova dancers, carioca dancers, and some brilliant musicians" (p. 1). Two years later, in the same newspapers, he would have seen, on January 3, 1965, the "610's Parade of Hits, the Week's Top Ten" listing the following tunes by local combos:

1. "Big Bamboo," by Ken Vaugh Bryan
2. "Sweet Adorable You," by Eddy Arnold
3. "Linstead Market," by Andre Tanker
4. "Wanting You," by the Bonaparte Brothers
5. "Santa Flora," by Trevor John
6. "There Is Nothing I Can Say," by Rick Nelson
7. "Heroes Never Die," by the Dutchy Brothers
8. "I've Got Sand in My Shoes," by the Drifters
9. "River Bank Jump Up," by Byron Lee
10. "Mutiny on the Bounty," by Ansel Wyatt

He would have learned that later on that year, renowned South African singer Miriam Makeba was going to perform a second concert at Queens Hall (in the capital, Port of Spain) on March 9, and would have attended the performance. He would have read one month earlier that the Jamaican band, the sensational entertainers Carlos Malcolm and his Afro-Jamaican Rhythms, would be coming soon to perform. And he would have become well aware how Jamaican Byron Lee and his band, the Dragonaires, were becoming remarkably popular in Trinidad, by seeing recurrent ads announcing their upcoming performances on the island.[12]

By reading the newspapers on February 2, 1967, he would have figured out which bands he was competing with by checking the Carnival Dance Diary.[13] The diary announced which bands were playing and where during that year's carnival.

CARNIVAL DANCE DIARY
- Casuals Club, Port of Spain, Joe "Chet" Sampson
- Canaba Drive-In Lounge, POS [Port of Spain], Art de Coteau's Orchestra and Shell Invaders, and Starlift Steel Orchestra
- Civil Service Association, POS, Five Fingers Combo, and Starlift Steel Orchestra
- Kowloon Restaurant, POS, Moon-rakers Combo, the Tops Combo, and Esso Tripoli Steel Orchestra
- Hotel Normandie, St. Ann's, Y. de Lima's Blue Diamonds Steel Orchestra, and Ray Sylvester's Orchestra

- Harvard Club, POS, Boyie Lewis's Orchestra, and Angostura Starlift Steel Orchestra
- Danny's Inn, Cocorite, the Souls Debating and Cultural Group, Gemeni Brass Orchestra, the Rockets Combo, Solo Harmonites
- Perseverance Club, Maraval (the Newallos), Ken Vaughn Bryan's Orchestra, and Coca Cola Silver Stars
- Paragon's Club House, Cocorite, Coca Cola Silver Stars, Ed "Little Roger" Watson's Orchestra
- Skinner Park, San Fernando, Ron Berridge
- Oxford Club, San Fernando, Watty Watkins "Combinders" Orchestra, and Leo John's Combo
- Habanera, San Fernando, Fen Fergus's Combo and Comancheros' Combo

After his return from New York in 1977, Roy would quickly learn which tunes were the favorites of the moment in Trinidad by reading the newspapers. On January 1, 1978, the chart prepared by Ivor Ferreira of Radio 610 "for the station's presentation to the nation during Old Year's Night and New Year Holidays" indicated that "the top 25 of the 100 chosen tunes for the year" were as follows:

1. "Wanna Make Love to You"—Nadie La Fond (T&T)
2. "You Are What Love Is"—Mave and Dave (T&T)
3. "Destruction"—Dorian Hector (T&T)
4. "Woody Midebar"—Gramacks from Dominica
5. "Hotel California"—the Eagles (U.S.)
6. "Dance and Shake Your Tambourine" Universal Robot Band (U.S.)
7. "Let's Do It Again"—Jenny Pakeera (T&T)
8. "Savage"—Maestro (T&T)
9. "Don't Trouble People"—Theophilus Homer (St. Vincent)
10. "Don't Tell Me Stories"—Saskie and Serge (U.S.)
11. "Torn between Two Lovers"—Mary McGregor (U.S.)
12. "This Time I'll Be Sweeter"—Wendy Alleyne (Barbados)
13. "When I Need Love"—Leo Sayer (U.K.)
14. "Love So Right"—Bee Gees (U.S.)
15. "Try Making Love"—Wild Fire (T&T)
16. "Disco Soca"—Joe Tempo Ceasar (T&T)
17. "I Don't Want to Go On"—Nazareth (U.S.)
18. "American Patrol"—Third World Steel Orch. (T&T)
19. "Sweet Soca Song"—Robin Imanshah (T&T)
20. "Give More Tempo"—Calypso Rose (T&T)

21. "Lovie Dovie" — Afro National Band (U.S.)
22. "I Like Your Style" — Tony Wilson (T&T)
23. "Ain't Gonna Bump with No Big Fat Woman" — Joe Tex (U.S.)
24. "Rock a Woman" — Little Caesar (T&T)
25. "To Love Somebody" — Claudia Fields (U.S.)

For a dance band musician like Roy, it was important to know about the eclectic repertoire that Trinidadians listened to. Indeed, this list and others clearly show that Trinidadians were listening not only to tunes from different countries (the U.S., the U.K., and other Caribbean islands), but to different musical styles (ranging from calypso to soul, funk, pop, rock, cadence-lypso, and jazz). Most important, to listen to music from different bands, styles, countries, and times would be one of the best ways to further one's musical training.

As Roy explained, when he grew up he learned songs by ear, listening to steelbands. He memorized lines by rote, as most pan players typically did—and still do—to learn their parts. At the Children's Home (the orphanage), Roy was taught, as he put it, "from a military brass band concept. So it had nothing to do with guitar and keyboards. So although we knew the scale, we were never taught chords. So you could improvise and maybe play around two chords then." Roy learned to read music at the Children's Home, but he memorized the lines so quickly that he did not need to look at the score after he read it the first time. As a result, he did not develop his reading skills until he left the orphanage and began to play in bands, particularly when he began to work with Frankie Francis at TELCO as a studio musician and as an assistant to write transcriptions for him.

As was the case in most British colonies, musicians who wanted to pursue their musical studies and play professionally would go to the Royal School of Music in England. In Roy's words, "Our world history [then] came from England. Under the Queen, we did very much things British." However, he added, "From the late 1950s, we started to see more about America. Young musicians began to go to Berklee or Juilliard schools of music in Boston or New York." But Roy did not pursue his musical education in any of these schools. He learned by observing the elder musicians perform, by playing, and, equally crucial to his musical development, by listening to music.

MOVING WITH THE TIMES IN SOUND AND STYLE

Looking at newspaper ads for shows, new recording releases, and parties helped me to trace the music that Roy was exposed to, which has been useful to relate Roy's sound and playing to a vast network of musicians, musics, and places. But exploring the socioeconomic conjunctures and musical trends that have marked his journey highlighted something else that I think has unquestionably contributed to Roy being a sought-after musician. I am referring here to what many of his fellow musicians describe as Roy's remarkable musical knowledge and memory (among musicians often referred to as "big ears"), and his ability to absorb many different musical styles. In this section, I address Roy's reputation as a musician with big ears and his musical flexibility. But I do so not only by focusing on Roy's recognized musical abilities, as is often the case with musical biographies of well-known artists. Rather, without underestimating Roy's personal musical talent, I connect his big ears and musical flexibility to his consciousness of sound as a musical worker.

As Roy remarks, musical tastes and styles change with time. Musicians—and dance band musicians in particular—have to be open to new aesthetics and new sensibilities, and to keep abreast of changes if they want to stay relevant in the highly competitive milieu of live music performance. From the late 1930s to the late 1960s, Trinidadian dance bands and calypso orchestras featured instrumental solos. Influenced by Johnny Hodges, an alto saxophonist who played in Duke Ellington's band, Roy points out, "I would have played a little bit of swoon and different types of embellishments then." Even though early in his career Roy had already developed his own sound and improvisational style, he would signal to his audience his knowledge of other saxophonists' acclaimed ways of playing and integrate it at strategic moments in his performances. The key here would be to integrate new musical knowledge and to be aware of new trends while keeping one's individuality. But by the late 1960s, as Roy puts it, "solos went out."

It could be suggested that solos went out by the late 1960s for at least five reasons: the impact of independence (1962); the increasing importance of the arranger in relation to the huge expansion of the local recording industry; the closure of many nightclubs; the increasing access to new home sound equipment and record listening; and the concomitant reorganization of radio formats.

In the aftermath of independence, state agencies focused on local popular culture, and on music in particular, to further nationalist sentiment. The Carnival Development Committee, the Best Village Competitions, and the Ministry of Education, to name only a few, encouraged younger and older Trinidadians to contribute to the nation-building process by performing and singing local music.[14] As Roy puts it, "With Dr. Williams [the first prime minister of independent Trinidad and Tobago] coming in, we started to be a little more nationalistic and more politically conscious of ourselves as a people." In this context, calypso, reputed locally and internationally for its witty sociopolitical commentaries, took on a pride of place in the national imagination. Viewed by Afro-Creole middle-class intellectuals and the politicians in power as representing Trinidad's worldview, its song lyrics became the locus of attention—at the expense, I would argue, of instrumental solos.[15] As Roy confirmed, the horn arrangements by the second half of the 1960s were transformed as follows: "You put a horn fill at the end of the line or if there is a space in the middle of the line, then we played a fill. But it is the words and the meaning of the song that mattered most. So everything was fitted into its own space in relation to the melody of the song and not to interfere with the words."

The fading out of instrumental solos in dance bands by the late 1960s in Trinidad may also be related to the growing role of the arranger, in the context of the huge expansion of the local recording industry. With the emergence in the late 1960s of several small recording studios, including SEMP, NRC (National Recording Company), SHARC, KH, Cook Recording, and Charlie's Records (Fulton Street, Brooklyn), to name only a few—most of which featured calypso, the privileged music of the time—came a new hierarchy among musicians.[16] Until the late 1950s and early 1960s, calypso music, as Roy explains, was not "documented" (i.e., written down); musicians would accompany the calypsonians by ear, and play musical formulas learned by rote over the years. "Just before he hit the stage, the calypsonian would sing eight bars of his song, and we would figure out when the singer had to come in and we would start playing. The musicians had to be able to play ad lib because there was no score." While calypso arrangements began to be scored more regularly by the early 1960s—thanks mainly to arranger Frankie Francis[17]—they became standards by the late 1960s. I link the increasing importance of the arranger and concurrently the consolidation of a musical hierarchy among local musicians to the need for greater efficiency and production values posed by the new environment in which many musicians found themselves: the country's proliferating recording studios.[18]

To record an album, calypsonians would hire an arranger and it would then be up to the arranger to select the musicians. If, in the past, some musicians in the calypso orchestras were given space to perform solos in the band chorus (termed "the ad lib chorus"), now the arranger would write the horn fills and would assign different musicians to do solos over a shorter number of bars. Could it be that in addition to seeking greater efficiency and production values in the recording studios, the arranger's approach also aimed to match the prevalent format of rock songs, verse-refrain, to be more competitive both in the recording market and on radio?

The fading out of solos in dance band music in Trinidad may also be related to the closure of many nightclubs during this period, and the concomitant migration of those musicians who could improvise.

RC: There were many nightclubs in the 1960s. The musicians in the nightclubs were not readers, but they could play solos. So the individual arrangers were not a focal point at that time. Many of these musicians left since many of the clubs closed down. The new crop of musicians was not trained to do solos. And as independence came, local musicians such as Joey Lewis started composing [songs] and having hits [with no space for soloing]. The individuals who could solo left and this type of talent dried up. From the late 1960s to now, calypsos have band chorus. We were taught from a military band perspective [and thus to listen to ensembles]. So these musicians would have listened to Glenn Miller, Tommy Dorsey, Duke Ellington, Count Basie, and many different bandleaders in America. The guys started to do their own arrangements. So we lost the soloing, but made back in orchestration and in collectiveness.

The fading out of solos in dance band music in Trinidad may also be related to two other interrelated factors: the increasing access to new home sound equipment and record listening, in tandem with the rise of the middle class in the country, and the reorganization of radio formats. The rise of the middle class in the 1950s and early 1960s, and during most of the 1970s, created the conditions for a new political economy of circulation. More people could buy home sound equipment and records. As several studies have shown, during this period, access to home sound equipment was highly related to class mobility and the larger accumulation of individual financial capital (Keightley 1996, 2003; Björnberg 2009; Anderson 2006; Danielsen 2010; Milner 2010). And as a study of Trinidad and Tobago's economy reports, an increasing portion of the Trinidadian population began to have the power to buy during at least two significant historical moments: "In the postwar era, the economy experienced two great boom decades. . . . Real GDP growth averaged 8 percent in the 1950s as the economy diversified into manufacturing and construction through the use of import substitution industrialization strategies." Even though, the report adds, "Growth in import substitution manufacturing and the economy as a whole waned in the late 1960s, exacerbating the social unrest at the end of the decade," by 1973, "the quadrupling of oil prices . . . revived the econ-

3.3 A telling 1962 record jacket confirming the importance of home sound equipment during that period.

omy and created a 9.6-percent real annual growth rate from 1974 to 1979" (Meditz and Hanratty 1987).

In conjunction with this new and sizeable middle class with purchasing power—and thus access to home sound equipment—the radio became intimately related to the local record industry by cultivating a market for record sales and simultaneously working to expand its listening audience. It is significant that during the huge expansion of the local recording industry, radio formats in Trinidad changed and stations selected shorter rather than longer songs in order to be able to play more per hour. I believe this is why recorded instrumental solos of dance band recordings also fell out of favor and how simultaneously they gradually disappeared in live dance band performances.[19]

While the solos gradually went out of style during the 1960s, other forms of musical expression and creativity emerged, spurred by nationalist sentiment after independence. In an effort to promote local music and, by extension, national pride, arrangers began to create cover versions of some of the best-known foreign songs on the radio and famous songs from foreign films playing in Trinidad. Hence, in the 1960s, the local musical tradition of calypso was not only hailed as the music emblematic of Trinidad and Tobago but also used to "domesticate" songs from any foreign musical style into its own time signature and syncopated rhythms.[20] Put another way, Trinidadian arrangers used the calypso style to turn competing foreign songs into local expressions for consumption in their own local market. For a dance band musician like Roy, this nationalistic musical attitude would leave a profound imprint on how he came to recognize the benefits, in his own words, of "being yourself" — of playing what you know best and what you are known for, in both local and international music markets.

Roy describes the cover-version era as follows.

RC: After we got independence, there was an effort to compose and write our own local music, and to have our own Hit Parade. There was a program called *610 Hit Parade* on the radio station of the same name. Musicians began to compose their own songs. Joey Lewis composed "Joey's Saga." I myself played with Clarence Curvan a song called "610 Saga," which stayed on the Hit Parade for fifteen weeks or something like that on Radio 610. We recorded songs like "Port of Spain," "Maracas," and so on [songs that all focused on the local]. At the time, we were playing foreign songs and calypso. And so we had songs like "Crying in the Rain," "Rhapsody in Blue" . . .

JG: So you would play everything!

RC: Yes, everything. But we used to take the American songs and British songs and even some classics and play them in calypso. For example, Sel Wheeler took "The Mockingbird" — which was a march that we [the brass band at the orphanage] used to play for the kids to go to school — and he did it in calypso. We were happy about it because we grew up with that [at the orphanage], and we knew it well then. [Later on,] Clarence Curvan recorded a song called "Teensville" — a song by Chet Atkins, who was a very famous American guitar player — that made the band very popular at the time.

It's not every song that we turned into calypso. Some tunes did not work well in the calypso style. And in those days, if you played dance music, you had to play a variety of music. So in one hour we would play boleros, Latin, samba, mambo, rock and roll, and so on. But as years progressed after independence, we began to play more calypso music. So Chubby Checker had a song called "The Twist" that we played in calypso. We did "The Young Ones," "Crying in the Rain," "Quando, Quando, Quando," "Minuet in G" — all of them in calypso. We did "With a Song in My Heart" — which was an arrangement from [the steelband called] Invaders. We did also "In a Monastery Garden" based on the [calypso] arrangement by the late Monty Williams for [the dance band] Casanova.

We also played songs from movies like *The Sound of Music*, *The Good, the Bad, and the Ugly*, and *Star Wars* in calypso style. We took big songs like "Tuxedo Junction" and "Take the 'A' Train" and played them also in calypso style.

As Roy's description makes clear, to be a wanted musician in the 1960s, one had to know a wide range of repertoire and demonstrate great flexibility. It was not sufficient to know only how to play calypso; one had to also play foreign tunes in foreign styles, as well as foreign tunes in calypso style. From 1959 until he left for the United States in 1970, Roy participated in a remarkable number of recordings.

RC: After getting independence, a lot of things happened. We started to do more and more our own local music. With Clarence Curvan and Ron Berridge, we did an [instrumental] album of ten to twelve songs every year for three or four years. With Ron Berridge, we actually did two [instrumental] albums a year. One album was for carnival with all the [hit] calypsos [of the season]. Berridge would treat some of them [the hit calypsos] a little differently, by playing them more up-tempo or a little slower [than the original version]. As Berridge became very famous, we had also [an] opportunity to record Kitchener's 1966, 1967, and 1968 albums. We were the first band to record with Kitchener when he came back to reside in Trinidad. In addition to this, we would do three or four calypsonians' albums. In 1968, we also did Sparrow's album with "Mr. Walker," and so on. Apart from recording all this, later on in the year we would play foreign songs, boleros, cha cha cha, or mambo, or samba—some in their original style and others converted in the calypso style.

While in New York, from 1970 to 1977, Roy continued to play calypso, and also Jamaican music. Playing with the Jamaican bands of Hugh Hendricks and the Buccaneers and the Blues Busters duo of Philip James and Lloyd Campbell, Roy was featured as the key soloist in the performance of ska tunes as well as in the calypsos. In addition, in these two bands, Roy said, "we were playing a lot of the North American hits."

Whether it is because of particular socioeconomic contingencies (political independence, new radio policies), technical possibilities (home sound equipment, proliferation of recording studios), new musical trends (increased role of arranger, emergence and popularity of ska), or market demands (playing "a lot of the North American hits" in New York to get more gigs), one thing is clear: what Roy played, where, and when, and his sound and musical aesthetics, cannot be addressed as merely musical issues. Roy's consciousness of the musical possibilities and challenges that have marked his career has been deeply informed by being—and seeing himself as — a musical worker. And in that capacity, as his musical journey attests, he has understood that to ensure his survival he needed, in his own words, "to move with the flow."

SOUNDING YOURSELF

Roy listened to and played as many musical styles as he could from a very early age, but by the time he came back to Trinidad in 1977, he had adopted another position. "As a matter of fact, I did not even use to listen to foreign music. Nothing. I had returned, and I wanted to be back, adjusted. And then living out abroad, you cannot be somebody else. I learned all of that in New York. You'd better be yourself. You're not going to get anywhere being somebody else."

Roy grew up in Port of Spain, where there are hardly any East Indian musicians around, compared to south of the Caroni river. So the live music that he listened to in Trinidad and later on when he moved to New York, as described above, was a mix of African, European, and Latin American popular musics and jazz. Correspondingly, the music that he played and continues to play, as his 2011 interpretation of the local calypso during the graduation ceremony at the University of the West Indies clearly attests, enacts in sound production and stylistic references his history of listening and contributing to Trinidad's distinct cosmopolitan sonic environment. Emerging from this mix, Roy now describes his playing as follows: "We play in cut time. We are not playing whole notes, but quarter or eighth notes. Our accent is on [beats] one and three, and we play a lot of syncopation." Speaking about the way he plays as a Trinidadian, he adds, "We are really legato people. Listen to our slang. We are a 'la la' people, very legato. So you would find we play legato with a light tongue for smoothness. But we also use the tongue not fully staccato but semi staccato. In contrast, hear merengue, for example. They have freakin' lines, like the sound of an accordion with lots of staccato. That is part of their cultural expression."

After seven years abroad, with only a brief interruption in 1975, Roy came to this conclusion: "All of us who [returned or] stayed here, we are champions then. Even with all the problems we have, we are staying. I like the people. I like who I am. And we have to take care of each other."

As is evident in this passage, Roy is at once highly conscious of the socioeconomic and political importance of sounding himself aesthetically, as well as ethically committed to helping his own people — Trinidadian musicians and singers — in the face of a highly competitive, cutthroat music market. As Brother Resistance, the president of Trinbago Unified Calypsonians

Organization and of the Copyright Organization of Trinidad and Tobago, points out, to make the decision to return home after several years abroad requires not only an inner strength but also a deep commitment to making a difference in your own country.

BROTHER RESISTANCE: When he [the musician who migrated] comes back, he is ready to make the adjustment. Getting back the name [one's reputation] is one thing, but to make the adjustment to the [socioeconomic] conditions is extremely difficult. Because when you are in a foreign country, even though most of the time things are rough, there are written standards: the contract for playing, the way they take care of you, the backstage facilities, all of these different things, including your necessity to be professional in your approach, your timing [showing up on time], and everything like that. And then you come back home to Trinidad and the attitude goes in the toilet, you know?

JG: It's tough. . . .

BR: For somebody who flies abroad and who comes back home and has to deal with that! Some musicians don't hold up—they snap. They get grouchy; they get grumpy. They find it too difficult to deal with [that], or they just simply surrender and go back out again to look for better conditions. So it is an amazing feat to make the adjustment and to stay [back home] doing the music.

So it is not surprising to hear Roy conclude, "All of us who [returned or] stayed here, we are champions then." However, he knows only too well that to continue to be a champion, the work will never be finished.

4 • LEADING THE BAND

From the time the All Stars opened their set with the appropriate "Get Up and Dance," it was a different story. Every line and nuance in the band's arrangement could be distinctly heard and the brass harmonies and riffs were at their sweetest. **TERRY JOSEPH, "KAISO ALL STARS SHOWS SUPERIORITY,"** *EXPRESS*, SEPTEMBER 25, 1996

Roy Cape and the All Stars was the band of choice for the launch of the carnival celebrations held last evening by the National Carnival Commission. And, the truth be told, there could have been no other. His is simply the aggregate which speaks to and about Trinidad music, the calypso, as no other can, or no other has in the last two decades or so. . . . Roy Cape has helped set the standard for calypso big band music. **"HATS OFF TO ROY CAPE" (EDITORIAL),** *SUNDAY GUARDIAN*, JANUARY 7, 1998

Shortly after his return from New York, Roy became a bandleader. The life of a musician and bandleader in Trinidad is markedly different from that in North America. Trinidad's musicians receive hardly any residual monies from record sales due to ongoing illegal dubbing and a lack of copyright enforcement, and there is no revenue at all from performing rights when the band provides the backup accompaniment on recordings of well-known singers. Most bands, including Roy's, make money as music laborers—on a performance basis. They are paid only when they play.

One of Roy's constant preoccupations as a bandleader is thus about economics. In the Caribbean context, and more particularly in Trinidad, Roy's story about how his band has not only survived but thrived over the past thirty years is thus exceptional and instructive.

If the sound of a band and the appeal of the lead singers contribute to the band's reputation and circulation, they do not tell the whole story about the band's commercial success and numerous performance contracts throughout the year. One of the key features that emerges from the exchange below, and that helps explain Roy's success as a bandleader, concerns his ability to manage relations—or, to be more precise, to manage multiple relations simultaneously. Roy is aware of the whole spectrum of relationships, while at the same time he is fully concentrating on the songs and quality of performance. Roy's discourse in this chapter is a bandleader's discourse. It is about the immaterial labor required to form and to keep a band together. What is addressed here is how, for Roy, the notion of being a bandleader involves working with, acknowledging, and caring about others. It is about social work and a social network. As one possible outcome of his tendency to avoid confrontation, it is at all times about managing relations with finesse.

In this vein, it is striking to see how and what Roy remembers as a bandleader. His memory works by marking out relationships as multiple conjunctions of time and space. The extent to which he acknowledges others in his narrative is no less extraordinary than the number of times he specifies "from that year, to this year, for that show." Why so many details? Because these are the things that Roy remembers and the way he remembers. They are central to the memory work of this musician. The details are not there to comply with some abstract standard of writing history. So the form of this chapter follows the form of his memory work. To read him—rather than just take his discourse and rewrite it as a typical text—it is important to align our understanding with Roy's memory process and to take his subjectivity seriously.

This chapter is based on dialogic writing and differs in many ways from the usual interview questions. It comes from talking together. So I am here for a conversation, not there just to ask questions. Sometimes after telling him what I know about something, the most important word Roy utters is "yes" after I finish. At other times, my questions are very open, allowing him to take me on a particular track that he finds important—and which I might not have considered otherwise. Our exchange greatly benefits from the cumulative process of listening, hearing, and learning from each other. So the stories that emerge would most likely not be the same if Roy was conversing with another interlocutor. By now, Roy knows far more about my interests and knowledge as a scholar and as a musician, and the different kinds of readership I have in mind when we converse together. And I know far more about his interests and the kind of knowledge he wants to impart to the different publics he has in mind during our conversations. We are both attempting to tune in to each other's respective desires in this project.

BACK TO TRINIDAD'S MUSIC SCENE: ROY'S EXPERIENCE AS A RETURNEE

After seven years in New York, Roy experienced the challenge of being a returnee to Trinidad. Emigration and the migrants' return, their experiences and societal interactions, have been a big subject in Caribbean studies.[1] Many scholars have reported how returnees have often been castigated as promoting conflicts through estrangement and the discouragement of being back home rather than contributors to positive social changes or economic growth. Few, however, have emphasized the importance of recognizing returnee "brain gains" as opposed to émigré "brain drains" (Potter, Conway, and Phillips 2005: 2, 4). The story that Roy tells about his return to Trinidad in our exchange provides a window on "return migrants as human agents" (Potter, Conway, and Phillips 2005: 8). It shows not only how he adapted to the changing circumstances of Trinidad after his return, but how his reputation—building on his recognized experience as a bandsman and his impressive sound on the saxophone—and his circulation in different musical milieus in New York led him to be viewed as an asset, as a source of cultural capital and transnational connections.

What Roy's story here also shows is that a successful return to one's country of birth is the result not only of the returnee's skills and agency but also of the particular conjuncture in which he returns—as Roy puts it, "at the right place at the right time." In contrast to today's musical scene, where live brass sections have by and large disappeared, replaced by synthesizers and samplers, brass sections in both calypso tent bands and party bands at the time Roy came back to Trinidad were ubiquitous and considered essential to most reputable bands.

Agency and the right conjuncture together make a powerful combination. What strikes me the most in Roy's story about his return to Trinidad is the determination he showed to use his musical skills and to seek opportunities to pursue his dream—to make music full time in spite of the economic hardships this would certainly entail. What is also revealing in his story is how much time and effort he dedicates to nurturing and continually expanding his collaborative networks—a preoccupation that cannot be overestimated in a musician's professional career.

Roy and I are now at his house, sitting at the dining table. We are both eager to continue our conversations about his musical journey after his return to Trinidad. This is how our dialogue unfolded in December 2010.

JG: [Brother] Resistance was telling me about how difficult it is for most musicians who have lived abroad for many years to come back home. The adjustment to the hard realities of Trinidad's music business—including the limited financial resources, right up to the new millennium, poor musical facilities (in terms of both number and basic equipment in performance spaces), frustrating cultural habits (for example, not showing up on time for rehearsals or performances), and until recently a lack of written contracts—has been for many too much to bear and made them snap, and leave again. And many of those who decide to stay, he was telling me, become grouchy and grumpy. How did it go for you when you returned from New York?

RC: After leaving New York in 1977, I landed in Trinidad with $125 U.S., and I was scared to death, because Trinidad is my country and if you don't have a way out in coming to Trinidad, life could be very sad. You could end up crazy or in a mental hospital or something. Anyhow, this was where my heart was, so I came home. When I came home, the elder people would have known me, but the younger ones did not know me because I was much older than them.

JG: So economically, how did you survive?

RC: My brother used to *casa* [someone who runs the gambling games] in a club. So I would go by him on a Friday evening and hang out with him at the club. You know where I used to live? I did ten days with the Unemployment Relief Program [URP]. But I wasn't from that area, so I was getting pressure for getting work there. The guys from the area where I grew up went to the director of the URP, and told him that I went to school and grew up in that area and that I needed help. He accepted to assist me and gave me employment. I became a tradesman assistant and worked on the road for six years. In the meantime, however, I kept plugging with the music. This is where my heart was, so I was looking for a way to find some gig that would allow me to leave URP. People like Fortunia Ruiz, Jude Bethel, and Michael Tobas, with whom I had played for years, were based at the KH [recording] Studio at Sea Lots.[2]

JG: But you were not able to join them?

RC: At this time, I was working with the URP. I learned there was a new tent opening named the Kingdom of the Wizards. [Calypsonian] Shadow was the leading star, and Leroy Calliste [known as Black Stalin in the calypso music scene] was the emcee.

JG: But Leroy Calliste was working at the Revue [Calypso Tent] before, no?³

RC: Yes, before that, during many years! I went to Mr. Munroe at his store named Cinderella on Frederick Street, and I said to him, "Mr. Munroe, my name is Roy Cape, and I played with Frankie Francis, Clarence Curvan, Ron Berridge, and the Sparrow Troubadours." "Very impressive," he said, "but I am not handling the music." Arthur de Coteau was handling the music. Well, I had known Arthur because we both grew up behind the bridge, so he knew me. Plus, when I was playing with Frankie Francis, he was the bass player. That was my boy, then. I went to him and told him that I needed work. He took me in. I played the '78 carnival season at the Kingdom of the Wizards, and the money was fantastic compared to what I had earned when I left Trinidad in 1970. By the next season, Shadow left the Kingdom of the Wizards and opened his Masters' Den and some members decided to support him and follow him. These include Funny, Rio, Gypsy, and many other calypsonians. But Leroy [Black Stalin] stayed with William Munroe.

JG: And you stayed with the Kingdom of the Wizards with William Munroe?

RC: Yes. The tent was based at the Port Services Club directly in front of where the Hyatt Regency is located at the present time. It was a wooden building where the port workers used to socialize after working. Around the month of August 1978, Munroe decided to record Black Stalin's first album, titled *To the Caribbean Man*. Earl Rodney was the arranger and the bass player, and the other musicians included Clive Bradley (keyboards), Fortunia Ruiz (trumpet and flügelhorn), myself (alto sax), Jude Bethel (tenor sax), and Fitzroy "Fitz" Jackson (guitar). This group of musicians was called Earl Rodney and Friends.

JG: You had known Earl Rodney for years before that, hadn't you? You played with him in Sparrow's band in the late 1960s, so was it through this old connection that you ended up in Earl Rodney's band?

RC: Yes. I had not really known Leroy before, but he had known me. Little did I know that many things would come from our collaboration. I was fortunate to play on Leroy's *Caribbean Man* album, not only because of the friendship we developed together from that time on, but also because this was a promotion and a chance for me to get back on track.

JG: He won the Calypso Monarch that year with his song ["Caribbean Man"], so that was truly a really big album. And you mentioned to me last time, a few months after carnival that year you went with [Black] Stalin to Carifesta in Cuba to perform in front of the whole Caribbean community of artists assembled there for the week-long festival. So you really came back in the music scene at the right time.

RC: Yes, I happened to be at the right place at the right time. And that same year, Shorty [Lord Shorty, calypsonian sobriquet for Garfield Blackman, who later renamed himself Ras Shorty I] came to Semp Studio, located on Mucurapo Road, and he needed the assistance from the musicians who worked at this studio. We all had great respect and admiration for his music.[4] I accepted to work with him and so did all the other musicians. We did the album *Soca Explosion* with "Om Shanti" (1978). So this is how my work in a recording studio began after my return from New York. And that same year, 1979, we did Explainer's *Positive Vibrations*, and Poser's "Ah Tell She" [1979 Road March]. The musical director for these albums was Carl "Beaver" Henderson, and the executive directors of this band called TnT Rainbow included not only Carl "Beaver" Henderson, but also Wayne Jameson, Frank Aggarrat (one of the most reputed and respected sound engineers and record studio technicians in the Caribbean), and myself.

ON BECOMING A BANDLEADER AND TAKING NEW RESPONSIBILITIES

Roy and I now discuss his transition from being a freelance musician to becoming a bandleader at a calypso tent. In the 1980s, calypso continued to be the local music that was most successful commercially, and thus to be working at a calypso tent and for the calypso competitions guaranteed bandleaders like Roy a substantial amount of work for a good portion of the year. This section provides a detailed description of how a bandleader comes to perform at some of the most prestigious calypso tents in the country. What it does not acknowledge—at least, not enough—is how, for a bandleader, to perform at a calypso tent is hard work. Since a calypso tent typically features as many as twenty-eight artists—based on the implicit motto "the more, the better"—at the beginning of the carnival season the bandleader must schedule many rehearsals with the artists and, along with his band, learn a vast repertoire. For the entire carnival season, which usually lasts from four to six weeks, working at a calypso tent also means working long hours, typically starting at 8 p.m. and ending usually no earlier than midnight or 1 a.m.

But Roy does not speak about this. Instead, he focuses on the pride of being able to work with the best musicians and artists in the country. Most important to him is to explain how—and this is perhaps where he derives his greatest sense of accomplishment—he was able to help musicians perform in better conditions and earn better incomes. From the outset, what the story below makes clear is that Roy as a bandleader becomes an agent of change for his musicians and also for the calypsonians his band accompanies, by promoting professional standards and cultivating mutual respect among calypsonians and musicians.

As can be deduced from the story below, the combination of Roy's initiative as a bandleader and the calypso tent named Spektakula where he worked for twelve years was felicitous. Both musician and institution work to bring change. Founded by music promoters Claude and Franck Martineau, the Spektakula calypso tent was managed successfully as a commercial enterprise with a cultural mission. It aimed to offer a modern conception of a show and to attract young and old alike by featuring veteran calypsonians alongside younger soca artists (soca, a musical offshoot of calypso, had begun to feature mainly up-tempo and light lyrics in the 1980s and, for that reason, it should be remembered, was not then welcome in every calypso tent). By organizing shows featuring local calypso and soca next to R&B, soul, reggae, or Latin music, its founders strived to de-ghettoize local music (even if only calypso and soca) and promote local artists. By organizing shows throughout the annual calendar in and outside Trinidad, in the Caribbean region, and in Toronto (Canada), the Martineau brothers fought the confinement of calypso and soca to the carnival season only—the legacy of both the colonial administration and the Catholic Church.[5] Working for the Martineau brothers at the Spektakula calypso tent, Roy could be said to have returned to Trinidad not only at the right time and place, but also with the right people.

Leading a Calypso Tent Band

RC: By that time the 1979 calypso season was approaching, William Munroe decided to refurbish the old market on Charlotte and George streets. After much time and investment in this venue, Mr. Munroe realized that the venue did not suit the acoustics for this venture. He had a building on Henry Street and in one week's time he bought the next-door building. And in one week's time he was able to prepare the building for the opening of the 1979 carnival season.

By then Leroy and me and [Brother] Valentino [Ellord Phillip's calypsonian sobriquet] had started to gel. In 1979 and in 1980 I did a lot of shows as the only horn with Valentino. We did the Rolls Royce Club in Port of Spain. We worked at Mackie's place at Sunshine Avenue in San Juan. We worked in Tobago and also in Grenada. Most of 1979 and 1980, I did a lot of shows with Valentino and with Leroy, who had won the crown [the 1979 Calypso Monarch Competition].

JG: Was this series of shows sufficient for you and your family to live on? Or did you have to take another job during the day to supplement your income?

RC: No, playing at these shows was not enough to live on, but I did not take a day job. By the middle of '79, I went to Mr. Munroe with Jay and asked him to hire the band [the TnT Rainbow band] to play in his tent [the Kingdom of the Wizards Calypso Tent] for the 1980 carnival season.[6] He agreed.

JG: So how did that work at the calypso tent? Did the band you played with become the tent's band, as opposed to your band?

RC: In 1980 I was the bandleader of TnT Rainbow at the Kingdom of the Wizards. At the end of that season, TnT Rainbow was disbanded and was replaced by the Kingdom of the Wizards band with me as the musical director. This band consisted of the musicians Clive Mitchell (trumpet), Noel Gill (trombone), Roy Cape (alto sax), Hayes Durity (keyboards), Junior Wharwood (guitar), Michael Nysus (bass), Joey Samuel (drums), and Carlton Braithwaite (congas)—most of whom were former members of the TnT Rainbow band.

In 1980, around the month of August, Mr. Munroe approached me to be the bandleader for the 1981 carnival season. "If I must accept the job," I said, "I must be in control of the salaries of the musicians. If I have that authority, I will accept the job." He agreed to my proposal. In the late 1970s up to 1980, the calypso tents were paying about $600 to $700 a week to the individual musician. I got him to agree to pay everybody $1,000. The following year, I asked for more, and every year after, I go up a little bit more. By the time I left the calypso tent, I had musicians getting $2,000 a week.[7]

Building Reputation through the Band's Name

JG: But during all this time, even though you were the bandleader, the band was still named after the tent, the Kingdom of the Wizards, to indicate for whom and where you played during the carnival season, right?

RC: Yes, that's correct. Sometime after carnival 1981 there was a change of tent ownership. Spektakula Promotions took over the Kingdom of the Wizards tent that was run by Mr. Munroe, and the new administration decided to call the band Spektakula Band led by Roy Cape.

JG: So when you changed the name of the band to Roy Cape Kaiso All Stars, were you still playing at a calypso tent then?

RC: I did not change the name of the band. When that year [1981] Stalin was having three shows at Sparrow Hideaway promoted by Eustace "Solo" Solomon, he decided to represent the band under another name. When I reached Sparrow Hideaway to provide the musical accompaniment for Stalin on the first night, I saw [on] the poster "Roy Cape Kaiso All Stars." Stalin did not think that I was looking out for myself, so he took it on himself to advertise me in the show under that name. In 1982, I asked Spektakula Promotions to be represented as Roy Cape Kaiso All Stars instead of Spektakula Band led by Roy Cape. My wish was granted.

JG: This name, Roy Cape Kaiso All Stars, put your band on the map as an entity of its own. But it would seem also that the Spektakula calypso tent gained in having your band named after you, since you would have been known as a very experienced musician by many people already.

RC: As you said, it put us on the map, but Spektakula put the food on the table for us for many years. It worked out for everybody. I stayed at the Spektakula calypso tent for twelve years [1982–1994]. By then, we had worked out for the musicians to be on a monthly salary all year long. In those years we accompanied many, many calypsonians. To name just a few: Arrow [Montserrat], Swallow [Antigua], Beckett [St. Vincent], Gypsy, Chalkdust, Relator, David Rudder, Tambu, Duke, Superblue, Black Stalin, Funny, Rio, Bally, and Lord Nelson [Trinidad]. From year to year the management would change the selection of the artists to produce variety and a show of top quality.

Through the years outside of the carnival season, Spektakula did many shows. We were the accompanying band for Shadow at the first and only showing of Michael Jackson and the Jackson Five in Trinidad in 1978. In 1982 we had a memorable show with Kool and the Gang at the Queen's Park Savannah during which we accompanied [calypsonians] Nelson, Explainer, and Chalkdust. The local artists impressed both the audience and the promoters to the point that the promoters decided to organize concerts featuring one prominent local artist with the help of supporting acts to open the show. The first one presented Nelson in Concert. This concert had a massive success and was held over many weeks at the Spektakula Forum. Before that time, the only person who used to perform in concert was the Mighty Sparrow. This situation changed radically with the initiative of Spektakula

Promotions. After Nelson in Concert, many other shows followed suit, featuring the Doctors in Concert, Black Stalin in Concert, David Rudder in Concert, Superblue in Concert, Baron in Concert, Sparrow and Sugar Aloes in Concert, and many other top exponents of the art form. Spektakula Promotions was then the premier promotional outfit of Trinidad and Tobago and in the eastern Caribbean as a whole.

JG: So Spektakula Promotions featured local calypsonians alongside foreign artists and presented a mix of local calypsos and other musical styles on the same show?[8]

RC: During our twelve years with Spektakula, we did shows with a great variety of artists, including Third World [reggae], Shalimar [soul-R&B group], Evelyn "Champagne" King [R&B, disco, and "post-disco"[9]], Teddy Pendergrass [R&B, soul], and Barry White [soul, funk, and disco]. Apart from performing in Trinidad, Spektakula did yearly shows in Barbados, St. Lucia, and Antigua. We also went to Tobago at every carnival. The support in Tobago was tremendous. We even went as far as Toronto and New York. I have been very proud to work with Spektakula, which I would say was in a class above the rest. Our band was very disciplined and whatever was promoted was always delivered at a very high standard to the people. In my twelve years at Spektakula we never started a show late.

Scouting Musicians

RC: I ran the band as a musical director from 1981 until 1995. The musicians that I grew up with were great musicians and this is where I got my music education from. Being able to produce a "self sound" on my saxophone, what I am looking for in selecting another musician is the sound that he possesses. The sound that he possesses creates a personality. And if you take five horns that can each have a distinct sound, you will get a sound signature.

Through the years and the many musicians with whom I have worked—as you can see from the bands and different musicians with whom I have been—I have always made sure after someone leaves the band that the next person who is going to replace him be of the same kind of caliber or even with superior musical skills than the one who left. Through the years, especially in the calypso tent, there were lots of movements with the musicians. For example, one guy may go to Berklee to study music in Boston; another one might leave to go to Canada, and so on.

JG: Did you ever hire a female musician for Roy Cape Kaiso All Stars?

4.1 Juliet Robin on keyboard, still performing to this day. Courtesy Juliet Robin.

RC: In all these years, I had only one female musician in the band from 1989 to 1992: Juliet Robin, a keyboard player. Juliet came from a music family.[10] In the 1950s or 1960s, there was an all-female steelband called the Girl Pat Steel Orchestra. But music was always regarded in Trinidad as a man's game. The music business was rough and tumble. So you did not have many females. One should not be prejudiced because of one's gender. Once someone is good, then . . . Juliet could read music, and [keyboard player and arranger] Leston Paul who had been playing with us had to leave the band. So I had to find someone who could play and who could join the band. I think that Juliet came to me. I agreed to admit her in the band, and Juliet played for two or three years in the tent. She is still doing her thing. In later years, she played with Shandileer, led by Eman Hector. Today things have changed. You are going to go to the Police Band and you are going to see females in the Police Band. That was not so ten years ago.

JG: Still, I have never seen any female musician in the dance hall.

RC: No, you don't see that. You may get female vocalists, but not musicians. But it is a little bit opening up because I am seeing now young people, female players, play saxophone and trumpet and trombone. I think that it was felt at one point that you had to be so physically strong to play an instrument.[11] But today the Police Band has quite a few females in it. It is going to influence.... In all cases, whether there is a female musician or not in the band, as a musical director, one has to understand the talent that is available to one. When one understands that, one will know the method that one has to use to have a good band. So you cannot treat someone as though he is in second grade, or as someone who is in sixth grade. I have been a stickler for a real soul.

JG: What does that mean?

RC: Okay, how can I put it: I've always been someone who understood how important real soul is. Without real soul, you don't have the sound. So you have to create an environment where people will feel comfortable. If you insult someone and you "paranoid" them, you will get nothing out of them. So you have to know how to talk to them, even if they made a mistake that has to be corrected. You have to know how to talk to them without embarrassing them in front of everybody and making them feel inhibited, feel small or ashamed. But then, for everything that we do, rehearsal is the key to the success of performance.

Rehearsing Democratically

RC: When we do soca music, there's no written music. What happens is this: after having listened to the material before and gotten on top of it, Juice [the band's arranger] takes the rhythm section and tells them the chords, and then the musicians run it, run it, run it.

JG: So Juice doesn't write the lead sheets for the chord progression, for example?

RC: Most times it's by ear, but there are things that he is going to write music for. For instance, when we performed at CLICO Trinidad and Tobago Jazz Festival, promoted in Tobago, and we did some R&B and some funk and things like that, for these songs Juice would write the music.

JG: So he would write the brass lines?

RC: The brass line, the bass, the guitar, everything. With soca, we don't really have to do that—although it is advisable to have music. Because if you don't

ROY CAPE (KAISO) ALL STARS MUSICIANS OVER THE YEARS

Trumpet: Clyde Mitchell, Fortunia Ruiz, Thomas Patton, Godfrey Williams, Roger Jaggassar, Neuman George, Hayden Robin, Ricky Clarke, Michael Lindsay
Trombone: Charleau, Noel Gill, Patrick Spicer, Lambert Phillip, David Jacob
Alto saxophone: Roy Cape, Frankie Francis, Jude Bethel, Selvon Sylvester
Tenor sax: Dennis Wilkinson, Curtis Lewis, David Phillip, Gavin Marcelle
Keyboard: Allan Oxley, Ivan Durity, Leston Paul, Juliet Robin, Kenneth Baptiste, Carlysle "Juiceman" Roberts
Bass: Eldon Oliver, Ron Reid, Gerard Rollocks, Albert Bushe Jr., Don "Sunshine" Diaz, Michael Nysus, Anthony "Bassie" Boynes
Guitar: Junior Wharwood, Tony Voisin, Clarence Charles, Arnold "Sly" Punette
Drums: Joey Samuel, Barry Howard, Stephen Jardine
Percussion: Winston Matthews, Kenneth Sylvester, Barry Howard, Don Craigwell, Stephen Jardine
Congas: Carlton "Jabbar" Braithwaithe, Kenneth McConey
Sound engineers: Wayne Jameson, Brian Morris, Treldon Thompson, Victor Donawa, Karan Mahabal, Marcus Ramsaran, Lyndon Kelly, Ray Roopnarin, Robert Cherrie
Samplers: Virgil Williams, Andrew Phillip
Stagehands: Michael De Freitas, Marlon Cudjoe

---

have music and you go out in the country, it makes life difficult for the musicians [out there who might join the band just for a show]. Worse, if they can read, they don't like to listen. So what Juiceman does is this: he takes the rhythm section [which, in addition to him on keyboard, includes the guitarist, bassist, and drummer], and he works them over. And when they [the musicians of the rhythm section] have gotten their parts, we come in.

JG: Okay, but Juiceman would have given you the [horn section] parts?

RC: What we do today is this: Juiceman doesn't take the music home, and he alone does the arrangement. After the rhythm section has mastered its part, then he goes to the band room. They [the rhythm section players] play the song, and he is then going to access our [the horn musicians'] suggestions. He would find the musicians suggesting the licks that they are going to play, and when we think we have it good, we are now going to write the parts into a score.

JG: So you go line by line, like that?

RC: Yeah. It's a little time consuming, but what it does is that it gives everybody an opportunity to contribute to the arrangement then. I think Juice's philosophy is that because the horn players are experienced, he should allow them to have an input. He understands that we would know what would be simpler or what may be more intricate for us. And as I said, it gives everybody a little chance to participate, so it makes the whole thing feel like it's the whole band that is contributing then, and not, you know, just one individual—even though it is Juice's responsibility. I guess I have my psychological way that I deal with him, and he has his own psychological way that he deals with the musicians.

JG: So during the normal carnival season, how many times a week does your band rehearse? What is your schedule like? And how long is a rehearsal each time?

RC: We rehearse for the jobs that we have. We are always in the band room every week.

JG: And how many times a week?

RC: Two times, three times a week.

JG: And how long are the rehearsals?

RC: We got about three hours.

JG: Every week, with the [very experienced] musicians you have?

RC: Well, the band is very tight. I give you an example. When we come out of Toronto where we had a month playing (until August), we've been working. So we haven't had a spell of time sitting around idle. And we've been working since we came back here [in Trinidad]. And working, like, last Saturday we played for BPTT [British Petroleum Trinidad and Tobago]. The week before, we played for the National Insurance Board, and we played also for Neal and Massy company. These were all Christmas functions with the ladies in long dresses. So we have to play not exactly ballroom, but a little bit of R&B, some slow music so that people can dance—because it's not a soca fete. Like the first session, we play cool, the R&B and things like that. In the second session, we start with light soca [moderate tempo], and we end up at the end of the session with the heavy soca [fast tempo]. By that time, most of the people had a few drinks. They had a little nice time, so they can now take the heavy jamming. Right now [January], we are already into carnival music. So we finish the Christmas music. So from here till maybe the fifth, sixth of January, we're gonna be working on carnival music. As a matter of fact we have done four or five songs already, recorded songs, songs that are popular already.

JG: So after Juiceman writes the arrangements, you rehearse two or three times a week to prepare these songs?

RC: During carnival, sometimes we may have to play in the night, and then come back in the band room and rehearse.

JG: To learn another song?

RC: You might find that a particular song came out after we stopped rehearsing, and it might be a hit. So we have to get on with it. Even down to the last week of carnival, somebody might come up with a bomb [during carnival, "bomb" refers to the release of a new song at the last minute], and it's looking like it is going to be the Road March.[12] So we have to have it [as part of our repertoire], so we go back to the band room. Like when we are doing the Soca Monarch competition—the Soca Monarch competition is on Friday—the whole of that week we play. Sunday night, three gigs, we have to come out on Monday, rehearse, work on Monday night; come out on Tuesday, rehearse, and work on Tuesday night; come out on Wednesday, rehearse, and work on Wednesday night; come out on Thursday, rehearse, and work on Thursday night. And then Friday is the final of the soca competition.

JG: Wow. And for the final, you often provide the accompaniment for the entire Soca Monarch show, including the groovy soca and the power soca songs.[13] So that means that you have been learning something like fifty songs?

RC: Yep. The amount of songs we learn, Jocelyne! In 1985, we did one calypso competition, the Biggest Universal Calypso King Show [BUCKS], which was organized by William Monroe. The first time the competition was held, the first prize was $100,000 TT [Trinidadian dollars]. Sparrow won that, and Leroy came second. We did over a hundred and something songs, because in the preliminaries we had thirty-something people. Count two songs apiece, and that's sixty songs. Then we get to the semifinal, we have twenty-something people with again two songs apiece. You're gonna find like twenty-something new songs because they are not going to sing all the songs they sang in the preliminaries. And then when you get to the finals, there are eleven people. They have two songs each. You could be getting eleven people with three new songs. So in one show, we could have crossed over 150 songs then.

JG: That's a lot of new songs.

RC: And music from people from all over the place, Barbados, St. Vincent, all the islands.

JG: Would the calypsonians come with their scores?

RC: Yeah, that makes it easier—if the music has been documented properly. In some cases the music is very shabby [not properly written]. It requires us to make corrections, and that takes up time. But once the music is readable, it's easier. Sometimes we may have to supplement the band, or augment it by a few players. As a matter of fact, in those competitions [BUCKS], I had two bands. I had eight trumpets, six trombones, eight saxophones, but I divided the band in two. And we had two separate rehearsals, so I knew who played what.

JG: Two bands so that you could handle all this material.

RC: Because to sit down, to play for thirty-something people, would have been too much.

ROY CAPE KAISO ALL STARS RECORD

For most Caribbean musicians, including Trinidadians, recordings have been more of a promotional device to obtain contracts for local shows or to be taken on tour than a means of making money. Local illegal dubbing, combined with the lack of resources to enforce copyright laws, have made recordings problematic financially, yet necessary for publicity. Hence the economic downfall of the recording industry, so often referred to in western Europe and North America, has changed little in the daily lives of Caribbean musicians. To this day, musicians earn most of their income through performance. Yet, for Roy, the first LP recording of his band marked an important moment in his career as a bandleader. It demonstrated the musical experience and ability of his band members to perform songs in calypso and soca by a great variety of artists—the ability to play a wide range of repertoire that is partly responsible for Roy Cape Kaiso All Stars' success as a band to this day.

In the story below, it is striking that even after he launched the first recording of his band, Roy continued in the 1990s (and still continues) to perform as a backup band for other artists in live performances and for recording studio sessions. In contrast to most soca bands from the 1990s onward, bands that perform with only a selected number of artists, Roy has opted to keep his band open to performing with many artists, and to becoming well known for a variety of unique musical skills. This includes both calypso and soca, and occasionally other genres, including reggae, R&B, and ballads. Could this choice, which continues today, come from Roy's sense of responsibility as a bandleader to secure performance and recording contracts, and thus ensure the livelihood and survival of his musicians and singers? His ethical approach to and care of his musicians may help to explain how he has kept many of his musicians for more than fifteen years in his band. But here I am getting ahead of my conversation with Roy. After we talked about his work at the calypso tent, I asked Roy to explain how his band was able to enter the recording market and to make the first recording of Roy Cape Kaiso All Stars.

Roy Cape Kaiso All Stars' First Time on Vinyl

RC: I was still working at Spektakula. I did this first album in 1990 with the help of Mr. Otte Mierez, entitled *Roy Cape Kaiso All Stars: 1990 First Time*. The album featured eight songs [three of which are played in a medley; see box] and was recorded at Muzik Kraft recording studios in Petit Bourg, Trinidad. In addition to the musicians listed here, the album also included steel pan by Earl Brooks.

JG: Did you make some money from this album or was it mostly used, as is frequently still the case in the Caribbean, as a promotion to get performance contracts?[14]

RC: We had already come to the conclusion that we were not going to make money out of records, except for very few exceptions. Even up to today, we are recording with the knowledge that records don't sell in our environment. For the past few years we have produced about ten songs each season, but we don't even release them in record stores. We give them to the radio stations and hope that they will play them. And out of that, we hope to get live jobs. It is an unusual situation, because all around the world, records make money, and they also serve to get live gigs.

Recording as a Backup Band

JG: I did not know about the first album with your band, the Roy Cape Kaiso All Stars. But in the 1990s I began to see the name of your band on many CDs produced in Barbados at the recording studio owned by Eddy Grant, and appearing on his Ice label. At the time Grant's Blue Wave Recording Studio was one, if not the, most sophisticated recording studio and Ice, the most prestigious label around, and many of the most reputed calypsonians wanted to be associated with both of them.

RC: I had known about Eddy Grant through the hits he had in Trinidad (e.g., "Neighbor, Neighbor").[15] Living in the United States, I also heard on sev-

ROY CAPE KAISO ALL STARS: 1990 FIRST TIME.

Rainbow Wirl, RC 0190 [on the vinyl itself], ELP009 [on the record jacket].

Keyboards: Hayes Durity, Juliet Robin, Godwin Bowen
Drums: Joey Samuel
Bass: Michael Nysus
Guitar: Arnold "Sly" Punette
Percussions: Barry Howard
Congas: Kenneth McConney
Tenor sax: Dennis Wilkinson
Alto sax: Roy Cape
Trombone: Lambert Phillip
Trumpets: Ricky Clarke, Clyde Mitchell
Vocals: Allan Welch, Ann Marie "Twiggy" Parks[16]
Background vocals: Patsy Holder, Maria Small, Ann Marie Parks
Arranger of Pan Night and Day: Clive Bradley
Arranger of Watch Out My Children: Frankie Francis
Arrangement of medley: Godwin Bowen
Songs:
   Nah Do Dat (Iwer George)
   Watch Out My Children (Lord Shorty)
   Medley: Gimme More (Crazy), Doh Bother Meh (Lennox Picou), Poom Poom (Blue Boy), Total Disorder (Duke), Pan Night and Day (Kitchener), and We Eh Going Home (Tambu)

---

eral radio programs several other hits of his, including "Electric Avenue." While most of his hits until then had been mainly in Europe, this one had crossed over. I have a big respect for him as one of the early Caribbean artists who had made it internationally. Apart from being an artist, I gave him big credit for being also a businessman. By the time I came back to Trinidad, Eddy had moved back to the Caribbean and was now living in Barbados. He had bought there the Baileys Plantation and had built his recording studio. In 1986 I met him in Trinidad, and we became very good friends. Eddy gave me a nickname, Royston—which tells you, you know, the friendship we developed.

JG: Did you record at Eddy's recording studio with your whole band?

RC: No, but with most of them. [Roy's drummer, for example, was not included because in the recording studio, drum machine instead of live drumming was used.] I selected all the musicians from Trinidad who went to Eddy's Blue Wave Recording Studio in Barbados to work on all the materials Eddy was then recording. Between 1994 and 1996, somewhere around there, we did Superblue's CDs and many of his hits; we did Duke and Calypso Rose's albums; we also did three albums of Black Stalin, including *Rebellion*, and *Highway to Kaiso* by Roy Cape All Stars. We did also Roaring Lion ("Papa Chunks"). We also did work for Barbadian artists, including Gabby ("Dr. Cassandra") and Grynner, Adissa, Viking Tundah ("Ringbang"), and Gillo from St. Lucia ("Bois Bande"). So I was part of the evolution of the ringbang rhythm originated by Eddy Grant.[17] In 2000 I also did the accompaniment for Eddy Grant's "Ringbang show" in Tobago, featuring [calypsonian] Terror, Gabby, Stalin, Rose, Duke, Superblue, and Kitchener in what would be his final performance.

In my whole career, I always worked with the guys that are said to be troublesome. In the young people parlance, they are said to be "music-sick." Working with them, I found that these guys were geniuses. Such was the case with Eddy Grant.

JG: I noted on the record jackets you did on the Ice label that most of the arrangements you played were either by Eddy Grant, who is from Guyana, or Carlysle (Juiceman) Roberts, who is your own band arranger from Trinidad. I also noticed that you played some arrangements by Frankie McIntosh, who is from St. Vincent, but who has been living and working as a performer and as an arranger in New York for years and years. To record arrangements written by so many different people, with quite contrasting musical experiences, must have been a treat, but also a challenge, no?

RC: No, they are all from the Caribbean, they know what works with the music. We were fortunate at some point to work with arranger Frankie McIntosh of St. Vincent, who came from New York to Barbados to record one of Duke's albums. We were supposed to do about four songs in the album. After playing for a while, the guys were getting tired.

JG: Because the music was difficult to play?

RC: No, because it was difficult to read it. I asked Frankie if instead of writing the music in common time [4/4], he could do it in cut time [2/2]. He said that to write in cut time would require more writing, but if the guys were patient, he would do it.[18] And he went upstairs and he wrote the scores in a master form and send them to us down at the studio. We then read our own ledger from the master score, and we ended up doing the whole album.

JG: This is telling of how important it is to recognize the many things—and I mean, not only musical but also material things—that can slow down a recording studio session. But also how important it is to recognize that the way scores are written is cultural, not universal—even when the music is composed within the same system (i.e., the Western tonal system). Maybe living and working in New York for years led Frankie McIntosh to adopt a North American way of writing scores in 4/4 instead of in 2/2. But returning to your recording career. For several years you released CDs one after another. However, since 2002, you have not released your own CDs, and instead you have recorded singles, and placed the carnival hit songs of your lead singers in compilations by various producers. Can you speak about how you arrived at this choice?

RC: You know, we never stopped recording full albums. We record enough songs each year to produce a CD. But being conscious by experience that there is no financial return from the CDs, by 2002 we just decided to do CDs for radio stations.

FROM THE CALYPSO TENT TO THE DANCE HALLS AND FETES (wuk)

To live exclusively from their playing, island-based musicians face at least two main challenges. Locally, band musicians must perform not only the music most in demand, but also in the spaces (venues) and times (seasonal activities) that are generating most of the work and income.[19] In Trinidad in the 1990s, this meant playing calypso, but increasingly it also meant playing more soca. It also meant playing during the carnival season—the most important period of the year for the release of new music and for performance opportunities. While the number of musical events throughout the year has increased—festivals held in different locations in Trinidad and Tobago, including the Plymouth Jazz Festival (now renamed the Tobago Jazz Festival), Borough Day celebrations in Point Fortin, and so on—very few musicians who perform only in the twin islands are able to make ends meet. Most are forced to take a day job to supplement their music incomes.

In the next section, Roy and I address the different playing opportunities that his band enjoyed in the 1990s, and also the consequential decisions that he made as a bandleader during that period.

On Leaving the Calypso Tent

JG: I do not know of many bands who, after playing for years in calypso tents, moved on to become dance bands (except for Ed Watson and the

4.2 Roy Cape All Stars at a dance club in Toronto, 2009. Courtesy Jeff Packman.

Brass Circle). In your case, you were playing at one of the top calypso tents in Trinidad and Tobago, quite possibly the most commercially successful tent in the country. But you left Spektakula Promotions to become a dance band. What motivated you to leave Spektakula?

RC: I had twelve wonderful years at Spektakula there with lots of memories. But I thought I needed fresh challenges, and I am still dealing with those challenges. I left Spektakula Promotions after the carnival season in 1993. Not long after, Mr. Gary Dore asked me as the bandleader of Roy Cape Kaiso All Stars to be the resident band for the Kisskadee Caravan [it was referred to as a caravan because it was a roving tent, circulating in different parts of Trinidad] for the carnival 1994 season. I immediately agreed. The Kisskadee Caravan was the brainchild of Mr. Robert Amar. My relationship with him had gone back some time before this, and I was very happy to be associated with his venture. Mr. Amar was deeply involved in music projects. In addition to the Kisskadee Caravan, he had built one of the most professional recording studios in the region. Things did not work out because I believe we were not ready for ventures like this in Trinidad.

JG: But the Kisskadee Caravan did not perform as many days in the week as Spektakula did.

RC: That is correct, but that gave us more freedom. In 1994, senior calypsonians such as Shadow, Sparrow, Superblue, Black Stalin, and Duke had an opportunity to mix with younger artists such as General Grant, Kindred, Homefront, Denise Belfon, and many others. This show is what I would call a stadium show—not the regular calypso tent. Because of its magnitude, the show could only be marketed at such a large venue. It could not either run nightly as the regular calypso tents. Since we were not working every weekend, Mr. Amar gave his approval for Gary Dore to do bookings for the band. We were offered to play at Mr. William Munroe Socathon at the Spectrum. It was a packed show and you had in this show bands like Sound Rev, Shandileer, Byron Lee, Charlie's Roots, and many other bands, ourselves included.[20] In 1994, Marvin and Nigel Lewis were the vocalists of the band, and we had a very good showing—which created many jobs [in the dance halls and fetes] apart from the Kisskadee Caravan. At the end of the season, we were still doing accompaniment for calypso shows.

JG: So by not having to play every night and every weekend, the schedule of the Kisskadee Caravan left you more free, and helped you make a smooth transition from playing in the calypso tent to becoming an independent band.

RC: Yes. After that season with the Kisskadee Caravan [1994], we were fully in the dance hall and fete [circuit].

Booking Contracts: On Making Choices and Taking Chances

JG: I know that soon after your band made the move to the dance hall, you began to play in dance clubs. I also recall seeing your band play in the Brass Festival.[21] I called Mr. Cliff Harris who, with the help of his associates, conceived and produced that festival. As he put it, "you became a fixture." He explained that the Brass Festival ran from 1989 to 2006 and that it was going on before your band entered the dance hall. But to enter that festival, as your band did when you moved into the dance hall, was important. As he indicated to me, the Brass Festival was in fact not really a brass festival, but rather a music festival with bands from the Caribbean.

RC: Yes, at these shows, you had about fifteen bands and maybe over fifty soca and calypso stars. At that point, that was the biggest annual carnival show. You had bands from all the Caribbean and all the top bands in Trinidad. This Brass Festival attracted the largest crowd you would have gotten in a carnival fete, thousands and thousands of people. And this went on for years.

JG: Mr. Harris remarked that the brass festival was the highlight of all the soca bands throughout the Caribbean. It included bands like Charlie's Roots, Shandileer, Sound Rev, and your band from Trinidad (to name only a few), the Moss International of Grenada, a Surinam band, one from the Bahamas, Burning Flames from Antigua, Byron Lee and the Dragonaires from Jamaica, Spice, Krosfyah, and Square One from Barbados, and Ellie Matt Swinging Stars of Dominica. One festival included as many as fifteen bands. The event was typically held on the Saturday one week prior to carnival. It would start at 5 p.m. and would end at 6 a.m. in the morning. Every band wanted to be part of this major highlight. As Mr. Harris put it, "In the same way that every cricketer dreams one day to play at Lord's [the most prestige cricket venue] in London, every band and soca artist dreamt to perform at the Brass Festival." But tell me, before you became a fixture in the Brass Festival, where else did your band have the opportunity to perform in the 1990s?

RC: Sometime in March of 1994, I was recommended by one of my musician friends, Errol Wise (a top drummer in Trinidad and Tobago) to meet Mr. Conrad Franklin, who used to take entertainment packages to Japan. He made me an offer to go to Japan, but I had to wait on his call for confirmation. Days and weeks went by. In the meantime we performed at the Upper Level Club in West Mall [a shopping mall in Trinidad].[22] One of the nights when we were performing at the club, Mr. Elsworth James [a Trinidadian living in Toronto, Canada, one of the premiere promoters of that era] came to the club. He loved what he heard and said to me, "Roy, come to Canada." In trying to keep the band working, I put Japan aside, and I told him, "Yes, I will come to Toronto for twelve weeks." Mr. James returned to Toronto and started immediately to put things in place. I then got a call from Mr. Franklin that Japan was on. I called Mr. James and told him that Japan was on and asked if we could cancel Toronto. He had already some confirmed bookings and thus answered that it would be very difficult to cancel. I agreed then that we had to do Toronto. To keep good relations, I recommended to Mr. Franklin the band Atlantik. Atlantik was confirmed for Japan. After the initial trip, the band returned to Japan on two other occasions. In the meantime, Roy Cape Kaiso All Stars has been performing in Toronto every summer since that year of 1994.

JG: In 1993, just before you launched your band fully in the dance hall, the Soca Monarch competition was created. I saw you perform as the backup band for the whole competition over many years. So playing at such an event must have helped your band build its reputation in the soca arena, no?

RC: Well, Charlie's Roots was the first band to do accompaniment in the Soca Monarch [competition]. And after maybe two years, we were offered the job by Mr. William Munroe. So we began to play in 1995. And we did the Soca Monarch until 2007. I have seen Superblue in the height of his glory mesmerize the crowd and win the Soca Monarch time and time again. I have seen Ronnie McIntosh as a force to reckon with in the Soca Monarch. Then you had Iwer George, who has been a dominant throughout the years and then reached his peak.

JG: After you left as the resident band for the Soca Monarch in 2007, did Mr. Munroe continue to hire one band to provide the music for all the singers, or did each singer come to the stage with his or her own band?

RC: Singers are always more comfortable with the bands that they work with. When we were rehearsing for Soca Monarch, we had many songs to play. But different bands have different specializations. So while we provided the accompaniment for all the singers competing for the Soca Monarch, some singers would ask to augment our band by adding some of their own band players.

Today [2011], Vincent Rivers is now the resident band for the Soca Monarch. Vincent had been doing the semifinals all along—which is the most tedious part of the competition. And it has been agreed with Mr. Munroe and myself that Vincent should do the finals, as our hands at this time are pretty much occupied for the whole carnival season for the parties and dances.

HIRING LEAD SINGERS FOR THE BAND

The hiring of lead singers is a complex affair for any bandleader, and for each musical genre there are particular demands. But until recently, lead singers in most Trinidadian bands, including Roy's, have been hired not through public media advertising and screenings, but following the recommendations made by friends or based on the traditional folk media of word of mouth. Soon after an initial meeting, the bandleader would set up an audition and the hiring would be formalized.

Since the 1990s, Roy's band has been performing mostly soca. Accordingly, Roy has followed the main trend in soca bands to feature two or three lead singers. Whereas in the 1980s and early 1990s most lead singers were male, by the mid-1990s onward having one female singer out of the three frontliners became almost the rule.

For a bandleader, the choice of a lead singer is key to the band's success. In contrast to the instrumental bands of the 1960s, whose fame largely depended on the musical skills of the players and arrangers, soca bands by the 1990s became recognized through the popular appeal of their lead singers. In soca, bandleaders are looking for a number of key features in their lead singers: first of all, a strong voice, not only to be heard over the high volume at which soca bands play, but also to last out the sets. (A set usually lasts from forty-five minutes to one hour, and can include as many as thirty songs.) Bandleaders must also choose a lead singer who will blend well with the other singers in the band, and at the same time offer contrast. And while the voices matter for obvious reasons, the physical appearance (sexiness, viewed as especially important for female singers) and dancing abilities (particularly vital in soca) are also of crucial importance—and therefore come into play in the selection of a singer. In soca, as with any other music, singers who have charisma, who have a big presence on stage, are considered an asset for a band—with the caveat, however, that they can still allow the other lead singers to take their place. Overall, the respective personalities of the two (or three) lead singers must complement each other.

In what follows, Roy and I discuss his experiences with lead singers since the 1990s. The story that emerges is partly historical, recalling the singers that passed through Roy's band, but it is also ethnographic, being based on both Roy's specific experiences with particular singers at a particular time and place, and my observations on how soca bands work. It also brings out the emotions singers go through before walking on stage, as Roy recounts his brief foray into soca competition as a singer contestant.

On Finding and Losing Lead Singers

JG: In soca, the lead singers have acquired a crucial importance. As you mentioned to me in one of our meetings, whereas before musicians in instrumental bands were the ones making or breaking a band, today, the lead singers greatly determine whether the band will tour or not. The financial success and recognition of a soca band now greatly depends on the relative success of the songs the singers premiere during carnival and the way the public responds to the singers' stage presence, looks, voices, and dancing during performances. So to select lead singers for your band and to work closely with them over the years must have been one of the most challenging and important tasks for you as a bandleader. Could you talk about your experience with lead singers in your band?

RC: In 1995 with Marvin and Nigel Lewis up front, we were fully in the dance hall. Performing amid bands such as Sound Rev, Shandileer, Machel Montano and Xtatik, Blue Ventures, Traffik, Atlantik, we were an instant hit with the public. We had a beautiful carnival season in Trinidad. I had a recording contract with Eddy Grant for Ice Records. So I could not get into another agreement as far as recording was concerned. While being in Toronto in that year during the summer, we were doing [the song by the band] Traffik, "Jump and Breakaway," nightly, and Nigel got the idea to write "Moving to the left, moving to the right." I was in my room when Nigel came and sang this thing for me. I said to him, "Nigel, I have a contract with Eddy. I cannot be involved with any other recording project." "Pappy," he replied, "I have a dream and I feel this is it." A few weeks later, in preparation for the 1996 carnival season, he and Juiceman and the band recorded "Moving to the Right." And for that season, this song "Moving to the Right" became like a national song, placing him second to Superblue in the Soca Monarch competition, and winner of the Road March.

With this huge success in 1996, we toured Miami, New York, Boston, and I think Atlanta. We also performed in Grenada, Barbados, St. Vincent, and Antigua. We [Roy Cape All Stars with Marvin and Nigel Lewis] went to London with Superblue and the United Sisters to perform at the WOMAD festival. On that same trip, we also played at the Hammer Smith Palais. In returning to Trinidad in September 1996, we had some problems in the band. We were informed by Nigel that after carnival (1997) he was going to do his own thing. We were forced to request of Kurt Allen to sit in with the band to fulfill the obligations that we were contracted for the rest of the year in 1996 and onward. Nigel actually left on Carnival Monday. When I sent a SOS that night in '97, the amount of singers who came and helped me [was heartwarming]! With Marvin and Nigel gone, we had only Kurt Allen left to play on the road [for Carnival Monday and Carnival Tuesday]. The artists were very kind to me and came to help. So Nigel went his way in '97, but we still won the Best Playing Band on the road that year. Soon after the 1997 carnival was over, Colin Lucas of "Dollar Wine" fame recommended to me that we should try Derrick Seales. Derrick stayed with us until 2007.

On Changing Roles: Roy's Singing Moment

JG: The sudden move of Marvin and Nigel must have been quite destabilizing for you and the band.

RC: Going through these changes in 1997 had an impact on us, so we had to reenergize our motivation. We did our normal tour through the islands and

ROY CAPE (KAISO) ALL STARS SINGERS OVER THE YEARS

Ann Marie "Twiggy" Parks-Kojo, 1987–present
Allan Welch and Kurt Allen, 1990 (for carnival)–1993 (after carnival)
Nigel and Marvin Lewis, 1994 (for carnival)–1997 (during carnival)
Kurt Allen, 1996 (circa October)–2000 (middle carnival)
Ajala, Daddy Chinee, Organizer, Gillo, Skunky, Iwer George, 1997 (during carnival)
Derrick Seales, 1997 (after carnival)–2007 (after carnival)
Dester "Blaxx" Stewart, 1999 (after carnival)–to the present
Destra Garcia, 2000 (during carnival)–2002 (October)
Esther Dyer, 2002 (October)–2005 (after summer tours)
Rita Jones, 2005 (circa October)–2006 (after carnival)
Trini Jacobs, 2007 (October)–2009 (after carnival)
Olatunji Yearwood, 2007 (late in the year)–2011 (after carnival)
Rita Jones, 2009 (after carnival)–2012 (before carnival)

---

our Canadian summer tour. In Toronto, we were staying at the Ryerson College, well located for our performances around town. This is when I came up with the idea for the song, "Jam Mih, Mr. Cape"—from wherever it came, it came to me. I kept singing it not to forget it.

When I came back to Trinidad, I went to Junior Telfer's house on Carlton Avenue, and Stalin and I met there. Stalin said, "I am not going to interfere with your topic or your melody." But for all of what I had done, I was not a professional with words. So I told him the lines I had composed, and he told me how they should be. Not being a composer, I had very long lines, and I did not have the skills to shorten them, so he did. The song ended up being composed by Leroy Calliste [Black Stalin] and Roy Cape. It feels very strange for me to be saying what I am saying, but the radio deejays and the public took a liking of this song. I think that their sentiments had to do with giving me appreciation for the work I had done so far in my life.

ROY CAPE'S SONG "JAM MIH"
Verse 1:
Long time in here in Trinbago
Ah start playing calypso
in so many different bands
and in many other lands
Clarence Curvan, Ron Berridge,

What a privilege
Now ah come to show
my version of calypso

Chorus:
Jam mih, jam mih, Mr. Cape
Let we get another take
Jam de music Mr. Cape
Dis jamming cannot escape
Soca music, yes we have it
Reggae music if yuh want it
Salsa music, we go jam it,
Kaiso music, All-Stars have it
Jam mih, jam mih, Mr. Cape
Let we get another take
Jam de music Mr. Cape
Dis jamming cannot escape

Verse 2:
With the Sparrow Troubadours
I opened so many doors
Playing music with the best
that was a serious test
Frankie Francis, Bert Innis
Is dey teach mih de business
My education
I got from these musicians

Verse 3:
Came back from New York City
to reside in TnT
Ah come with ah kaiso band
to jam in de land
Every calypsonian know
my business is kaiso
In de street or in de fete
is one cry yuh going to get

Verse 4:
Ninety-six, ninety-seven
Ah teach dem ah good lesson
Masquerade thru the land

4.3 "Mr. Cape" (also dubbed "Jam Mih") by Dr. Roy Cape and Dr. Leroy "Black Stalin" Calliste. From Roy Cape's collection.

Learn that All-Stars is the band
From de street to de dance hall
I respond to every call
Everyone, no matter who
This music is just for you

As I said before, Kurt Allen and Derrick Seales were the band vocalists. We did record that year a CD and it so happened that "Mr. Cape" got more airplay than the other two singers' songs.

JG: So once a song during carnival gets a lot of radio airplay, you already know that this is your ticket to get bookings for the band during and after carnival, yes?

RC: Correct. So I entered the Soca Monarch in 1998 and did the preliminaries, the semifinals, and I qualified for the finals. The finals were held at the Queen's Park Oval. I remember being at the bottom of the steps that take you to the stage in queue to be ready when I was presented by the emcee. There again with me was Leroy. Just before they called my name, he asked, "Are you nervous?" I was but I said, "Nah." I was introduced to the audience and was given a cordless microphone. I started to do a Iwer George antic and to run on the stage singing. I was about to do that when the microphone stopped working. So everything stopped and they had to give me a microphone with a cord. It took me a little time to readjust, but I could not let that incident distract me. I performed the song and was pleasantly supported by the audience. Results time came, and I was declared ninth position. I was a bit surprised, but very humbly happy. It was exceptionally satisfying because I had always been playing with the whole band. And here I was, standing up front and singing.

During the 1998 carnival season, I made an appearance at Spektakula calypso tent to present my song to the press on Thursday and on the Friday, I performed for the public at the Spektakula Forum.[23] When I finished performing I went to the dressing room to change from my show clothes to my street clothes. I heard a knocking on the dressing room door and when I looked out, I saw Gypsy, who said, "They callin' back the Mighty Cape outside!"—which meant that I was being encored! For that season, as the band was heavily booked, I sang nightly. After singing at the tent Spektakula on a Friday, I went to Chaguanas. I got wet in the rain, and I lost my one throat. So I had to forget singing at Spektakula and concentrate to keep the one voice for the band.[24]

JG: So after your song, "Jam Mih, Mr. Cape" in 1998, your band had another great year in 1999, with many bookings with Kurt Allen winning the Soca Monarch and ranking runner-up in the Road March with his song "Stampede." So between 1997 and 1999, your band was very active. At that point, you had two lead singers, Kurt Allen and Derrick Seales. No women, correct?

RC: Not yet. In 1999 we went to Jamaica for carnival, and I was very happy to be there. We did an all-inclusive, a regular carnival fete promoted by some of the carnival bands, and we also played on the road in Jamaica. This was history to be playing on the road in Jamaica [carnival parade only began in Jamaica in 1989]. We had put on a serious mix session, and Kurt was also the current Soca Monarch with the song "Stampede." We had the partygoers stampeding out the exit on their way home.

After the party someone told me, "Pappy, we can get Blaxx." I said I did not like to poach on other bands but I knew that Bobby Quan had two of the big artists on the scene at that time. So I asked Bobby for forgiveness. He was strong, and we needed some more fire and an all-round performer. And that is what Blaxx is. We have been together since then.

Since 1998 we have produced a commercially released CD for the season every year until 2002. In 1999 we were happy that the media acknowledged us with the song "Stampede" [official name, "Dust Dem"]. We enjoyed the media support as we did in '96 and '97 with Nigel, "Movin'" (1996) and "Follow the Leader" (1997).

JG: The song "Stampede" was a song based on high energy—with 155 beats per minute. I remember indeed that it was hugely successful.

RC: We had a hectic 1999, again through the islands and then our normal Toronto summer tour. We did New York that year, and we returned home to get ready for the 2000 carnival season. During the 2000 carnival Kurt was not happy and we agreed that he would move on. I was recommended by Brian Morris to see Destra Garcia, and I said to Brian that I don't think that the business is ready as yet for a female singer. And he insisted, "Pappy, you must see her," to which I agreed. She came to the band room, and we asked her to sing something she could sing. And that was all she had to do. She immediately was admitted to the band.

JG: The timing to include a woman in your band was perfect. Just around that time, women were starting to be more and more prominent in the soca scene. I remember Alyson Hinds [from Barbados] was then recognized as the leading female soca artist throughout the Caribbean. In Trinidad, Sanell Dempster had just cupped the Road March (1999), and Denise Belfon, who dubbed herself the Soca Queen (as the equivalent to the Dancehall Queen in Jamaica), had been developing her own following since her success with "Kaka Lay Lay" (1995?). Singing Sandra had also just won the calypso monarch title just the year before (1999) [some twenty years after Calypso Rose, the first woman to win that competition]. So women were starting to be more visible in the calypso music scene, but most particularly in soca.

RC: That's true. Many soca bands began then to have one female singer at that time. But since Destra came into the band smack in the middle of carnival [2000], we could not really record her because the time for recording had already gone by. We did our tours in the Caribbean, and we went to Toronto for our normal summer tour. Destra was instantly a hit with the public. While in Toronto, Kernel Roberts used to visit us, and one day he sang part of "Tremble It" for us. He mentioned that when he would get back to Trinidad, he would complete the song. We recorded the song and it instantly was a hit. It became, at that time, Destra's signature. Destra stayed with the band until 2002 carnival. She had resigned a very good job at McEnearney Business Machine (computers and equipment). Destra stayed with the band from 2000 to 2002. During that time we did our normal travels and we went to Belgium for the Hoogstraten Festival.

After carnival 2002, Destra said to me that she appreciated the opportunity to be a member of the band and she would always be there for me if I ever need her. But she wishes to move on because there were things that she wanted to accomplish. I requested of her to stay until October of that year after we finish the Miami carnival, and after that, I told her, she can do what she has to do with my blessings — our friendship staying intact. In October of 2002, regrettably Destra left.

JG: At this point, did you feel that it was important to replace her with another female singer or did you consider hiring another male singer then?

RC: No, we wanted to have another female singer. There were many songs around that should be sung by a woman.

JG: So you hired Ester Dyer and she stayed for three years, right?

RC: Yes. After three years, again we had to make decisions that were very painful but, as you are aware, Destra was not an easy act to replace. In trying to keep the band at the highest level of the competitiveness vis-à-vis the other bands, we decided to try something new.

My son Roy was getting married in 2005 and Rita Jones, who happens to be the first cousin of Roy's wife (Arlene), was invited to sing for her cousin's wedding. We were ecstatic about the strength of Rita's voice. So we invited Rita to join the band and she agreed. She joined the band sometime in 2005, and stayed with us in 2006.

On the Challenge of Keeping Lead Singers

JG: To keep singers in a band is complicated, isn't it? If they are very, very successful, they want to leave the band and start a solo career. And if they are not successful with the band, they may also want to leave the band to try something else.

RC: This is what happens. So Derrick Seales exited the band in 2007 after carnival. At that time Olatunji was singing with the band Traffik, but he was not too happy. His father, Eddy, called me and asked us to take Olatunji into the band. I advised him to call Juiceman [the musical director by then] and to speak to him. Juice recommended that we take Olatunji as we were focused on youth. Olatunji joined the band later in the year 2007. Olatunji's first record with the band was "Get Wild," which was Tunji's personal production. He stayed with us until 2011.

JG: Since the singers are now the focal point of soca bands, you have had to put a lot of effort into finding good singers, ones that work well with the other singers and the band.

RC: Jocelyne, it is a constant challenge. Sometime in 2007 we were having some problems in the band and in the best interest of everyone involved, we decided to make a change and replace Rita. Many people who are very close to the band suggested that we try Trini Jacobs (daughter of Carl Jacobs, who has been very famous through the years in Trinidad and Tobago music). She joined the band in 2007 and stayed with the band in 2008 and 2009. As usual each year after carnival, we did the Caribbean islands and our annual summer tour in Toronto, and went also to the Miami carnival. When we returned to Trinidad, we were once again looking for that blend with the two male vocals. Our musical director, Juiceman, saw Rita, and apologies were given by Juiceman to Rita, and by Rita to Juiceman. Rita returned to the band in 2009 [and stayed until the beginning of 2012].[25]

PERFORMING ON THE ROAD IN AND OUT OF TRINIDAD

Playing at different sites and for different lengths of time brings different sorts of challenges for musicians. Performing on the streets of Port of Spain (Trinidad's capital) during Carnival Monday and Carnival Tuesday (commonly referred to in the United States as Fat Tuesday) for hours on end, after having performed every night (often twice a night) during the previous four to six weeks, not only demands that musicians be physically fit, it requires the band arranger to prepare medleys of hit tunes from the carnival season to keep the revelers moving through the streets. Regardless of weeks of lack of sleep, this in turn requires the band musicians to go back to the band room and rehearse the new arrangements before they can perform in the streets—often on the back of a truck overlooking crowds of masqueraders, ensuring that the sounds they produce irresistibly move everyone forward, in great spirits, in style, and on the beat. On Carnival Monday, the band must be in the streets by 7 a.m. and play until midday. After a few hours of rest, the band resumes its playing on the road for a few more hours in the evening. On Carnival Tuesday, the band has to be set up on the back of the truck, ready to play by 8 a.m. until 6 or 7 p.m. — and sometimes later — in the evening. The demands of playing on the streets during the two last days of carnival could be described as excruciating. And they are. And yet they can also be exhilarating. Still, the bandleader must judge whether the musicians are willing to meet these demands and whether these performances are worth the efforts — musically, financially, and emotionally, both for themselves and for the communities they serve.

Playing abroad in a North American city for several weeks at a time brings other kinds of challenges for a bandleader. As the conversation below indicates, these challenges are not simply musical. The band has already played the hit songs of the carnival season — the hit songs of the band and those of other bands and singers — countless times during carnival, and is thus very tight. The challenges concern the economic profitability of the tour. The focus for musicians is thus on finances, the number of bookings, and the revenues for the band. For the bandleader, however, the challenge is not just financial. It concerns the well-being of his band members and his willingness to reach out to new crowds and reinforce the reputation of the band with previous audience members. As explained below, Roy's preoccupation as a bandleader is to be accountable at all times to his musicians — a preoccupation that has undoubtedly played a great role in his ability to keep his musicians for a remarkably long period of time. (In 2012, the average time that his musicians have remained in the band is sixteen years.)

A Test of Fitness: Playing on the Streets on Carnival Days

JG: As you explained earlier, Roy, a band that is on the road can mean two different things in Trinidad. Whereas in North America, being on the road for a band means being on tour, in Trinidad it can still mean being on tour, but it can also mean literally to be playing in the streets during Carnival Monday and Carnival Tuesday.

RC: On the road, yeah. In 1986 and '87, I went and jammed with [the band] Charlie's Roots. So I was able to see the kind of operation there was on the road now. In the past, we did not have a big PA system like that. So I was able to see how things are organized on the road for two years before I myself went on the road with the band. So by the time [the reputed masquerade bandleader] Wayne Berkeley came and asked me if I wanted to play on the road, I agreed. And then when I did it the first year, it was all right.

JG: That was 1989?

RC: Yeah, then we did '90. It was tough! All went well in '89. So I don't know if it was going back on the road, and the interest of everybody was no longer there. . . . But in '90, it got hard! Because we were in the tent, we didn't have the time to rehearse that music, then.

JG: What music are you referring to?

RC: The dance music. You know, the road is not just playing and stopping. There's formatting and playing song into song and things like that. So I realized by 1990 that if I had to do good on the road, I would have to go to the dance hall and meet the other bands squarely. After the carnival season 1994, I left the calypso tent and went to the dance hall.

JG: So you could then concentrate on the band.

RC: You know, the musicians have been always touring. It is part of the work. When you're young, you enjoy the challenges of going all over the place and meeting different people and getting different experiences. That was part of the attraction for going into the dance hall. And there was another reason. Playing in the calypso tent, people used to regard us like the old man's band. But I don't want somebody to put that on me. Plus, I wanted not even money, because I was never thinking about money, but I had more desires then and was attracted by the challenge.

I went back on the road. I went to [the masquerade band] Poison. I played with Poison for three or four years until we [the Poison masquerade bandleader and Roy] both decided amicably to make it a quit. We [Roy and his musicians] had gotten disgusted at playing on the road. The work is laborious. If you talk to foreign musicians, they would tell you that no foreign musician will ever play for eight hours. No way. Worse, in the sun! They won't do it. And at times when we were playing on the road, I could see that we weren't satisfying the people. Because after we play thirty-five nights, the guys are tired. Some of them want to go off the truck and jam with the girls. Alone in the truck! I came to the decision after listening to the players that instead of being miserable and having the band members also make me miserable, to leave it alone. When we played the young people's music, the elder people would sit down at the pavement and look at us. We could see that they were looking at us in resentment because we were not making them happy. All of that made me come off the road. So after coming off the calypso tent, I later on also came off the road.

Very few bands play on the road in Trinidad today. There are now more deejays on the road during carnival. The deejay can mix; he can do all kinds of things. No one gets tired. It's easier to amplify a record than to amplify a whole band that has x amount of microphones.

From another angle, we are not playing on the road because through the years, every time a mas' [masquerade] carnival bandleader is put in charge by the authorities, the first thing he talks about is that the cost of the music band is getting so high. Little does he seem to realize that whatever price you get, 50 percent of it goes to the logistics, for example, the PA [public address system], the generator, to have the truck ready, to have railing, roofing against the rain and sun. The money that goes to the musicians, I am telling you, a good musician from England, Canada, America would never play for that. You couldn't pay them.

Again, too, you think about sports. A sportsman could only run x races a day in the Olympics. Otherwise, the muscles would go. It's the same thing with the face. This is muscles. If it gets overwork, it gets tired. And if it gets tired, you're not going to get no notes. Once those muscles get tired . . . and if you don't practice an instrument or perform often, you won't get notes. Worse if you're playing trumpet. With saxophone, same thing.

I played with Wayne Berkeley for nine years, from 1989 to 1998, and then I played with Poison, founded by Michael Headley, from 1999 to 2004.

On the Effort of Reaching Out: Planning Performance Programs

JG: You spoke about the importance of planning the sequence in which you play songs when you are performing on the streets during Carnival Monday and Carnival Tuesday, so that you keep the energy going. Do you prepare the playing you do at a party in the same way?

RC: A calypso show is a completely different show to a party. What you get in a party, it's an unrehearsed production, what evolves in a session for the night. We have songs and a program, but we don't have really a format.

JG: You don't have a preplanned sequence in which songs will be played?

RC: No, you can't plan the order of the emotion, because emotion is going to happen as things develop. We can't say what the vibes are going to be on this boat ride tonight. You have to listen to the response between the audience and the performers and decide which songs we are going to play when.

5 • REMEMBERING WITH PICTURES

It is far more complicated to find visual images of the musicians behind the popular music in the recording studios and backup bands than the lead artists. This is a clear example of what Deborah Poole names "visual economy," as opposed to "visual culture." For her, culture suggests consensus and homogeneity. Instead, she speaks of visual economies to stress the inequalities that characterize representational domains. As she explains, economy "suggests that this organization [in our case, newspaper photo archives] has as much to do with social relationships, inequality, and power as with shared meaning and community."[1] In the same vein, speaking about the ways the Navajo have been photographically depicted, a remark by anthropologist James Faris is highly relevant to the impoverished visual representations of musicians not only in Trinidadian, but in Caribbean popular music at large. Referring to the enduring stereotypes that seem to represent the Navajo [or more broadly, indigenous populations] in archives, he writes that while they may appear as distorted or objectionable, they are not "flaws in an uneducated, unevolved, unenlightened West, [rather] they are the necessary conditions of existence of the Navajo to the West" (quoted in Pinney 2005: 9). In the same way, it could be suggested that the invisibility of musicians in representations of Caribbean popular music (and popular music at large?) has been the necessary condition of existence of the dominating position of the star—the song leader onstage.

The few photographs of musicians that do exist in the Trinidadian archives I consulted, to use the words of anthropologist Christopher Pinney, point to "creator[s] of culture, rather than simply . . . its reproducers" (Pinney 2005: 11). Looking at the selected photographs that follow, I asked myself: what kinds of stories do these images tell of Trinidadian musicians, of Roy, of his friends, or of his colleagues? What kinds of popular aesthetic do they produce (or suggest) in a saxophonist and a bandleader like Roy? What situations do they foreground? What types of politics of representation do they enact? The sociology of photographs invites one to go to the edge of the frame and to take note of what is cropped, indexed, or edited out. It is a sociology of selection, of what is included and of what is not, of what and who is featured, of how the selected photographs tell stories about Roy's reputation or circulation in various milieus.

Roy and I began selecting the photographs at his home, searching through his own collection. Roy would pull out photographs and briefly explain the importance they had for him. The majority of the photographs were taken by friends, and there were only a few taken by photojournalists. Others were reproductions of album covers. And a few commissioned by Roy were taken by a professional photographer for his press book. From the outset, I was fully aware that the sequence in which the photographs appeared would tell a certain story. Such a sequence has the effect of creating a narrative of social life by providing contexts and connections for "what might be going on in the frame, both socially and visually" (Feld 2007: 11). While each grouping serves as visual documentation of the particular times, places, people, and events that have marked Roy's journey, they also serve as a kind of aide-mémoire to Roy's comments and feelings about the worlds he has inhabited, often launching stories about "what was, what is, what may be, what wasn't, what could have been, what could be" (Feld 2007: 11).

The first group of photographs tells several stories about Roy's journey with different bands, musicians, and singers he performed with between 1961 and 1977. Here the images chronicle the changes that Roy went through—playing with different bands, in different places, with different hairdos and styles of clothing. The second group covers Roy's deep affinity for the saxophone and his love of playing in horn sections. In the third group of photographs, we can witness the close relationships that Roy built with calypsonians, and many of the events he shared with them. The emotional registers that Roy and the calypsonians express in these photographs attest to the long-term friendships and the many connections Roy has established in the calypso music scene. The fourth group focuses on Roy's own band, Roy Cape All Stars, and the many tribulations and pleasures that come with being a bandleader. The fifth and last set of photographs focuses on Roy's journey, and how he has circulated not only by traveling in the world of music but through his expansive career reach and reception in general.

As Corinne Kratz writes, photographs can act as mnemonic devices, as a medium for negotiating social relations, and as testimony to situations and events. They can also help to define particular practices. "They [can also] provide resources through which people might create, foster and advertise social relations, imagine, shape and show identities, values, personhood; and bridge past, present, and future" (Kratz 2012: 242). Photographs are powerful in their immediacy and in the way they affect the play of memory. In what follows, Roy, several journalists, and I recount the stories that the selected images prompt us to tell.

ROY'S NETWORK AS BAND MEMBER

FIGURE 5.1: "Here we are at TELCO recording in Champ Fleur. We are either recording or we are getting ready to record, and someone decided to take a photograph."

The photograph in the middle has been reproduced many times by local newspapers, but was never accompanied by the two other photographs that were part of the back cover of the record jacket on Clarence Curvan's album *The Artiste*. Roy selected this photograph, given to him by friends, because it documents his playing with Clarence Curvan's band.

The three photographs present rare snapshots of an ongoing recording session in the early 1960s in Trinidad. Whether or not the physical position of the players or their body movements were scripted by the photographer, the photographs reveal the conditions in which the recordings were taking place. They acknowledge the musicians as workers, playing, recording, discussing the cuts, starting all over again. They recall the time of the direct-to-stereo ¼ inch tape recording technology that was most demanding for all musicians. One mistake in the next to last bar, and they had to start the recording all over again. In the photograph on the right, the musicians seem to be discussing the score. In the photograph in the middle, some of them run through the tune. In the photograph on the right, two of the band members are listening to a take of the tune they just recorded. All the band members appear to be concentrating on their respective tasks. Were these photographs meant to show the professionalism of the musicians? Were they taken to educate the public about the different steps involved in producing a recording? Were they taken to help increase the public's respect for the work they do? Were they

5.1 Clarence Curvan's band, 1963. In the middle photograph, from left to right: Conrad Little (bass), Roy Cape (alto sax), Scipio Sargeant (guitar); behind him from left to right, Kenneth Sylvester (percussion), Clarence Curvan (drums), Mervyn Callender (congas), Missing (bongos), Ron Berridge (trumpet), Colin Dennis (tenor saxophone). Beverly Griffith, pianist and arranger, appears only on the left side of the photograph subtitled "Everyone looks to TELCO."

taken to show how, even though musicians may love making music, their recording studio sessions nonetheless required considerable hard work?

As these photographs reveal, in the early 1960s, recording studios in Trinidad were still equipped with only one room to record everyone at once. While the multitrack recording technology already widely used for popular music in the United States by the late 1950s was visibly not yet available in the newly independent nation-state of Trinidad and Tobago, the world of fashion seemed to have reached the Trinidadians, including the musicians, much faster.[2] The skinny, narrow pants made famous by the Beatles are visibly worn by everyone in the band. As Roy's son explains, "Music is sound and

5.2 Younger Roy with Ron Berridge's band, 1966. From left to right, standing: Roy Cape, Scipio Sargeant, Ron Berridge, and Clem Berridge; behind the fountain kneeling, Neville Oxley, Michael Tobas, Ulric Sobian; behind them, Kenwyn Hunte, Terry Moe, Joseph Alexander, Kenneth Reece, and Conrad Little. Courtesy *Trinidad Express*.

sight. If you sound good and you look good, people will admire you." Even in their daily lives, Trinidadian musicians playing popular music dress the part: they adopt the international mainstream style of modern fashion. Even only one year after Trinidad and Tobago gained its independence (this album was released in 1963), the reputation of bands and musicians, including Roy Cape's, was not built solely on sounding Trinidadian and showing cultural independence, but also on looking and sounding modern. Hence, even without resorting to the latest recording technology, TELCO saw the recording studio sound quality as an index of modernity and as a way to position itself in relation to the global popular music industry of the time. On the back of the jackets of each recording it produced, the recording studio thus boasted, "Everyone looks to TELCO for the Best in Sound Reproduction."

FIGURE 5.2: "We had photos taken of us in the Botanical Garden for our upcoming album titled *The Big Songs of Ron Berridge*. Here we are relaxed, enjoying each other's company and the environment we are in. And as you can see, our dress code is in effect. We had a tailor who made our outfits to complement the functions where we performed."

This photograph is part of a series that were taken for the album titled *The 'A' Train*, released in 1966 and named after Duke Ellington's song. Typical of the time, dance bands were composed of male instrumentalists only. Also typical, even though not visually signaled, the horn section was composed of band members who all came from the orphanage and was thus built on long-term friendship. Roy grew up with Ron Berridge and his brother Clement, and with Scipio Sargeant.

Even though there was considerable interaction between Afro-Trinidadians and East Indians in the popular music scene from the 1930s onward—often in the form of partnerships with East Indians in charge of equipment rentals or financial assistance and Afro-Trinidadians in charge of the music making—little of that partnership was visible (or audible) in bands until the 1990s. Accordingly, bands like that of Ron Berridge included musicians of mostly Afro-Trinidadian background.

Deeply influenced by American jazz big bands and small combos of the era, Berridge's band members all wore the same outfits, as Roy puts it, "to complement the functions where we performed." Echoing his son's remark, Roy explains how sound and sight work together to produce a sensual aura of respectability and professionalism. In articulation with each other, sound and sight make a band appear local, while at the same time internationally connected.

FIGURE 5.3: "This photograph, I believe, was taken at Queen's Hall because in those days this was really the only performing center; but it could also have been at the Hilton [hotel]. As was typical of the time, all the band members were wearing a suit. We all had also music stands. In addition, our band had portable lights. As this photograph clearly demonstrates, Sparrow shows by his expression how he is at home performing onstage with the Ron Berridge Orchestra.

"Ron Berridge's orchestra also went with Sparrow to Grenada in 1969 for Expo 69. The event, which was held at a place called True Blue, was the early beginning to what is known today as Caricom. The politicians then were talking about economical federation."

This photograph is important to Roy. With the Mighty Sparrow, Roy performed in some of the most prestigious venues and at the most important musical and political events in Trinidad and the Caribbean region. Performing in a band accompanying this most acclaimed calypsonian unquestionably helped Roy build his reputation and expand the compass of his circulation.

Since the photographer here clearly focuses on the Mighty Sparrow in the midst of performing, he (I use "he" here because women were not recognized as photographers in Trinidad, as in the rest of the region, in the 1960s) only catches a glimpse of the musicians—actually only half of the band members.

5.3 Sparrow with the Ron Berridge Orchestra, 1967. Courtesy *Trinidad Express*.

Yet, as the backdrop ironically reminds us, "one hand don't clap." Even for an exceptional artist like the Mighty Sparrow, the musicians accompanying him are essential for his performance to take place. Standing up to play, they inject rhythms and dynamics into his performance.

FIGURE 5.4: "We are at the Flamingo Hotel in Jamaica, and we were just loving up each other when this picture was taken. We were in Jamaica with the Mighty Sparrow and his Troubadours. On that trip, we worked at the Flamingo Hotel in Kingston and we also played at the [campus of the] University of the West Indies, the Brown Jug in Ocho Rios, and at Yellow Bird in Montego Bay. So we did four gigs during our stay there.

"Harold De Freitas's nickname was Vasso, short for Vaseline. He played like Vaseline, meaning that his sound was very smooth and fluid; that's why they call him Vaseline or Vasso for short. He was such a loving guy that anything he did sounded sweet. Vasso was with Sparrow for many years. When a calypsonian would come up to sing in the tent [the Original Young Brigade], he would sing something for Vasso, and Vasso would immediately play it back to him identical to what he had just heard. He would tell him, 'Bum bum!' [*Roy claps twice*]. That is when you will make your entry. And that is how it went until music started to be written."

In the Mighty Sparrow's band, Roy performed for tourists in some of the best hotels in the countries he visited and also for the locals in prestigious places recognized nationally, including the campus of the University of the West Indies, in Mona (Jamaica). After playing mostly in Trinidad with previous bands, Roy gained a new kind of knowledge by accompanying the Mighty Sparrow on tour not only in the Caribbean, but also in major cities in the United States and Canada. He learned how to circulate among audiences with different kinds of knowledge and musical sensibility. He learned about how to pace a performance and how to choose not only which songs

5.4 From left to right: Harold De Freitas and Roy Cape in Jamaica, 1969. From Roy Cape's collection.

but also in which sequence they should be played for this or that particular audience. As Roy proudly recognizes, professionally, "doing the whole of 1969 with Sparrow brought me to the greatest part of my career at that point in time."

If Roy's selection of this photograph leads him first to acknowledge his touring experience with the Mighty Sparrow, more importantly it also enables him to recognize his good friend and colleague Harold De Freitas. It grants him the opportunity to speak about his remarkable musical skills and also about how his loving personality translated into sweet sounds on the instrument. For Roy, this has been an important lesson. Throughout his career, Roy has also aimed to translate his love of people through his own sound on the saxophone.

This photograph captures a moment outside of the music, a moment of affection between two kindred souls in musical thinking.

FIGURE 5.5: "Harold 'Vasso' De Freitas grew up in the same home with me. He was my elder. He is one of the people who loaned me a horn and who told me that whenever I could have gotten a horn for myself, I could then return it to him. Joseph Alexander came from a triplet of three brothers, Joseph (tenor saxophone), John (trombone), and Joshua (trumpet). We were in New York, and we were launching the band, and we wanted the band (Ron Berridge) to look nice."

Roy's story about Vasso growing up with him in the same orphanage and lending a horn to him speaks loudly about the deeply affective relationships, the "brotherhood" in Roy's wording, that developed at the Chil-

5.5 From left to right: Harold De Freitas, Roy Cape, and Joseph Alexander, 1970. From Roy Cape's collection.

dren's Home. Even if they are not from the same orphanage—the Alexander brothers grew up at the St. Mary's Children's Home, the orphanage in Tacarigua—they helped each other throughout their careers. They recruited each other to form bands. From the outset of Roy's musical career, this tight network has played an important role in the ways he has been able to play, move from one band to another, and access different musical circuits.

The posture of the three saxophonists in this recorded moment illustrates the pleasure of being in the music together as section mates.

FIGURE 5.6: This photograph captures a private moment that Roy shares with Neville Oxley, a trombone player, older than Roy, who had vast experience playing with top bands in the country, including Fitz Vaughn Bryan's, one of the premier bands in the early 1960s.

Here again, Roy selected this photograph to focus on social relationships and places. Photographs taken backstage in particular are among the favorites of many musicians. They record and help remember the more private and personal side of music making than what is more typically found on stage and in the public record. Roy did not make any comment on this photograph. Could it be because this image appeared to him simply as a record of his friendship with Oxley?

An additional way of reading this photograph, however, would be to address what Roy's hairstyle says about his relationship to the cultural politics and politicized fashion of the early 1970s, when this photograph was taken.

5.6 From left to right: Roy Cape and Neville Oxley cooling out at a party in Brooklyn, around 1973. From Roy Cape's collection.

5.7 From left to right: Fortunia Ruiz, Philip James (one of the singers of the Blues Busters from Jamaica), and Roy Cape, around 1973. From Roy Cape's collection.

Even though he is of mixed race, Roy clearly emphasized his African heritage by sporting an Afro—a hairstyle that visually indexed his support of the Black Power movement, which at that very historical moment had reached an unprecedented height worldwide.

FIGURE 5.7: "In my age group, Fortunia Ruiz played a very serious part in my career. I was able to ask him questions and he explains many things to me. I always have had respect for Señor as a trumpet player. He is very efficient, punctual, and all the things that make up a very professional person. We have had a musical history that goes way back. I remember when I tried to instigate him to write dance music for Sparrow Troubadours, as Earl Rodney dealt mainly with calypsos. I gave him a song and I recommended to him to arrange it for the Troubadours. We spent lots of time together musically and we also spent time together in New York in one or two bands.

"In the middle of the photograph is Philip James of the Blues Busters from Jamaica, famous for many songs, including 'Wings of a Dove,' 'Behold,' and 'Wide Awake in a Dream,' which were recorded and performed with Byron Lee in the '60s. Here we are in New York City working with the Blues Busters in the company of Philip, who was a fantastic vocalist and performer and, I would say also, a consummate entertainer."

This image is a portrait. Fortunia, Philip, and Roy are all looking directly at the photographer. It is visibly taken to be a record of the working relationship between reputed Trinidadian musicians and a Jamaican singer, and of their pleasure in performing together in New York—in prestigious places, judging by their bow ties and elegant suits. Roy's selection of this image is about pride of work—to have been working with, and learning from, Fortunia Ruiz for years, the leading trumpet in Trinidad during this era, and to be able to perform together with Philip James of the Blues Busters from Jamaica. His great admiration for James is clear from the moment he speaks about him. He smiles, remembering fondly the sweet tone of Philip's voice and his expressive phrasing. This collaboration between the Blues Busters from Jamaica and Trinidadian musicians is a good reminder that collaborations between artists from the two islands are not new. They have been going on for many decades, but have remained, for the most part, unacknowledged in Caribbean local and regional media.

The question is, to what extent is New York responsible for this collaboration between these two Trinidadian musicians and the Blues Busters from Jamaica? Would the legendary rivalry between the two islands have made it more difficult for this collaboration to take place in their respective home countries in the 1970s? Even though, as Roy remarks, Caribbean musicians migrating to New York end up playing mainly "for their own kind"—simply because it is easier to find support from the diasporic associations of people from their own islands—has the need to rally forces for Caribbean musicians arriving en masse in New York been an important strategy to attract a wider public during that era? More research is needed to acknowledge the close and complex relations among Caribbean artists living in diaspora.[3]

FIGURE 5.8: "I had known [the late pianist and arranger] Clive since about 1960. I first met him at Club 48 on Park Street. We would have seen each other through the years. After [arranger and pianist] Beverly Griffith migrated to the U.S., Bradley was the replacement for Griffith in Clarence Curvan's band. [In addition to being the arranger for Clarence Curvan's band], Beverly Griffith was the arranger of Desperadoes. With his migrating, [inventor of some of the current steel pan instruments and the bandleader of the Desperadoes Steel Orchestra] Rudolf Charles, who was my very good friend, sought my assistance in finding a replacement for Beverly. And I recommended Clive Bradley. I don't think that there is much that I can add to what has already been said about the success that Clive Bradley brought to Desperadoes. He is regarded as one of the all-time best arrangers for the steelband—a fact that has been documented in various ways. To talk about Clive and his work would maybe take a whole book."

Soon after the United States changed its migration policies in 1965, some of the best Trinidadian musicians moved there. This exodus would become even more intense during the 1970s, and included Roy himself, who went to live in New York during that period. While the departure of these key musicians put great pressure on those who stayed in the country, it also gave the opportunity for others to shine and thrive. For example, Clive Bradley, a math teacher during the day, was an outstanding pianist at night, playing in jazz clubs. As the opportunities to play locally increased with the departure of many musicians, Bradley abandoned his teaching to become a full-time musician.

FIGURE 5.9: "As a young man, I had known about Frankie as he grew up in the same Home as me and I had heard so much about this great man. By the early 1960s, he requested me to join him as one of the members of the TELCO recording band. In 1962, I had my first experience playing in a calypso tent. It was at the Original Young Brigade, which was situated (and is still there up to today) at the Good Samaritan Hall on Duke Street.

"Frankie had been one of my mentors from very early. I would visit him every day and admire him arranging music. And I would make coffee for him. In those days, he was smoking cigarettes very often. So I would also go out and buy cigarettes for him. [In] later years, being responsible for the band at Spektakula, I felt that it was a decent thing to ask him if he would like to play in the tent. He said yes. And it is how we come to see him at the end of the horn section playing the tenor sax."

5.8 Clive Bradley, during Panorama 1981. Courtesy *Trinidad Express*.

5.9 Roy and Frankie Francis, 1988. Courtesy *Trinidad Express*.

This image gives a good sense of the conditions in which calypso musicians were working. The space is typically cramped, with chairs offering a minimum of comfort. By 1988, the outfit calypso musicians wear was simple, and in many ways far more adapted than before to playing in a tropical climate. No necktie or long sleeves, but just a simple T-shirt, as is the case in this photograph, or a loose or comfortable tailored shirt. For musicians, playing in a calypso tent is hard work. It means accompanying calypsonians for four to six hours with only a brief intermission. The audience might barely see them. And yet numerous journalists, as well as calypso aficionados in public media, have regularly acknowledged the tightness and the sound quality of Roy Cape All Stars at the calypso tent Spektakula.

ROY'S LOOK AND PLAY AT WORK

FIGURE 5.10: "And one time with the Jamaicans, once they see your hair . . . it's very long and they see gray, they know that's an elder, then. It pays that kind of respect. Even Barbados, St. Lucia, anywhere I go, the Rastas see my hair and pay me respect, because they see that I'm their elder. They see my hair and they see the length of it. So, they know the journey has been long."

In this comment Roy was speaking about a show he did with Superblue in which Buju Banton was also performing. In an interview for the *Sunday Guardian* in 1999, the topic of growing locks came up: "How old are you? I will be 57 in April. And your dreadlocks? Twenty-two years. Why did you decide to grow them? I was living in New York City at the time. . . . I was exposed to Edgar Fitzgerald, a musician, and he and his whole family had ras. He was a very good friend of mine and I found they were living a really beautiful family life. . . . Then coming to Trinidad . . . it (Rastafarianism) was already here when I came back home."[4]

This portrait of Roy, taken by a local professional photographer in 1994, originally accompanied the article, "Soca's Cape of Good Hope" (Blood 1994: 41). This article speaks about Roy's decision to leave the calypso tents and have his band "focus all of its attention and energy to the fete circuit for Carnival." It is about the glowing reviews he received for the band's performances in Germany and Belgium; Eddy Grant's telling selection of Roy's band to provide the horn tracks for all the soca recording releases on his Ice label for three years; and Roy Cape All Stars as the contracted resident band to provide the music for the following year's Soca Monarch competition. This article is a tribute to Roy's many achievements. A press kit with

5.10 Roy's Rasta look, 1994. Courtesy *Trinidad Guardian*.

articles and photographs like these offers yet another layer of work to explain his reputation.

While nothing is said about the portrait of Roy that accompanies the text, the image composition is striking. It has little to do with just being a documentary portrait. It is in stark contrast to the few photographs of musicians that one typically finds in the local newspapers. It is photography as promotion, in the highly commercial register of press kit material; photography to create, reinforce, confer, and confirm star status. It demands that

Roy strike a pose. The upward tilt of the camera toward Roy's face emphasizes his largesse and suggests a gesture of deference by the photographer. Roy's eyes, looking above and beyond the photograph, suggest that he is a musician with a vision. His long, thick, and impressive locks, brought to the front for the camera, frame Roy as a Rasta and as a spiritual man and, at the same time, a man of conviction not easily deterred by normative looks and behaviors. This image does its own cultural work to amplify the tribute article on Roy's impressive stature in music.

FIGURE 5.11: In her 2004 article, "Driven by the Music," Sateesh Maharaj reports that Roy would not trade his instruments for anything: "I love my instrument. What motivates you to certain things is God. I really think it was Him who sent me to play that instrument. It is me. The sound of it . . . it is a loving instrument and I have to say, I am a very loving person. It's a gentle instrument. I am a gentle person. There are things that happen when you choose things that suit your character."

Speaking about getting his own instrument in a conversation with me: "You had to struggle [to get your own instrument] if you grew up in an institution, or even if you learned to play it outside [the orphanage]. Your parents would have not been able to buy you an instrument. See, what this means is that you had to get an instrument loan from this person and from that person and from this other one until years would pass. But some people never make it so that they could buy their own instruments."

Recalling the days at the orphanage: the major impact that the Children's Home had on those who learned music went beyond the nuns' expectations. Even if he had not gone to the Children's Home, Roy would most likely have been a musician. However, by living at the Children's Home during his formative years (eleven to sixteen years old), Roy was exposed to instruments he would not have been able to afford to play otherwise—instruments that would ultimately give him a life.

FIGURE 5.12: "I am playing my horn, and I am enjoying the masqueraders. After weeks of playing every night—two or three gigs per night—I am still playing on the road on Carnival Tuesday. The joy of playing and seeing the people enjoying themselves is what we live for. The exhaustion will come only after you leave the venue. As long as you are in the venue, that vibe is still going to be flowing."

I took this photograph on Carnival Tuesday, a particularly heightened moment during carnival. My aim was to portray both the pleasure of the audiences dancing in the streets to the sound of Roy Cape's band and the plea-

5.11 Roy Cape playing his saxophone, late 1990s. Photograph by Jocelyne Guilbault.

5.12 Roy playing his saxophone on the truck on carnival day in Trinidad, circa 2009. From Roy Cape's collection.

sure of the musicians playing for and interacting with the crowds. I wanted to capture the synergy that arises between the two.

In 2009, Roy's reputation was well established, and yet it was still furthered by the hit song, "Tusty," featuring Blaxx (one of his band singers) in that season. By Carnival Tuesday, Roy already knows how much work (shows and tours) he can expect to have over the next months before the band returns to the studio in November and December to record new songs for the next carnival season. The news about the success of his singer's song circulates at lightning speed across the region, North America, and Europe. A reveler calls London, England, to make sure that everything is okay at home and at the same time signals to her friend the hit songs of the season. A deejay from Toronto transmits from his cellular phone the news about the latest hits to his audience. A show producer tells Roy he wants to see him before going to the airport to sign a contract for next Mother's Day in New York. This last gig on the truck on Carnival Tuesday is thus the crowning achievement of the band's season. It marks the closure of the carnival shows and parties and, apart from a few local shows, the beginning of the touring season a few weeks later.

FIGURE 5.13: [*From the left*] "On tenor sax Dennis ['Big D'] Wilkinson, a stalwart in calypso music, too much a history to mention. Next to Dennis is your humble servant, Roy Cape, on alto sax; on first trumpet, Thomas Patton, a fantastic trumpet player; on second trumpet, Fortunia [Señor] Ruiz, a complete musician all round; on trombone, Noel Gill, one of the better trombone players of this era; on piano, Junior Ruiz, the son of Fortunia, who was taught by his dad—young and brilliant, a very good job done by his dad. On guitar, Arnold [Sly] Punette. We can say so much about Sly, but I would choose to say that Sly has been a member of the band for the past twenty-five years [as of 2012]. On bass, Michael Nysus, a very intelligent human being and if not number one, one of the top bass players in Trinidad and Tobago. On percussion, Kenneth McConney. Kenneth and myself grew up in the same yard. I used to call his mum 'Miss Ivy' and his Dad 'Uncle Ranny.' On drums at that time was young and energetic Joey Samuel—a very humble and loyal friend. Joey has paid his dues and today he stands out as one of the top drummers in our country. Not in the photograph, Carlton [Jabbar] Braithwaite, who also I grew up with and one of our better congas and percussionists of all times. From my sight here, it seems to me that this is at the auditorium at the St. Joseph Convent or at St. Mary's College."

This photograph, taken in the midst of playing, does not give any indication of who the bandleader is. From an audience's perspective, Roy keeps such a low profile onstage that no one could guess that he is the bandleader—unless people know him as a friend or from seeing his photograph in the newspapers.

5.13 The whole horn section sitting down at Spektakula, early 1990s. Courtesy *Trinidad Express*.

FIGURE 5.14: [*From the left*] "Here on trombone, you have Patrick Spicer; on trumpet, Kenny John and Roger Jaggassar; on alto sax, Roy Cape; and on tenor sax, David Phillip. In the past, I would be either second or second to last in the formation of the horn section. In recent times, because of the proximity of the PA system, some of the guys could not take the thunder of the system. So to accommodate harmony among us, I chose to be at the extreme end of the row. In my way, I am trying to make the musicians as comfortable as is their desire."

The spatial disposition of the musicians onstage matters for several reasons. It allows a musician to best hear the instrument with which he wants to lock in, or to marry his own tone to the instruments similar to his. And perhaps most importantly, it greatly influences the overall sound production. It is thus significant that Roy is willing to modify the disposition of the musicians onstage to favor harmonious relationships. For him, harmony and well-being in the group take precedence over aesthetic concerns.

Looking at Trinidadian musicians' bodily posture onstage quickly gives away tips about the music they play. Typically, musicians accompanying calypsonians perform sitting down. They occupy the back of the stage, while the calypsonian they accompany receives the limelight, occupying the front line closer to the public. In contrast, musicians playing dance music — and soca music in particular — stand up. They stand close to the singers and often move their bodies from right to left with the music beat. In Roy's band, however, the bass player, Anthony "Bassie" Boynes, goes far beyond these simple movements and caters to both the ears and the eyes. Son of

5.14 Roy Cape All Stars full horn section standing up, late 1990s. Photograph by Jocelyne Guilbault.

Aldwyn Boynes—the professional dancer, choreographer, and founder of a reputed Trinidadian dance company—Bassie performs dance moves that his audiences find both mesmerizing and contagious.

ROY'S RELATIONSHIPS WITH CALYPSONIANS

FIGURE 5.15: "This photograph was taken near the Parish Hall in Diego Martin. We are performing outdoors, and Stalin is listening to what I am playing.

"For the longest time in Trinidad, you know, we have separated the calypsonian from the musician—which does not make sense because a calypsonian makes music. But we will not fight with that. As you would know and as most people in Trinidad and elsewhere where we traveled know, Black Stalin and myself possess a special relationship. Coming from a similar background and having the same type of love for people, we have been able to bridge the gap between the calypsonian and the musician in spite of the slogan I often heard when I was coming up as a musician: 'All dem calypsonians, the same thing.' So when you had a bad experience with a calypsonian, that slogan would be used: 'All dem calypsonians, the same thing.'

"When I left New York to come back to Trinidad, I came back with this as one of my objectives: to bridge the gap between the calypsonian and the musician. I think I have been able to achieve it. The people know about Stalin. They know about the type of work that he does and that he is not a quitter. He is not a man that compromises on any compromise. When he com-

5.15 Roy playing and calypsonian Black Stalin (Dr. Leroy Calliste) sitting, around mid-1990s. Black Stalin received an honorary doctorate from the University of the West Indies (St. Augustine, Trinidad) in 2008 for his exceptional contributions to calypso. From Roy Cape's collection.

promises, it's because it fits the philosophy of his way of thinking. Together, we have been able to bridge that gap between the calypsonian and the musician. I am the godfather of one of Stalin's grandkids. So we have elevated our relationship to a whole different level, not just of friendship, but like family. I am sixty-six and he is sixty-seven [at the time of this 2008 interview], and he could take me across the charcoal [give me a hard time]. You know, he could reprimand and discharge me, and if I'm wrong, I accept it.... If I was doing something off-key and he spoke to me about it, I don't feel bad at all, because there's no ego [no battle of personalities] between him and myself. I know, it's love then. If it's somebody you do know who is going to try to humiliate you or dehumanize you, then you would put up an arrogance against it. But when it's someone who loves you and cares for you, it's a whole different thing. I got love and respect from Leroy. He is very influential in calypso because he's one of the all-time greats. And because of that, some of that has rubbed off on me. Because if you are my friend, and I bring you to him, he has to understand that you are also my friend."

The story prompted by this picture makes it clear that no man is an island. If Roy's career and numerous opportunities to perform have been greatly enhanced by his deep connection with one of the most internationally reputed calypsonians, Black Stalin, in turn, has also benefited from being confident that with Roy's band his music will be played at its best. As he puts it, "I can't think of how much countries we've been to, and I was able to just stay inside and Roy go and rehearse the band, you know? You know for sure that you have somebody watching your back then, you know? Yeah . . . positive about that, for years Roy watching my back."

Since the late 1960s, Trinidadian musicians have rarely been given the opportunity to play solos in the midst of accompanying calypsonians. The arrangers' increasing role from that time onward has typically left little space for musicians to improvise and show their individual musical skills. However, the close collaboration and mutual respect that Roy helped establish between musicians and calypsonians has produced tangible effects that Roy himself could not have anticipated. One way that Stalin has shown his admiration for Roy's musicianship has been to regularly ask him to play a solo during his performance. Today, this is a rare occurrence in calypso performance. According to a horn player I interviewed, even if given the opportunity, most younger band musicians have not had the chance to hone their improvisational skills and would thus shy away from playing solos.

FIGURE 5.16: "Stalin and Sly [Roy's band guitarist] are having some fun during a cool day in New York, probably hanging out just before going somewhere with the band.

"What I have done is to give the band players an opportunity to get together with the calypsonians. Stalin has his personal relationship with Sly and with other band members because

5.16 Calypsonian Black Stalin and Arnold "Sly" Punette outside a van, Brooklyn, New York, 1987. From Roy Cape's collection.

they have performed together on many occasions and in many situations. Sometimes, when Stalin performs with Juice [Roy's arranger] alone, Juice gets all the love for the night then."

Stalin and Sly are clearly aware of the photographer and strike a pose to show how much they enjoy each other's company. Roy's selection of this photograph reveals how he values collegial relations. For him, the friendship between calypsonians and musicians not only makes weeks on tour away from family more enjoyable, it also makes everyone strive all the more to perform at their best.

REMEMBERING WITH PICTURES 157

FIGURE 5.17: "We gathered for some sort of rehearsal. My eyes are really on [calypsonians] Brigo and Baker. We are probably talking about something related to music or what the rehearsal is all about.

"Around that time, I was probably the only musician with long dreadlocks, which was the name at that time—today it would be simply called locks. The locks today is not a curiosity for people; it is just [understood] to say, 'We are Rastas.' Sparrow had sung about the outcast, which was describing the perception of the image of the pan men by the population as a [vagabond]. When the Rastas came, they took their place at the bottom of the social order. Through the years Rastafarians have proven that they are not just ganja [marijuana] smokers and unproductive. They are making a serious contribution to the society in the form of music, arts, and crafts, not only in Trinidad but also in the whole Caribbean and wherever they settled."

At the calypso tent Spektakula, Roy as a bandleader assumed a position of authority. He decided when the band would rehearse, which calypsonian songs they would play, and in what sequence. Was this professional journalistic image, which positions the calypsonians seated and looking up to Roy, aiming to reaffirm the divide between musicians and calypsonians or to show Roy's burgeoning relationship with them? Was this image taken to comment on the length of time calypsonians have to wait before being able to rehearse their songs with the band? Or conversely, was it aiming to show how Roy began to talk to the calypsonians on the importance of being on time for rehearsals? In 1982, Roy had just started to assume his position as bandleader at Spektakula. It was an important moment to communicate his musical standards in the calypso milieu and a sensitive time for him to establish his reputation.

FIGURE 5.18: "Chalkie and myself are speaking to someone, and we both seem to be in a very pleasant mood with whatever discussion is going on. Being responsible for the band at Spektakula from the year 1981, my relationship with the artists is wonderful.

"Chalkie—who was a senior member of the cast of Spektakula—and I had a special and professional friendship. Chalkie was invited by Krister Malm, who was then the concert tour producer for Rikskonserter [a government concert bureau organizing tours in Sweden].[5] Chalkie chose me to travel with him to Sweden, and he gave me the option to choose one person to travel with us. For the type of work that we were going to do, I chose deceased guitarist Junior Wharwood."

By 1989, after having worked for nine years at the calypso tent Spektakula, Roy's reputation as a bandleader was well established. In this picture, even

5.17 Roy receives the attention of calypsonians Brigo (Samuel Abraham), Lord Baker (Kent King), and Crazy's manager, January 1982. Courtesy *Trinidad Guardian*.

5.18 Calypsonian Chalkdust (Dr. Hollis Liverpool) and Roy, 1989. Courtesy *Trinidad Express*.

though Chalkdust was a highly reputed calypsonian in the Caribbean, the photojournalist chose to feature Roy as the star and the focus of attention.

FIGURE 5.19: "The telethon was initiated by Mrs. Lynne Murray. She asked me to organize the first telethon for the Family Planning Association of Trinidad and Tobago in aid of Sai Krishna Children's Home and Rebirth House, which is a home for rehabilitation of substance abuse. The funds raised in the telethon were distributed to the different organizations to assist with their programs. Mrs. Lynne Murray got the generous support of many of the top artists in the country. Many, many names were part of this event. In this picture, we have the late Lord Kitchener performing at the telethon. The accompaniment band is Roy Cape All Stars. As part of the show, you would have had also Black Stalin, Denyse Plummer, Superblue, David Rudder, All Rounder, Brother Mudada, and Brigo. This telethon went on for about ten years. During that period, we played for different types of charitable organizations that deal with the underprivileged and people with physical disabilities. The last one I did was at the Savannah in aid of the calypsonians. On hearing Mrs. Murray's idea, I had no hesitation to participate [in these events], as I was very aware of one of the famous telethons hosted by Jerry Lewis—which I would call the father of the telethon."

The mixture of social associations, musical performances, and transnational influences evident in this photograph is typical of the different milieus in which Roy Cape All Stars perform. On the one hand, the Sai Krishna Children's Home next to the Children's Home on the banner foregrounds Trinidad's multicultural milieu—the presence and spiritual influence of East Indians in Trinidad together with institutions run mainly by Afro-Trinidadians. On the other hand, the performers—including Lord Kitchener headlined here, and the many other artists that Roy mentions—are all mainly of African descent, and they are all recognized as calypsonians. While this telethon was organized for a wide range of social organizations and for people of various ethnic groups, the music it featured was calypso only—still the most prominent local music at that time. Yet, as Roy explains, the telethon, which responded to some of the most pressing local needs, was transnationally connected to (and influenced by) an American televised initiative hosted by the American comedian and movie actor Jerry Lewis.

FIGURE 5.20: "That picture represents ninety-three years of friendship—when I take our friendship to each other into account. We have known each other for thirty-one years each. So in Trini saying, we have ninety-three years of friendship all together. That is a hell of a friendship. It is not for today, or for tomorrow alone, but until we pass away. We can say all

5.19 Calypsonian Lord Kitchener (Aldwyn Roberts) and Roy Cape All Stars, 1992. Courtesy *Trinidad Express*.

5.20 Black Stalin, Roy Cape, and Junior Telfer, 1995. Photograph by Jocelyne Guilbault.

sorts of fancy words, but thirty-one years is a lot of years. The value of the friendship we have developed is even past friendship; it is more like your family then. Our individual well-being is being protective of each other—by each of us to each other."

The recognition and commercial success of calypsonians like Black Stalin and of musicians and bandleaders like Roy depend on a network of support. But on a day-by-day basis, this success is facilitated by someone like Junior Telfer—a music aficionado, dancer, and philosopher in his own right, former manager of Black Stalin and owner of a nightclub in London, England, for several years, as well as a highly respected cultural observer locally. The steadfast support that he provides to both Black Stalin and Roy is as much about providing a place for them to cool out, giving them feedback on their artistic ventures, reflecting on the lyrics of one, commenting on the musical performance of the other, reminiscing on some of their respective feats, as it is about critically reviewing and laughing away at the unpredictable twists and turns of everyday life.

FIGURE 5.21: "The fingers pointed to Superblue and Stalin mean number one. Here it is Carnival Day, 1995. I was playing with Wayne Berkeley's masquerade. When we reached Victoria Park, we usually stop[ped] here for lunch. Seeing Superblue and Stalin here and later on Junior Telfer, one would gather that it was preorganized for us to meet here. And they would be right because this is our every-year custom. As I just confirmed with you, Stalin won the Calypso Monarch with 'Sundar Popo,' and Superblue won the Road March with 'Signal to Lara.' And I am giving both of them the number one sign which they so richly deserve. It is a lovely picture and a privilege for me to be around such huge talents."

On this Carnival Tuesday in 1995, I felt very privileged to be hanging out with the winners of the main national competitions of the season and with Roy, whose band had provided the instrumental accompaniment to both winners. It was a day of celebration for Black Stalin, who had defeated not one but two Calypso Monarchs, the cowinners of the national competition the year before. It was a day of celebration for Superblue too, because even though he had just lost his title of Soca Monarch, which he had held since the inception of the competition in 1993, he had won the Road March—a coveted title that reflects the people's choice. It is won by the highest number of times masquerade bands choose an artist's tune to accompany them during Jouvè morning [Carnival Monday] and the Carnival Tuesday parade. It was a day of celebration for Roy too, for he knew that his band had carried the tunes of the two winners of the season.

When I mentioned that I was going to take a photograph, Superblue,

5.21 Superblue (Austin Lyons), Roy Cape, and Black Stalin, 1995. Photograph by Jocelyne Guilbault.

Roy, and Black Stalin took a position of their choice. Typical of Roy, he directed the attention toward the two winners. Yet his position, standing between the two icons of calypso and soca, was inadvertently felicitous, by allegorically reflecting the central (musical) role he played in their respective victories.

FIGURE 5.22: "With Marvin and Nigel Lewis as the Road March winners that year, we had gone to Boston. As we were on a truck just vamping because at that time we were standing stationary, I decided to jump off from the truck to go to the bathroom before going back to hit the road. I jumped from the truck and in jumping I injured my right foot. So when I reached Brooklyn, one of my friends, Kenneth Cardinal, gave me this walking stick. I was somewhere at some function and hanging out with the two calypsonians. We were booked for the Customs fete in Brooklyn around Labor Day. I recall that when I was backstage and I saw Machel [Montano] in the audience, I went down and walked through the audience to greet him. But I could hear one of the patrons at the dance call me. So I turned and he said, 'Roy, I did not know you had a stroke.' I quickly answered, 'No, no, no! I jumped off the truck in Boston and hurt my feet!'

"Here Poser has a cup in his hand—which does not really mean alcohol. I have a bottle in my hand and Scanty is gesticulating to me with his hand and his smile, seemingly saying, 'Look de man, boy.' And you can see Poser studious of the situation.

"Rehearsal is the key to the success of performance. I think it's one of my strengths. It is about my sincerity to give calypsonians my finished product, as they like to hear it. It is also about a show of tolerance toward them. I am keeping their music so that even if they lost their

5.22 Calypsonian Poser (Sylvester Lockhart), Roy with a cane, and calypsonian Tunapuna Scanty (Michael Scanterbury), 1996. From Roy Cape's collection.

5.23 Calypsonians Gypsy (Winston Peters), Black Stalin, Penguin (Sedley Joseph), and Roy, 2001. From Roy Cape's collection.

scores, they can come back to me and get a copy from me. A guy always feels very great about you because he knows then how much you care about the music."

FIGURE 5.23: "This here really reflects my friendship with Leroy. They were having a function at the mayor's office in city hall in San Fernando for Leroy's birthday on the twenty-fourth of September 2001. I am in the company of Winston 'Gypsy' Peters [calypsonian and friend], Sedley 'Penguin' Joseph [former president of the Trinidad Unified Calypsonians' Organization], and Black Stalin."

This is a formal portrait, and its subjects are aware of its historical potency. That a calypsonian's birthday would be celebrated at a mayor's office is telling of how politicians came to respect calypso celebrities and how they understood what the artistic reputation of a calypsonian like Black Stalin could bestow on his city of origin. On Black Stalin's birthday, powerful representatives of the calypso fraternity are invited and represented at the celebration: Winston "Gypsy" Peters, a reputed calypsonian, but also, in 2001, a politician and member of Parliament, and Sedley "Penguin" Joseph, himself a calypsonian and in 2001, the president of the calypsonians' organization.

ROY'S BAND FAMILY

FIGURE 5.24: "At the time I was thinking to do the first LP with the band, none of the people who were then producing and recording music seemed interested. But I am a self person who usually does my work and who lets time take care of things. So I simply continued to do recordings at Musik Kraft recording studio for the owner, Otte Muriez. While doing a session, Otte told me that he would produce a record for me. I then made preparation for the songs that I was going to record.

"Not included in this photograph were the following musicians who also played on this LP recording: Dennis Wilkinson (tenor sax), Lambert Phillip (trombone), Ricky Clarke (trumpet), and Clyde Mitchell (trumpet)."

This album marks the beginning of a new aspect of Roy's career: recording projects with his own band. As this photograph clearly shows, it is a happy moment for him. All of his band members are young and project lots of energy. For this album, Roy enlisted the help of top arrangers to make his band sound at its best. His guest artists, pan player Earl Brooks and singer Allan Welch, were and still are well-known artists. The backup singers included on this album had considerable experience as vocalists in calypso tents. His choice of tunes featured classics of calypso (e.g., by Lord Kitch-

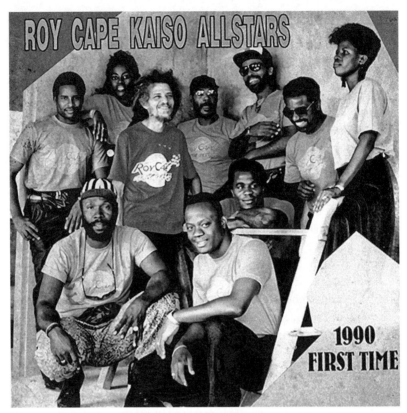

5.24 Roy Cape Kaiso All Stars, 1990, *First Time*. Front row, right to left: Joey Samuel, Kenneth McCommey, Michael Nysus, Juliette Robin, Ivan Durity, Arnold Punette, Barry Howard, Ann Marie (aka Twiggy) Parks-Kojo, Allan Welch (stooping), Roy Cape.

ener and Duke) and some of the latest hits of soca (e.g., by Iwer George, Superblue, and Tambu) — the type of wide repertoire with which Roy Cape All Stars earned its reputation and that has put Roy in great demand locally, regionally, and internationally.

FIGURE 5.25: "In trying to give freedom to the members of the band, we would choose uniforms pertaining to material and color and I would allow the players to decide how they would dress [the design of clothes they would choose]. In this picture, the bass player, Anthony, and the guitar player, Arnold, had chosen short pants. It was not a policy to say that everybody had to wear short pants. All members were free to decide how they would want their uniforms, and I would comply with their feelings and with the fashion designer."

I took this picture in Toronto at an HMV store, where Roy Cape All Stars were promoting their new CD and also advertising their upcoming con-

5.25 Band members wearing short pants, 1995. Photograph by Jocelyne Guilbault.

5.26 Nigel and Marvin Lewis on Carnival Tuesday, 1996. Photograph by Jocelyne Guilbault.

cert during Caribana (the largest Trinidad-inspired carnival outside the Caribbean). To the group of listeners assembled around the band, the soca sounds Roy's band members produced left no doubt that the band was from the Caribbean and, for those in the know, from Trinidad in particular. But as this photograph shows, Roy's band members are highly aware of the image they project by the way they dress. For the occasion, they wore the short pants that were then highly popular and part of a transnational fashion— a fashion that was deeply influenced by African American artists.

FIGURE 5.26: "This is Marvin and Nigel Lewis and this was in 1996 when we won the Road March with 'Moving to the Left.' Nigel and Marvin had been with the band from 1994 and Nigel was always looking to do things different and to do things that would create some sort of frenzy or comments. And this was his way to create these comments. They are wearing body suits and a jock. This picture shows that we are on the road on Carnival Day."

Nigel and Marvin Lewis, the first singers in Roy's band, looked hip, had strong voices, and produced a winning song with "Movin'" (more popularly known as "Moving to the Left"). As Francesca Hawkins puts it, "Roy was elated. He had the number one tune for the carnival, whereas before he was always backing up. . . . So suddenly, Roy was a star, he was the man. And then they [Nigel and Marvin] left [the band]. It was a terrible period of anxiety, terrible." Since then, Roy's band has featured several singers.

FIGURE 5.27: "This is Destra on the road on Caribana Day (in Toronto). We are on the truck. She looks very cool, mature and also content. 2002 was a hectic year for her, as she had many performances with the band and also without the band. This is the year when she made an exit, after she agreed to hold on with me until after Miami Carnival in October. Had she moved on in February, which I explained to her, it would have killed the band's promotion for the whole year. I was grateful for her kindness and understanding and that still remains up to today."

Destra Garcia is today one of the most recognized female soca singers in the Caribbean. Nearly ten years after she left Roy's band, Destra was there in 2010 to celebrate Roy's achievements for his fifty-plus years in the business. Such a gesture speaks highly about the long-term relationships Roy has been able to establish in the soca milieu.

FIGURE 5.28: "Esther came into the band as Destra exited. This picture is a picture that was done for promotional use. As you see, Esther and myself are up front and I think that you can see affection in the picture. In bands and also in calypso in Trinidad and Tobago, it was gener-

5.27 Destra Garcia wearing a Roy Cape All Stars 2002 Canadian Tour red T-shirt. From Roy Cape's collection.

5.28 Roy and Esther Dyer (front), and in the second row, Derrick Seales (left) and Dexter "Blaxx" Stewart (right), around 2003. From Roy Cape's collection.

ally a man's game. Even with people like Calypso Rose and Singing Francine, the environment was not always female friendly. But as time passed, the women in calypso and in soca have been given the attention that should be given to them. Some of these people are Ella Andall, Singing Sandra, and in the soca scene today, you have Sanell Dempster, Lima Calbio, Alison Hinds, Destra Garcia, Fay Ann Lyons, Rita Jones, Denise Belfon, and Nadia Batson."

Until 2011, Roy Cape All Stars featured two male singers and one female singer. It is a formation that allows the flexibility to perform different kinds of songs and styles. It is also a formation that complements the powerful sound of the band with its horn section, samplers, and rhythm section. To have more than one singer in a soca band performance is also welcome because soca is vocally and physically demanding for a singer. While they project their voice at full volume, they also dance and move across the stage in sync with their energetic songs.[6]

FIGURE 5.29: "It is normal from time to time in a band that you will have changes. Any time there are changes, you have to take new photographs, clean up your bio, and bring it up to date. This photograph here includes Olatunji and Trini Jacobs as part of Roy Cape All Stars family.

"To keep musicians together in a band, you have to understand each individual. And you have to understand the likes and the don'ts of each individual, the things that make them [the band members] happy and the things that they are not happy with. At one point, I probably would have seen me [would not think as much about the band members]. For some time now, I am not seeing me, I am seeing them. Because I have learned now that if I see them, God is going to see me. And so far, it has worked for me. In all my difficult times, he has always shown me a way out. I have a son today, and he has acquired a whole lot of my temperament. He looks after people. Right now he is the one—he and Juiceman—who runs the band. Musicians don't like talk and promises. Give them action. If you want to give them something, give them something. But to promise them? We have been promised our whole life, and nothing much has ever materialized.

"I have been a musician for fifty years. I have been a bandleader for the last, let's say, thirty years. This puts me in a position to appreciate what Joey Lewis, Byron Lee, Ron Berridge, Clarence Curvan, Sparrow Troubadours did, what it took to keep the band together. In most of the bands that I played with in my younger life, we never really stayed in a band long, maybe two years, never felt like your desire was being satisfied. So you had to move on, still looking for the satisfaction of that desiring. The economics wasn't great enough to keep us for long in a band. What we were not seeing is that the leader's responsibility is the survival of the people underneath, and that's why he is named leader. This is why the guys choose him to be their leader. This is why they come from here to here under his leadership. He has proved to them his caring and his sincerity and his love for them.

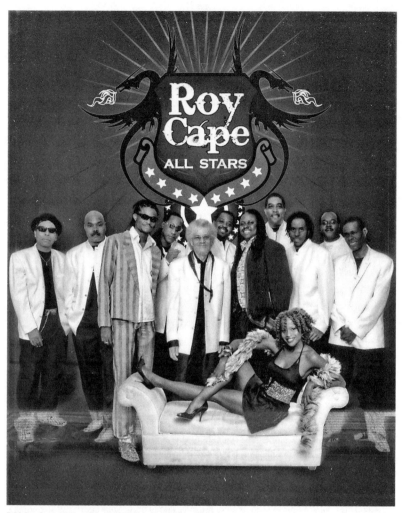

5.29 Roy Cape All Stars band, 2008. Courtesy Anthony Moore.

"The guys in the band call me 'Pappy,' they call me 'father,' they call me such lovely names. They call me 'the boss.' However, I don't let these things become an attachment to me, because if it comes an attachment, then the open relationship I have with them doesn't exist—wouldn't exist—although there's a lot of things that they hide from me. Things may be going on, but they would not let me know because they don't want to worry me. They don't want me to be unhappy, so they hide a lot of things from me. In the past, when things went wrong, I would have gotten angry. I have learned now not to get angry, because time and age have made me see that you do what you can do. Yeah. So as Stalin would say, 'We came here and met the world one way, and we would hope that in our going from here, we should be able to leave it in a better condition than how we met it for those who are coming.'"

FIGURE 5.30: "I am not biting my lips, but I have a special expression like I was examining something that was going on out of concern. If I had been in a critical examination, you would have seen exclamations with my hands.

"When I am onstage, I attend to everything going on during the performance. Orchestras usually have a conductor. In our case because of [the] size of the band, there is no need for a physical conductor but there will always have to be someone who oversees the flow of either the song or how the program has been designed. In rehearsals, we tried to rehearse so that when we are on the stage, there is not too much looking as though there was some teaching going on in a performance. This means that the band has been properly rehearsed."

In an interview with me in June 2009, Black Stalin commented on how Roy responds to his band members when their playing is below his musical standards, straying away from what has been rehearsed in the band room. In his own words, "And you wouldn't believe that one little fellow could get so bad then, you know? I saw when the band had not [been] playing good, and Roy pack up and go home, you know, and leave the band [laughs], leave the band [behind] to play then [laughs]. No, you would never see Roy backroom the night that the band didn't perform well. He don't make joke with that. He don't make joke with that, you know? And when I cross a brother like that watching my back, what more then [would you want]?"

FIGURE 5.31: "In this photograph, we are outside of our band room on Church and George Cabral streets in St. James. You can see that we have taken a break from rehearsals, and we were just chilling outside of the band room. In the photograph, there are the members of the band and you can see Carlysle, my son Roy, and Kerwin Dubois in a conversation. Kerwin has given us songs [such] as 'Breathless,' 'Tusty' [Thirsty], 'Huntin',' and 'Good Times.' All these songs to our standards in Trinidad have been hits. As you see here, we are a group that hangs together when we are finished rehearsing. The guys like to drink their beers and sometimes, there are cases of beers there. In this picture, I am just cooling myself, and Blaxx is on his iPhone. Blaxx is the lead singer for the band for the past thirteen years [as of 2012]—a fantastic vocalist and performer."

Roy's demeanor here, sitting on the back of a bench and looking relaxed and very low key, is telling of the relationships he has with his band members. The importance of socializing among band members and especially between the bandleader and his band cannot be overestimated. Besides the weekly salary that Roy's band members earn and that provides them with a decent living, spending time together after rehearsals as friends has been declared by all band members in interviews with me as one of the most sig-

5.30 Roy looking sideways at one of his horn players in Toronto, 1997. From Roy Cape's collection.

5.31 Roy and his band members after a rehearsal, 2010. Photograph by Jocelyne Guilbault.

nificant factors in making Roy Cape All Stars sound musically tight and feel like a family.

FIGURE 5.32: "I was in Toronto during a show, doing a provocative, playful gesture. From my eyes' expression with a smile but no smile, I am looking at someone with whom I was playing or someone in the audience. I am very silent about marijuana, and I am aware how misguided today the youths are. So I would never want to be an influence for things that are illegal."

This picture speaks volumes about how Roy communicates with small gestures and in intimate ways with people. Is this communication style precisely what has enabled him to manage relations with finesse?

FIGURE 5.33: "Here is me with a microphone and my saxophone strap hanging from my neck. I am singing. This is the year 1998 and for whatever reason, God sent his intuition to me in the form of 'Jam Mih.' I competed in the Soca Monarch semifinal and qualified to be in the grand final on Carnival Friday that year. There were some thirty-something contestants, some with very much experience. And in this competition, I was placed ninth. It was very gratifying to me as I am accustomed to play with the band, and here I was upfront doing lead singing with my usual lead singers."

For Roy, no doubt, singing was about exploring another creative space. It was about creating for himself a challenge, to experience the thrill and the stress of singers he had observed during his entire life as a musician.

Musically, "Jam Mih" puts together many strands of Roy's musical career. Revealing the deep imprint that the calypso music scene has had on him, Roy wrote his song as a tribute to the many people with whom he played, in combination with a certain bravura, two narrative styles typical in calypso. Hear him boast in verse four:

> Ninety-six, ninety-seven
> Ah teach dem ah good lesson
> Masquerade thru the land
> Learn that All-Stars is the band
> From de street to de dance hall
> I respond to every call
> Everyone, no matter who
> This music is just for you.

But "Jam Mih" also demonstrates the musical style of soca in which Roy has immersed himself since the 1990s. While he sings a calypso melody—in terms not only of form but also of melody—Roy moves, and makes the

5.32 Roy in Toronto, around 1997. From Roy Cape's collection.

5.33 Roy singing at the Soca Monarch National Competition in Trinidad and Tobago, 1998. From Roy Cape's collection.

audience move, to the rhythm of soca. "Jam Mih" musically sums up Roy's career and specifically his work in calypso and soca.

ROY'S OUTREACH AND REWARDS

FIGURE 5.34:

RC: We just returned from the World Cup in Germany and the whole team of the soca warriors was on the plane. The plane was like a carnival. They fix the first class to make it like a lounge for the team. We were invited to join in. So we were singing calypsos, and having a fete on the plane on the way back to Trinidad.

I have in front of me a picture here of myself and our little magician, Russell Latapy. I left Trinidad in 1970. And before that, I was very much a spectator of local football. Recently I met my old captain of Maple, Sedley Joseph, and I spoke to him and I showed him, you know, I was always a Maple. In the institution, I was in the house of Maple (which was yellow). Coming out from there I was a supporter of Maple. We had people like Alvin Corneal, Lincoln Philips, Tyrone De Labastide (he was called "the tank"). In my elder of years, Russell [Latapy] has been one of the brightest football stars in Trinidad and Tobago. Russell has been playing in the Scottish League in England. He has just been signed on by the Trinidad and Tobago Football Association with a contract for the next two years. Russell and Dwight Yorke, I don't have a picture of Dwight, but Russell Latapy goes hand in hand with him. They are a combination as two veterans on our national team at this point. So we were returning to Trinidad from Germany after the World Cup on a plane, and even though I hadn't known him personally I had heard so much about him from my younger friends. He came up to me and he gave me a can of Carib beer, and this is us here posing for a picture. You can see I framed it because he is one of the younger people that I'm very impressed with.

If there are two people from poor backgrounds who young people can relate to and emulate, they are Russell Latapy and Dwight Yorke. Dwight Yorke played for Manchester United when the team won three successive championships.

JG: Yes. Do both of them come from the orphanage as well?

RC: No. But I never remove myself from families of people who have been going through the same kind of economical struggle that my parents went

5.34 Roy with Trinidadian soccer player Russell Latapy, 2006. From Roy Cape's collection.

through. So even though Russell didn't grow up in an orphan home—he grew up with his parents—I would consider Russell as having the same type of background as me. Although Russell might have had a mom and dad, it was a struggle. A struggle, yeah. Dwight Yorke is from Tobago. Again, even though today we are into money, growing up in those days these guys had no money. They had ambition and desires, and they pursued something that could make a meaningful contribution to the country and to their own lives.

A young person could watch Russell or Dwight and emulate them. It can give them hope. They can see that Dwight and Russell, and probably people like myself, and maybe Stalin or David Rudder or Gypsy or Valentino or Shadow or Sparrow or Kitchener—that all of these people came from very humble background and they were able to make something. These guys are very famous. I have a little popularity in Trinidad and in the Caribbean and in little pieces, parts of the world, but these guys are world renown[ed].

FIGURE 5.35:

RC: In 1987 or 1988, Machel came to sing at Spektakula. He was still a child and at times he would come in school uniform. He was doing the song "Too Young to Soca." And I had to organize with his parents times for rehearsals. And we had to do his rehearsals in a timing so he could get back home at a reasonable time to go to school in the morning. You would understand

5.35 Machel Montano, Roy, and the members of HD and Roy Cape All Stars at the Antilliaanse Feesten [Festival] at Hoogstraten, Belgium, 2011. Courtesy Elizabeth Montano.

from the title of the song, "Too Young to Soca," which some in the society would have felt that he was really too young to soca. He has proved to us that those comments were totally wrong. It is a memory in Trinidad and Tobago in seeing this young boy in the Calypso Monarch competition of that year.

Through the years, we have met on different stages and different functions. We have had always a very cordial relationship—which still exists today. Again, to talk about Machel, it may take a whole book to talk about his growth and the contributions that he has made to our country and to our people. But I would like to boast and say that, apart from Machel's own band, Roy Cape All Stars band is the only band that has performed for Machel through half of the season in 2003. And this has continued when we are in Toronto. If he is around, he would come and do a few songs with us. I had the privilege of doing a track on *The Collectors Riddim* CD.

I would say that our country and myself are very proud of our boy wonder. He has now grown to a full man and is the leading and most sought-after artist from the Caribbean. He has been fantastic and will be always fantastic. God blesses his health as long as he lives. He is very thoughtful, and he is always trying to make a difference. Again I would like to say here that it has been proven by this young man that hard work and dedication seldom fails. My apology that this is as much as I could say for now, as it would take a whole book for me to write about Machel Montano.

5.36 Roy receiving the Hummingbird Gold Medal award from President Professor Maxwell Richards in Trinidad, 2004. From Roy Cape's collection.

FIGURE 5.36: "This medal is awarded to people for national service and contributions to culture. Awards are given to the category of service to the nation. As a national of your country, it is always with pride and humility that one accepts [a] national award. This national award was very distant in my mind. In being awarded it, it made me realize that I had reached the age for awards. With thanks to the people who nominated me and the nominating committee."

In Trinidad, artistic recognition comes mostly in the form of winning a competition. Since most associations—including the Republic Bank Limited, the Trinidad and Tobago Electricity Commission, the Carib Brewery, National Flour Mills, Queen's Park Oval, and Petrotrin (Petroleum Company of Trinidad and Tobago Limited)—hold an annual musical competition in either calypso, soca, chutney, or chutney soca, or several other genres, it could be concluded that Trinidadian artists receive more attention and more recognition than is the case in many other countries. However, many local artists complain that they do not receive the rewards and official recognition they deserve from the state government. The state-sponsored awards that do exist are indeed few in number and thus considered very prestigious. The artists who are bestowed such awards are recognized for their life achievements and contributions to the nation-state. They are considered national assets and part of the national treasure.

The question of who is granted these state-sponsored awards and who is entitled to receive them often raises controversies. This question is particularly sensitive for those who left the country at a relatively young age, had brilliant careers as professionals abroad, and returned to Trinidad at the end of their careers to find themselves in nearly complete oblivion. For musicians who chose to pursue their entire musical career or most of it in the country, the state of affairs for those returnees is sad, but unfortunately the fate of many migrants. It is the musicians who have faced the challenges and hardship of living on the island, in both its physical and postcolonial conditions, who have helped nurture and expand the vitality of the arts in the country that are being rewarded. In this sense, the Hummingbird Gold Medal is a nationalistic award. It is attributed, explicitly or not, to those who contribute to the nation-state locally and internationally while living within the confines of its geopolitical entity. After living for nearly seven years in New York and having the choice to go to Europe to pursue his musical career, Roy decided to come back to Trinidad. Little did he know that this decision would lead him years later to earn the prestigious award of the Hummingbird Gold Medal.

CONCLUDING REMARKS

The focus of this chapter has been on visual economies, how the conjuncture of musical work and photographic work perform memory work. For Roy, the visual economies of the photographs included here perform a double task, one that could be viewed as highly personal and the other as pedagogical. Our selection of photographs helps him remember his own musical journey and at the same time acknowledge with pride and admiration his colleagues and the musicians from whom he has learned and with whom he has had long-term friendships. Speaking with and about the photographs for this chapter, Roy focuses on social relationships, on people, and on places. His selection of the photographs emphasizes the cumulative and the collective dimension of music making, rather than stars and celebrities. As Roy kept saying throughout this project, "This book is not just about me; it is about the many people who have taught me, the people with whom I played, and the people through whom I have learned what little I have learned."

In addition, as Roy has often emphasized (even though not in these words), the visual economies of the selected photographs provide a pedagogical document of Trinidad's musical history. They inform older and younger generations about the past. They illustrate some of the distinct ways musicians have produced and performed calypso and soca locally and internationally, and they present a visual record of key musicians from Trinidad and Tobago. They also recall key interrelationships among musicians and artists that were transformative musically at specific moments in Trinidad and Tobago's history.

In contrast, my comments underscored the substantive materialities of what is inside the photographic frames (literal to the images) and what is outside the frames (historical-social-political-affective contexts of the images). Some of the photographs were indeed replete with information concerning, for example, the recording technologies used at a certain historical period and the performing conditions (at times cramped space) in which Roy and his band performed. Musically, the images of Roy's musicians sitting down or standing up gave cues to people in the know about the contrasting traditions in which calypso and soca are played. Other images were highly telling of how fashion helped Roy and his band connect global trends to a local and regional music.

In addressing the substantive materialities of what is inside and outside the photographic frames, I emphasized also the politics of representation inherent in the photographs' compositions: how, for instance, the inclusion of some individuals and not others spoke about race, ethnicity, gender, and class politics in the musical milieus in which Roy works; how images foregrounding Roy's self-fashioning (the construction of his own persona) through hairdo revealed the taking of a specific stance, in this case, in relation to African diasporic politics. I highlighted how Roy's selection of a great number of photographs featuring him in the company of many calypsonians, soca artists, other musicians, and friends also loudly communicated the importance Roy gives to relationships and support networks, and to the pride and pleasure of playing with and for people across borderlines.

My comments also paid attention to another type of visual economy, this time undertaken by the photographers themselves. I indicated how the photographers' framing of the images also produced their own narratives. The angle at which a photograph is taken (e.g., the upward or downward tilt of a camera) and the image composition (e.g., the frontal or sideways figure profile), reveal not only some of the local conventions through which musicians are usually portrayed, but also how individual photographers worked to construct the aura of a star visually for a saxophonist and bandleader like Roy.

The cumulative effect of all the photographs included here cannot be overstated. They speak to each other and they do cultural work. The distinct visual economies they enact produce many different kinds of stories. When I now think of Roy in the 1960s and Roy in 2012, I have a better understanding of his vast experience with different musicians and singers, spaces and places where he performed, the variety of people with whom he hangs out, and the many different kinds of people—including photographers—that have helped him build his reputation.

6 • WORKING WITH ROY
Musicians and Friends Speak

In the Caribbean calypso culture, a typically critical attitude is found in everyday conversation. Things are frequently not taken at face value. A positive comment can instantly be responded to with a sharp dismissive one. Reactions can be suspicious and quite defensive. Rivalries and jealousies abound. Judgments can be harsh. Words can sting. While reputed Trinidadian novelists such as V. S. Naipaul and Earl Lovelace have long recognized this vocal habitus of the place (Trinidad) in their writings, few academics have addressed it.

In this cultural context, to ask for testimonies about Roy's band leadership was tricky. Musicians are well known everywhere for complaining about the conditions of their employment. One expects this. However, some bandleaders are quite successful in keeping their musicians for a long period of time. Everyone knows the story of world-renowned pianist, composer, and bandleader Duke Ellington and his longtime band member Johnny Hodges, himself a star saxophonist. Testimonies about such long-term relationships are important (Dance 1970). They bring out noteworthy exceptions in an industry well known to be the subject of many complaints about employment—including not being paid on time (or not enough or not at all), having erratic schedules, and working for bandleaders that are self-centered, uncaring about others, stingy with due credit, or who abandon others to pursue their own careers, in other words, that have no time for affective labor or care for others.¹ In a discourse replete with sniping, mean-spirited comments, bitchiness, and bitterness about the boss, it is significant to hear the variety of positive ways in which not only calypsonians, rapso and soca artists, but also Roy's own musicians speak about him.

While social commentaries and critiques are part of everyday speech in the West Indies, praise is also typical to express one's relationality, positionality, and sociality vis-à-vis others. Like criticism, praise is a speech act that can have far-reaching effects.² Praise elaborates on and confirms a reputation at the same time that it contributes to its circulation. It is the counterpart of *picong*—the ability in calypso singing duels to utter stinging words and witty remarks to destabilize one's adversary in order to win a singing contest, to win an argument, and to demonstrate one's cunning abilities and superior command of elocution. In contrast, praise establishes a different relationship between the one who speaks and the one who is spoken for (the Other). It should not be confused with flattery (locally referred to as *mamaguy*)—complimenting excessively or insincerely to win favor. Praise gives approval as much as it expresses admiration. While it establishes hierarchy, it does so positively—as in, "I feel good and better off knowing you."

The testimonies I gathered come from individuals who have had many different kinds of interactions and exchanges with Roy over the years. In this sense, the comments included here are not presented as a promotional press release about Roy. Even though their force is to valorize and praise achievement, their placement and purpose here aids us to analyze exactly what accomplishment means in a local music industry. These testimonies come from experience. They also come from the heart.

In reading through the interviews with Roy's musicians and other artists, I was struck by the number of themes that repeatedly came up to describe Roy as a bandleader. Many of the stories that emerged from the testimonies referred to Roy's reputation and magnetism as a bandleader. A number of others addressed the ways in which Roy handles openly the sensitive issue of salary. Several others discussed his ethical care vis-à-vis the music and his coworkers. And nearly all of them made reference to Roy's character as a bandleader.

The image that came to my mind as I thought about how I would produce a montage of these voices, and the similar themes they addressed, was a documentary. Based on this idea, the chapter is laid out as if I had filmed and then edited the musicians' and artists' interviews.³ The opening shots establish the pedigree of the speakers; the medium shots address particular relations with Roy; the close-ups feature recollections of particular experiences; and extreme close-ups acknowledge personal sentiments. Throughout the chapter, I use jump cuts: by compressing the time of the interview exchanges I can highlight the different themes that the same speaker addresses. At other times, I leave some of the speakers' statements with an ellipsis at the end, drawing on the movie technique of fading out to let the statements resonate and create emphasis. At still other times, I resort to the dissolve approach used in documentaries, allowing one speaker's assertion to be taken up simultaneously by another voice.[4] I also use the documentary feature of title cards, which quickly perform a sort of discourse analysis by highlighting in one word or a single sentence the main theme of what follows. The choice of themes is not evident: in many cases, I could have called attention to other themes that are embedded sometimes in the same stories. But regardless of the selection, the chosen themes featured in documentary title cards help assemble a great number of voices and provide a wide range of perspectives on a given subject.

As in a documentary, I left most of the repetitions intact, including not only the words, but at times complete sentences. I also incorporated in words most of the expressive vocal gestures, including onomatopoeia, that accompanied the storytelling. These speech markers help establish emphasis, reveal emotions, and share important moments of one's embodied memory. I also retained most of the discourse frames—the positional, relational, or evidential expressions like "you see" or "you know?"—that are abundantly used in Trinidadian speech. They help call attention to and establish particular positionality among interlocutors and demonstrate knowledge (e.g., "you know?" used to establish either the complicity that we both know, or that I am just about to tell you something that you may not know). In the same way, I left the quoted speech (he said, "—"), the reported speech (he said that Roy always says, "—"), and what is referred to as embedded speech—the number of layers of reported speech, quotes, or thoughts (he said that you told me that he would go)—intact. Apart from conveying the informality and the speaking style of everyday verbal exchange (rather than formal or journalistic interviews), these different kinds of quotes are performative. They serve not only to authorize an opinion on a given subject but also to produce the evidence or the justification for it.[5]

OPENING AND MEDIUM SHOTS

At the time of this writing (June 2012)

Bassie: Anthony "Bassie" Boynes
(seventeen years with Roy's band)

Before joining Roy's band as a bass player, Bassie had had experience on many other musical instruments. In his first band, Earth Worms, composed of his brothers and himself, he played the vibraphone. In the next three bands—T&T Sunblast, Sound Revolution, and Shandileer—with whom he performed during the 1970s and 1980s, Bassie played the keyboards. While he was playing with Sunblast, he began to play the bass. Shortly after leaving that band, he focused on the pan and became the director of Pan Vibes at Petit Valley. After playing on a cruise ship for five years, he joined Roy's band in 1995. Son of a reputed dancer and dance company founder in Trinidad, Aldwyn Boynes, Bassie has been recognized in Roy's band not just for his remarkable musical talent, but also for his dancing skills while performing on his instrument.

Royie: Roy C. "Royie" Cape (Son of Roy Cape)

Since 1987, Royie has been working in various capacities with the band, and in 2002 he was promoted to the position of manager. He oversees the contracts, the performance scheduling, the purchase and maintenance of the electronic instruments (e.g., the keyboards, the monitors) and the larger instruments, such as the drum set. He is also in charge of purchasing the performers' outfits and the setup of the band's instruments on stage.

Jakey: David "Jakey" Jacob
(eight years with Roy's band)

Jakey joined the Trinidad and Tobago Police Band in 1986 as a trombone player. Over the years, he also worked for the Police Band as a sound engineer. In 1989, he began to play in Machel Montano's band, Xtatik, where he stayed until 1994. From 1994 to 2004, Jakey played the bass and sang at his church. His love for singing led him to take voice lessons, and he is now close to obtaining a diploma (equivalent to grade eight) as a singer. He is currently completing his bachelor's degree in music, with a focus on pan and voice, at the Creative Arts Center at the University of the West Indies, in St. Augustine, Trinidad. In Roy's band, Jakey is often asked to use his musical training to transcribe melodies and riffs that the horn section would like to play, as well as his knowledge of musical notation software to produce computerized, professional-looking transcriptions.

Stephen: Stephen Jardine
(twenty-one years with Roy's band)

As a drummer, Stephen began playing with the steelband named Dixieland. He later joined the dance band Sound Rev (short for Sound Revolution). After playing briefly at the Mecca calypso tent, Stephen joined Roy's band, and he has been playing with them ever since, first as a percussionist and then as a drummer.

Lion: Michael "Lion" Lindsay
(twenty-one years with Roy's band)

In 1968, Lion enrolled in the apprenticeship program of the Trinidad and Tobago Police Band as a French horn and trumpet player. For years, however, he was simultaneously moonlighting with many other bands, including the Gemini Brass band, Ed Watson's Brass Circle orchestra, Shandileer, and Charlie's Roots until 1990. From there, he went on to freelance in recording studios. Since 1991, Lion has been performing full time with Roy's band, with the exception of two years during which he studied and earned a certificate in music, with pan as his main instrument. No longer a member of the Police Band, in his spare time he teaches trumpet at Trinity College (in Trinidad).

Curtis: Curtis Lewis
(former band member, played in Roy's band for twelve years)

Nephew of well-known tenor sax player Randolph Lewis and of Joey Lewis—the bandleader of one of the most respected and certainly the longest-lasting band in Trinidad and Tobago (for about sixty years)—Curtis learned musicianship (music theory and reading) from his uncle Randolph, as well as how to play piano and saxophone, all from an early age. He later taught himself to play pan (the double second), guitar, and flute. After playing with several other bands, he joined the band Kalyan in the late 1970s. Curtis performed with Kalyan for several years before moving to Boston to study at the reputed jazz center, the Berklee College in Boston, Massachusetts, for two years. He returned to Trinidad to perform as a freelancer until he joined Roy's band in 1990, as both an alto and tenor saxophonist until 2002. He is now a freelancer, actively involved in recording studio sessions and in live performance with different bands.

Garvin: Garvin Marcelle
(eight years with Roy's band)

At age eleven, Garvin began his musical training as a saxophonist at the Petrotrin Cadet band in Fyzabad, a small village in the south of Trinidad. After five years in this junior military unit, he graduated to the Trinidad and Tobago Cadet Force. On the side, he pursued his apprenticeship with the Watty Watkins Orchestra and with Vin Courtney's dance band. Reputed as a tenor saxophonist, he also played with several other highly reputed bands, including Boyie Mitchell's, Ed Watson's, Sparrow's, and Cummings and the Wailers (the resident band of Mas Camp—a club known for its nightly entertainment featuring calypso and steelbands, and that also serves as a main gathering place for calypsonians). Garvin also served as a Police Band member in Barbados (for three years) and in St. Vincent (for seven years), after which he returned to Trinidad, where he has been a member of the Police Band ever since.

Mitch: Clyde "Mitch" Mitchell
(former band member, played in Roy's band for fifteen years)

Younger by only six years, Mitch has known Roy all his life, even though he was raised in St. Mary's Home, the orphanage based in Tacarigua. From early in their lives, the musicians who grew up in the Belmont and St. Mary's orphanages formed a tightly knit group. As a trumpet player, Mitch joined the Trinidad and Tobago Police Band in 1968, and left in 1973 to go to the United States. After playing with numerous Trinidadian, Jamaican, and American bands in different parts of the United States, Mitch came back to Trinidad around 1989. However, during his entire stay in the United States, Mitch kept coming back to Trinidad to play regularly with the top bands in the country, including the Mighty Sparrow's band in the mid-1970s. In the late 1970s, he was a member of the TnT Rainbow band initially led by Carl "Beaver" Henderson, and later on by Roy himself. Mitch continued to play in Roy's band at the calypso tent called the Kingdom of the Wizards, and then at Spektakula, and on numerous tours with him. He still performs with Roy when the occasion arises. He is now a freelancer, performing in recording studio sessions and on live shows. He also teaches trumpet at the Birdsong Academy of Music.

Lambert: Lambert Phillip
(former musician, played in Roy's band in the late 1970s for one calypso tent season, in 1990 on the first recording of Roy Cape Kaiso All Stars, and throughout the years on several other occasions as a freelancer)

Lambert is a trombone player who joined the Trinidad and Tobago Police Band in 1975. During the 1970s and 1980s, while he was still in the Police Band, he was also actively working as a studio musician and appeared on countless recordings during that era. In 1991, he was the first Trinidadian to become a fellow of Trinity College in London, specializing in wind instruments. In 1999, he completed his bachelor's degree in music at the University of the West Indies. Since then, he has served as a judge in several calypso and steelband competitions, including the Calypso Monarch competitions and Panorama, the national steelband competition. In 2001, he left the Police Band, and shortly after he began to teach music at a secondary school in Sangre Grande. After nine years, he moved to the Valsayn Teachers Training College as a music instructor. He still occasionally plays as a freelancer.

Sly: Arnold "Sly" Punette
(twenty-five years with Roy's band)

Sly had never played in a band until Stalin and Roy noticed his talent as a guitar player. Every time they met him, Sly was playing on his own. Needing to replace Junior Wharwood (one of the most respected guitarists at the time), who could no longer continue to be part of two bands—Roy's band as well as Charlie's Roots—Roy asked Sly to join his band in 1987. Sly has been a full-time member of the band ever since, and on the side he gives private guitar lessons.

Juiceman: Carlysle "Juiceman" Roberts
(twenty years with Roy's band)

At the age of ten, Juiceman was encouraged to learn to read and write music and to play piano, so that he could play at church. A few years later, still performing in church, he became the musical director of a choir called Conversionites. In 1987, he joined the Trinidad and Tobago Police Band as a keyboard player. Soon after, he began to do arranging for several calypso competitions organized by private institutions such as British West Indies Airways and the Republic Bank. At the same time, Juiceman was moonlighting, playing with Charlie's Roots from 1989 to 1991. Roy first met Juiceman rehearsing at Charlie's Roots band room in 1992. He called him and asked him which orphanage he grew up in, because he was sight-reading. After learning that Juiceman had learned through private lessons, Roy asked him to join his band. In 1994, Roy called on him to do the arrangements for Black Stalin's *Rebellion* album, which was to be recorded at Eddy Grant's studio in Barbados. Since then, Juiceman has been the arranger of the Roy Cape All Stars and subsequently its musical director and record producer. In addition to his work with Roy's band, Juiceman is a sought-after arranger with many of the top calypsonians and soca artists like Superblue, Brother Marvin, Iwer George, Singing Sandra, Colin Lucas, Denyse Plummer, and Anselm Douglas of Trinidad and Tobago and other artists from many Caribbean islands. Introduced by Roy, Juiceman has also written arrangements for the famous Desperadoes steelband, and for several other steelbands, including Solo Pan Knights, Exodus, and Skiffle Bunch.

Blaxx: Dexter "Blaxx" Stewart
(thirteen years with Roy's band)

Blaxx is an experienced lead singer in many musical styles, including not only calypso and soca but also reggae, ballad, soul, R&B, hip-hop, and chutney soca. He began to perform in his teens with a band called Succession Brass, in Santa Flora, located in the deep south of Trinidad. He quickly became a sought-after lead singer and moved on to perform with some of the top Trinidadian bands, including Atlantik, Blue Ventures, and also with the internationally well-known Jamaican band Byron Lee and the Dragonaires. In 1999, he joined Roy's band as a full-time member. However, Blaxx continues to perform regularly as a guest artist in and outside the Caribbean region.

Black Stalin: Leroy "Black Stalin" Calliste
(has known Roy since 1978)

One of the most respected and much-loved calypsonians today, Black Stalin has won the Calypso Monarch national competitions five times, and the Calypso King of the World competition. He worked in the calypso tents from the late 1960s to 2000. His experience with bandleaders over the past fifty-some years enables him to address Roy's musical skills with considerable credibility. But having worked with him since 1979 in the calypso tents, in calypso competitions, in special shows locally and internationally, and in recording studio sessions, Black Stalin (now Dr. Leroy Calliste, after having received an honorary doctorate in 2008 from the University of the West Indies, St. Augustine, Trinidad) is in a particularly privileged position to address Roy's musical style and personal character as a bandleader.

Chalkdust: Hollis "Chalkdust" Liverpool

(for twelve years, between 1982 and 1994, worked every night with Roy as the bandleader of Roy Cape All Stars, the accompanying band at the Calypso Spektakula tent)

Chalkdust is the only other calypsonian who has won eight Calypso Monarch crowns, as many as the Mighty Sparrow. His long experience as a calypsonian in numerous calypso tents, combined with his role as stage manager of Spektakula for many years, makes him particularly suited to comment about Roy as a calypso bandleader. Highly respected throughout the Caribbean both as a calypsonian and as a historian (he earned his PhD in history at the University of Michigan, Ann Arbor, in 1993, and he now teaches at the University of Trinidad and Tobago), Chalkdust's assessment of Roy comes from long experience as both an artist and a scholar.

Brother Resistance (or simply "Resistance"): Lutalo "Brother Resistance" Masimba

Brother Resistance has known and worked with Roy since the late 1970s, as a leading rapso artist, social activist, and later on as the secretary and current president of the Trinbago Unified Calypsonians Organization, vice president of the Copyright Music Organization of Trinidad and Tobago, and member of the board of directors of the National Carnival Commission of Trinidad and Tobago—unquestionably the three most important artistic-related organizations in the country.

Brother Resistance's numerous performing experiences with Roy's band and exchanges with Roy as a bandleader, coupled with his long experience as a spokesperson in Trinidad's calypso milieu and the music industry in general, give him a unique perspective from which to speak about Roy as the leader of a soca band and an accompanying calypso band.

Sister Paul

(a Trinidadian sister who has known Roy since 1954)

Sister Paul was a teacher at the Belmont Children's Home when Roy was living there from 1954 to 1958. As one of Roy's teachers who was and still is close to him, she is able to trace many traits of Roy's character that seem to have marked his career. Her assessment of Roy as a youth adds a historical perspective to Roy's recognition and reputation as a bandleader.

What Attracts Musicians to Play in Roy's Band

The Force of Reputation

GARVIN: Strange enough that you should ask that question—when I was about fifteen years old, my dad took me to the Petrotrin recreation grounds in Fyzabad. That's when Roy was still in the tent backing up the singers.... So when I heard the band play, I was cognizant of the fact that ... well, I told my dad, I said, "Look, I will be playing with that band one day." I never would have known that it would eventually come true. I have to say, thank God for that.

STEPHEN: When Roy Cape Kaiso All Stars was in the tent, I used to go and listen to them. I used to tell my wife (well, my present wife now), I had to join that band now. I have to join that band. I loved that band.

MITCH: When Roy was a young fellow, he had such an outstanding personality. We would just admire him and want to be just like him. You know? He young and he playing with his band. Everything about him was rounded and we always say, "Ay, this is a good guy to follow." Yeah.

LION: I can let the world know that for anybody joining the Roy Cape Band, it's a world of experience. And being a member of the Police Band, I knew exactly what sort of experiences to expect when I join Roy's band because we share the same common knowledge in the Police Band. We encourage the Police Band members to join bands on the outside so that they can get a different feel of the music, not only the merry-time music; we should be interested in all aspects of music. And the one band that affords you that opportunity is Roy Cape All Stars, you know?

LAMBERT: So how does he succeed keeping his musicians for so long? To me, I would say several factors. You have to give a very competitive wage scale, right? So you have to show well, at the end of the month, when you compare my wage with other bands, my wage would be higher. That's one. Another way is to show longevity, that your band has been there for a long time. Two, you have to more or less give a guarantee for a number of gigs. So if you can say, this year we won't get any lower than this number of jobs. Then when you compare that with other bands, it comes out better than the other bands, right? So that's what comes to mind: wage scale and guarantee of the number of jobs. Well then, Roy Cape band has a certain prestige. When you compare it to other bands, relatively speaking, as a calypso band it is more respected than other bands. And then you know, the ring of "All Stars": it makes you feel that everyone in the band is a star. So it has a good name and people are looking at it now. I mentioned the prestige—people regard the band with a certain respect. There's a certain kind of quality associated with players from the band. If you play with Roy Cape band, they consider you of a certain competence level, you know? And the way the tone [in which] the band is described [in the media], it [the band] is very visible. Roy Cape All Stars is visible on the print media, and it's also heard a lot on the electronic media as doing a lot of jobs.

The Pull of Magnetism

BLAXX: Maybe if I was not in the band [Roy's band], I would have think of quitting and opening up a restaurant or something, but something about Mr. Roy Cape . . . I cannot put my finger on it. I don't know if it's his aura, if it's his halo, if it's his magnetism—he draws good people. Mr. Roy Cape always draws good people. Being that he has that pulling power as we call it, we have a very tight unit, a unit that is very cohesive, and we could operate with one another. So I believe it's because of Mr. Roy Cape and his good aura, his good spirit, that attracts these types of people to the band. No matter if it's old members or new members, it's always good people that come.

LAMBERT: He has an experience—the experience that I refer to is fraternizing with other people, with other practitioners in the performing arts. Roy can fraternize with them better than the others—he has that skill. He has a different language, and he [is] more broad minded and all that than the others.

BROTHER RESISTANCE: To this day, Roy, for me—you know, I might be biased—but when I go to a party, Roy Cape and the All Stars is to me one of the best bands to party with because of the variety of music that you get and the quality of music that you get, you know? I just feel good. . . .

• *Exhibiting a Sense of Ethics* •

Open Books: Accountability and Transparency

CHALKDUST: When I was in charge of Spektakula, when I would do the shows, Roy would do what Art de Coteau used to do—he would have learned from him. Roy would buy fifteen little envelopes and put everyone's salary inside there. Everybody gets the same thing. Once you come to all the rehearsals, the same. He treated them well, he treats musicians with respect. That's

Roy. They won't leave Roy. And some of them could form their own band if they wanted to.

CURTIS: When I went into that band, what shocked me is that when Roy gets money, Roy would have the money in his hand, and he would give you your money right there. He was not, you know, getting the money and then cutting corners and taking out yours and give it to you after all the cuts—no, no, no. He tells you how much money he gets, you see the money, yeah, and he shares that with all the band members. . . . The books are open. I could never say, you know, I'm uncomfortable because I don't know how much he gets, no, no, no. If you have problems, whatever it may concern, he comes and explains. And he'll say, "Well, guys, so-and-so hasn't sent the money yet because so-and-so, and so-and-so. And when he gets it, he goes straight to you, and he gives you all of what you're supposed to get.

JAKEY: Pappy looks out for his men. He makes sure we are comfortable. If Pappy buys champagne for himself, his men have to drink the same thing. He's not buying champagne [for himself] and water for the guys. No. If he is eating fish and this type of fish, all of us are eating that type of fish. He is not buying that, and the cheaper thing for the guys. And he hates to buy no-name drink [for] himself, you know? If he drinks a nice juice, all of us drinking the same thing.

JUICEMAN: Financially, I am well taken care of in the band. I told Roy that I don't have a problem. You know? I don't have a problem. I told him, I am settled here for life. I tell my friends, now when I finish with this band, I go do farming or something else, man [*laughs*].

SISTER PAUL: Roy is very honest. And actually, what strikes me about Roy is his interest, his interest in other people. His readiness to help. Years ago we were having a fund-raiser at the church. He said he would come and play. So I said, "What do I have to give you for that?" He said, "What? What? I will be the most ungrateful if I asked you for something."

Work Ethics: Right on Time, Right in Place

BROTHER RESISTANCE: I had a show to do, and Roy Cape was the band. I said, okay, this is the band. Well, he calls me up, he says, "Meet us this Tuesday for one o'clock at the band room." I say, "No problem Tuesday whatever." I don't turn up. Whatever. I got too busy. So the show is Sunday, so I turn up at the show on Sunday. I know, maybe I didn't bring the bell or whatever [for his song, "Ring de Bell"], but Roy and them must know that [tune]. So I turn up at the show on Sunday, and Roy say, "What happened?" I say,

"We're friends—we have known each other so long." Roy say, "We have a policy: if you didn't rehearse, the guys and them won't play for you because they know that it could embarrass the band and everything." And I had to take that.

CHALKDUST: How would I qualify Roy's band? Well, I really boast about it. Even today, when I have rehearsals, when I have to play out, I boast about Roy Cape, and I use Roy as a standard measurement for bands and bandleaders. One of the things about Roy Cape at Spektakula was rehearsals—emphasis on rehearsals. Chalkdust, you're on at seven o'clock. Sparrow, you're on at 8:15. And for all Spektakula people, that became a norm that Roy decided on time. How much songs you're doing? One song, seven o'clock. Therefore you come on 7:00–7:15. How much songs you doing? Two songs? Therefore, you are 7:00–7:30. . . . Plan in advance. So that made a big difference in the band. Secondly, if you found that your rehearsal wasn't good, or you didn't feel comfortable, well, there'd be another rehearsal.

On the whole, Roy set that kind of standard for us. Secondly, Art de Coteau used to say, "You know a musician by the way he looks after the music sheets, how he treats music sheets." Some musicians bring the wrong music sheet sometimes. Not Roy. Long before the show begins, Roy comes in, and Roy has all the music in order. He is prepared. And if there's a change in the program, they'll come and tell him before, because Roy would get very, very angry if you come and tell him [at the last minute], "Chalk isn't singing, so-and-so, so-and-so." Because when you change that program, he has to deal with the music. [Roy then has to rearrange the sequence in which the scores are prepared, which slows down the show and can disorient the musicians.] I learned a lot from Roy about tempo, keeping that rhythm. And there're some fellas, when you want them to bring another tempo [for your song], they go, "I don't know, I don't know [what should be done]." Not Roy. Roy had it down pat. So when we go up on Spektakula night, it would be tight!

CURTIS: When Roy was at Spektakula, Roy changed the sound, the [calypso] tent sound. He changed the tradition of that sound of the fifties when you're getting that . . . a kinda . . . da da daa da da daa, you know what I mean? When Roy['s] band came on the scene, it was like an American band. What would make the difference was that the music, the musicians, they were more tighter. He raised the standard! Roy raised the standard of tent playing in this country. This is not my interpretation or yours—it was very, very evident.

And I always say, wow, I would love to experience that playing. That's a band I would love to play with. I used to say that because I had never played in a tent. No! Because I didn't like it. I didn't like what I was seeing. But when I heard Roy [his band play] ('cause I lived very adjacent to where the tent was, that's considered behind the bridge), every time I get the opportunity, I would pass up and listen to that band. And when I heard who the band was, I say, wow—this man, this man's done a lot for the industry where calypso music is concerned. He has lifted the standard for all the players.

All right. I can safely say, his past experiences with good bandleaders and also his experience he had in New York, right, helped him develop his standards. And two, he's a bandleader that doesn't really take mess. You come to work. For some reason he had the American international principle, because when he says, the tent starts at eight o'clock, we have to be there one hour before. Roy will be there from about six to put all the music together for everybody. It's a way of life for him.

Roy's work at the calypso tent has been respected to the highest. And when Marvin and Nigel came to the scene [and Roy went into soca], it was a smooth transition. The band kept the standard.

So because of the standards that he always kept, in order to be in this band you have to be tolerant, you have to be good obviously, and you have to be dedicated to your instrument. And it wasn't different when we go on tour or preparing to go on tour, you know? We have to be in the airport at a certain time. He says the time, and you have to be there. He wasn't a guy, like he would bully you. But if you're consistently breakin' the rules, it means you don't want to be a part of this, you don't, you're not trying to, you don't love this band and you don't love the standard of this band. That is, if you continue doing things, then it won't work.

JUICEMAN: Roy does not take anything for granted. If we have a show, like if the show is the Saturday twentieth, we start rehearsing from the second of the month just to make sure that when comes the time, we don't have the rush. So we always leave room for the unexpected. I learned a lot from him, including to come to practice on time. And this whole life discipline is important because if you are disciplined at your work, basically you are disciplined at home.

Roy loves to rehearse. He wants to go into a show, and he wants to lick off the air. He wants to lick off the air. So the band is tight. For real, I love to come to rehearsal. I love to come to practice. I love seeing the guys.

MITCH: That discipline, it has a lot to do with the Homes, growing up in the Homes. And I will tell you why. When I was a young guy, there was this guy, we used to call him Mr. Thomas Elias Marcus, and he used to rule with a rod of iron fist. He used to have a leather belt in his back pocket about four inches thick. You know, and he always used to tell us, "I will carve you for the outside world." But at the time, I was pretty young and I never really understood what he meant by "I will CARVE you for the outside world." And we used to look at this as though he don't like us, and he brings in pressure on us. But it's when I grew to be older, I understood what he meant. He will make us and mold us, so that when we leave the orphanage, we'll be able to stand on our own two feet without depending on anybody. You understand? And this is the discipline I think comes out from the Homes. I'm not trying to be prejudiced or anything, but I have met a lot of guys who didn't grow up in the homes, and the discipline that we have, they don't have it, they don't possess it. The leadership qualities? They don't have it.

But you know, at one time in Spektakula, my life wasn't going as it should, so musically, I started fall back and the other trumpeter told me, he say, "You gotta be careful because Roy listens to how we play, and if you continue like that, he gonna get somebody else." And I was real troubled by it. I never told Roy about it. You understand? But it was a wake-up call and I decided to let—whatever problem I have cannot get in the way of this music and I learned from that. I bucked up and fell back right in the groove.

SISTER PAUL: At the Children's Home, there was certain amount of discipline attached to the band because they had to come for hours of practice. And when they went out—because people asked them to come to play for different places, and so on—they had to dress in uniforms. But of course there was a tailor shop where the boys were learning to sew, and therefore all the clothes were made right there—right at the orphanage. They would look really sharp! Therefore they had to be really disciplined to be part of the music band.

Against All Odds: Problem-Solving Attitude

SLY: One of my best tours was when we went with Stalin and Denyse Plummer all over Scandinavia. Well, [what made it] most memorable, the challenges of staying together, trying to make things work right. We were not the entire band, just six of us. So most of the band players was doing background work 'cause we had one horn man, right, he was blowing and singing. I was playing guitar and doing background vocals. Everybody had to put in their two cents to make it work. So Roy had to sing, direct the band, save all the money, everything, and still play his horn. Yeah. And he managed that with broken ribs [after slipping on a wet floor], and he hang in there, and we did it! Very few bandleaders would have gone through that, like, for a whole month.

MITCH: We were in Toronto. One night, the guys went out and on their way back, they got into an accident. The trombone player, he was unconscious, he lost a tooth, and all kinda thing. And Sly and them, they were injured, but the drummer only very slight[ly]. But we had a job the night after, and Roy had to come up with something. Thank God, he was able to get somebody who was capable to fill this slot, and we went on and did what we had to do. Along the way, there was always little problems. But Roy has a way he could always solve it. Yeah, he could always solve it. I don't know how he used to do it, but he used to always solve it.

• *Being an Ace Player* •

CURTIS: When you have a section of five horns, and a spread-out harmony—even though I'm a strong player, I'm a musician first. So when I play, I listen. I wouldn't push my harmony note louder out to show them [the other musicians], I'm a powerful player. We're talking music. Before I play what's on the sheet, I'd look at it. I would come down, and drive with the melody, and give him that melody. And that is what me and Roy share in playing.

I just miss playing with that guy. I miss playing with Roy because, like I say, I freelance and I play with a lot of other horn players. So now it boils down to get a job, do it, and collect what you all agree upon, and move on—because there's no musical connection. But with Roy, you don't have to tell Roy to listen—he does. I've done some recording with him by Eddie Grant's studio [in Barbados] . . . oh my God, man! That time we smile, we make love, we love up each other in music! And we just watch each other and smile [*laughs*]. Without saying anything. Just watch each other and smile because we just play something there that was so . . . wow.

GARVIN: As I said earlier, I've been a military person for almost all my life and I've played with a lot of people. Playing with the guys from Roy Cape is a different level of discipline from playing with the guys in the Police Band. There's togetherness, there's a spontaneity. It's knowing what comes next without it being spoken by anybody. It's a matter of a glance, a nod of a head, and you know what's happening next. But in the case of the Police Band, everything is scripted, you know? You have to go according to the plan. But playing with Roy has developed me as a musician in so many ways, you know? Being able to interact with guys without having to speak with them verbally . . . you get certain things done.

Roy has served as a serious mentor to me for the past six years that I've been here. Most of my playing and improv[isation], as I said, I would have gathered a lot from him. My only one regret, honestly, is that I was not a part of the band for a longer period. I would have liked to meet him when he was a lot younger. I know he had a lot in him then, but as age comes on, the onset of age, you know, he would not be as flexible [in playing] as he was then. But that's my only regret; I would have liked to meet him many years before and to be associated with the things that he was part of then.

JUICEMAN: Being the arranger, you know, and working with him on a daily basis over the years, I talk to him every day. Every day. Because I would always ask him, where the alto sax would be, where the tenor, where this, where that. Although I learned [arrangement] before, coming here it's a different flavor. When you listen to our brass, it's a different kind of flavor. Our harmonies are spread differently. So, in music, you can never stop learning. Every day as you go along, you learn something new.

BLAXX: In Roy's band, I have a lot of freedom. I have freedom to stop the band when we're rehearsing to discuss things, to add, or to take out things. That is a part of Roy Cape All Stars. We don't have no restrictions on who should talk or who should do this and who should do that. It's done by every single individual. If the bass man finds it's not all right at the top, he says, "Wait, wait, wait: we can do this like that, and we can do this like this." And I have a lot of freedom to travel on my own as long as I don't interfere with the band's business. Roy gives me that.

JAKEY: With Roy, it is all a collective thing. You have a tune, and you all can put your idea. And then we will agree what licks will work and which ones wouldn't work. And that is the thing about the band that I love: everybody has an input. Other horn players will travel and say, "What, look at dem licks!" And it works, you know? So all I can say is that it really is a beautiful thing that we can do something like that in the band.

JUICEMAN: Roy gives everybody their chance. Each individual in the band, he gives them their space. He's not like, "I'm Roy Cape, so I say we do it so." No. He has been in three separate eras—Joey Lewis time, Clarence Curvan time, and now he is in this time with the youths Bunji [Garlin] and Machel [Montano]. And although he knows that the music of today does not have the substance of the years gone by, this is today what the people want. As he said to me yesterday, now it's the time of Jay-Z and Beyoncé and them. But many people still want to live in the past. But you have to live now! Yes, our band will . . . go and play back-in-time music like "Best of My Love," "Johnny," "Gimme the Ting," "Ladies Night" to make everybody feel at home. But we have to play the modern music. Roy is very open. And, you know, working with Roy is easy. Trust me. As he gets older, it's like fine wine [*laughter*]. As he gets older, he's just graceful. You know, there's no headache, no hassle. Once the guys are happy, he's happy.

• Providing On-the-Job Training •

BLAXX: A lot of musicians and entertainers have passed through Roy Cape All Stars in their school uniforms on lunchtime. I recall Kernel Roberts. Kernel Roberts used to come sit down here at the drums in his school uniform. Kernel Roberts is now a musician extraordinaire, drummer, keyboardist, writer, singer, writer, you know. Look, Destra has passed through here, Kurt Allen, Nigel and Marvin, Derek Seales (he's the front singer for Dil E Nadan). So you know, everyone that passed through Roy Cape All Stars got their training on the job. Roy Cape is the on-the-job training station. And when you graduate from there, you can go out and kick ass.

BASSIE: Roy showed me how to read. I learned everything from everybody here. The band took me to another level. It is really a college of music here. I am still learning from them.

MITCH: There are some bands that might call me to work with them as a freelancer. I will take out my horn, warm it up and things, and when I look at the other horn players, they are not warming up their horns! Now with Roy Cape, now, when you go to Roy Cape, you see everybody warming up their instruments, and then we take a tune in together. They are the same Trinidadians [as the other players]. But this is Roy. He's a professional.

CURTIS: If Roy fusses, it's not a negative. It's a positive because of the fact that the standards he has set. He would hear if you're not tuned, so you must tune. You must tune your instrument where he's concerned. And he will know your sound before he accepts you in his band. He will know your sound. If he calls you to replace one of the members in the band—like, for instance, a trumpet—he will have been lobbying before. Before you get in the band—whether it's trumpet, saxophone, bass—he will have been scouting. So he knows you before you come in.

ROYIE: He likes everything to be perfect. He's a perfectionist.

SLY: Well, Roy would always say, "Stick with it and try to learn as much as you can because here you are and you can learn everything." So I took the advice and used to come from the tent and go home and practice and try to be on top of everything. Yeah, because those guys were top class. I was like the last man to come in then, so I had to speed up to meet the criteria of the band.

I learned to read with Roy. Yeah, you know, this is the university here, the university of the local music. So a lot of people came, a lot of people go. But I'm still here.

STEPHEN: I'm a dedicated person. I don't really jump ship like that unless something is really not happening. And I learn a lot here. I mean, I can't read and whatnot, you know, but musically I can hear. And I learn from Roy and them teaching me: "Stephen, you got to do this and that," or "You have to look at so and so." In the tent, it wasn't just like going in and play. You had to be listening and, you know, those calypsonian were not easy. They wanted things exact. I mean, I learned from that, and that just built my career playing-wise.

BROTHER RESISTANCE: Roy put on a number of young artists and gave them [a] platform from which to address the world, you know? And the amazing thing is that he does all this without, "I did this, I did this." No! He brings them, they grow, and at some point they say, "You know, I think that I don't want to be playing as a band singer. I'm a star. I need to go." And he says, "Okay" [laughs]. "Okay, go ahead. I wish you all the best" [laughs]. You know? No bitterness, no nothing. Maybe once or twice it happened where the singer will try to create some sort of antagonism. Roy would not respond. "Well, we wish you well," and send you on your way. I've seen it.

• Caring Character in Words and Deeds •

LION: Roy is more like a family person to all of us, you know. You could have a problem and you could rest assured, Roy would try as best as he can to solve it. . . . He can't fix everything. He's just one person. But it's a group where we all enjoy a family life with each other, and by the end of the day, you have to go back to your personal space. But whenever we get together, most of us make much of it. Working with Roy is a beautiful experience. He always treats us as family, puts himself last, and makes sure everybody is well taken care of.

SLY: Looks after everybody. Leaves himself for last. You can't get a better leader than that.

JUICEMAN: You see other bands traveling and the airline tickets they want. Some people will travel first class, and the rest of the band in the economy class. No, not Roy. He says, no, no, no, put me with the guys—because he just likes being around the people.

Roy is my father, yeah. And once I'm around the guys, this is my family. Brothers here, we family because other than my wife and child and grandchild, these are the people I spend most of my time with. Every day I see these guys, every day. Every day, like today, we finish rehearsing. But it is now seven o'clock—just old talking. Because I always say, you are a musician on and off the stage, and if you are together off the stage, when you come on the stage, it will reflect. So you will be together on and off.

There are some bands, when they're done, the door slams—bang—and everybody's going—vroom-vroom—everyone's separate. Not us. We just sit down and enjoy one another and talk a lot of rubbish. We have one another, each other, laughing, and just having fun. And each of us go home to our families. It does spill off to the family too. So if you leave here in a nice, bright mood, you're always in a nice, bright mood. You know?

GARVIN: That [family unity] could only help to serve as a secure platform to advance more musically, that togetherness. That only serves as a platform to advance the music.

STEPHEN: Sometime, if we don't practice for, like, two or three days, we get frustrated! Sometime we call some of the other guys, and we just get together, cook, do some sports. That does keep the love and the tightness and that does keep the music tight.

MITCH: Roy used to always make sure I'm pretty cool, I'm all right. If I have any problem, I could call him and say, "Roy, so on and so on." He has come like a big brother too, you know? And seeing the road we [have] travel[ed] on from young—he grew up in Belmont, I grew up in Tacarigua [orphanage], there was a connection with us, which was and is beautiful.

While I was in America, I used to come back and always work in the calypso tent with Roy. Because many times around carnival time, if things are rough, I'd call him and say, "Roy, things are rough, could you get me some work for the carnival season with you all?" He say, "No problem." And he would organize a [plane] ticket, and I would come down. And maybe by Ash Wednesday, I would leave and go back to America, and so on.

LAMBERT: When I interacted with Roy in the early times, there was something that endeared me to Roy, which wasn't common. Roy had a passion for referring to people as family. And then he would refer to people as "King." I didn't get that from other practitioners in the performing arts, you know. So even that little greeting, that initial greeting, if he would address members in his band like that, that would have some resonance, huh? And that was unique to Roy. I can't recall anybody like that.

ROYIE: Roy is a people's person, you know. The fame hasn't gone to his head. And that's why generation goes, generation comes, and you'll still see the same person. Someone doing a business like this for fifty-four years and still at the top level and surviving, it has to be because he is doing something right.

CHALKDUST: Roy was a bandleader [at Spektakula] who people could talk to. [But] there are some bandleaders you can't talk to. Like Art de Coteau was a great musician, but you couldn't talk to him. You would say something to him and Art would say, "You could write this?" [*laughs*]. I saw [The Mighty] Duke—and this is a good friend, [a calypsonian] who could answer a musician. Duke wanted to change something and said to Art, "Art, that piece of music there is bugging me." And Art said, "Which piece of music?" Duke answered, "That part there." So Art said, "This piece of music is bugging you?" Duke said, "Yeah." Art said, "Oh, you can write this?" And Art took the piece of music and he tore it up! He tore it up.

You see, what you have to understand is that calypsonians are not the easiest people to deal with, you know? Calypsonians are very difficult to deal with. But you are talking about individual creators, and many musicians don't understand at all.

- *Overseeing Roy Cape All Stars Organization*
  Interview with Royie, the band manager, June 2009 •

JG: At the moment, your band carries how many musicians in all? And when you travel, how many band members do you take with you?

ROYIE: All of us go. We travel with fifteen people. We have four horns, bass guitar, guitar, drums, keyboard, programmer, three frontline vocalists, and two engineers—front house and a monitor guy—and me. We are the biggest band onstage because bands today in Trinidad hardly use horn, but that is Roy Cape's sound. That is the strength of Roy Cape, our horn section. So [it's] hardly likely you'll ever see Roy Cape without horns.

JG: And when you play abroad, do you hire a roadie?

ROYIE: No, the two sound engineers do that work. We just remain within the family. In Trinidad, we have two guys that do that part of the business. Their portfolio is to see about the equipment and make sure it goes from venue to venue to venue. We also have a van driver. We also have people like security and people who are close to the band and who will put [out] a hand to help us. For example, if we have two or three jobs in a row, they will assist us. Yeah, because of the tightness and the bond we build with people. Like we have one of our good friends in Toronto, Claude. He comes every year for carnival; he's up there seeing about things for us right now. So we have different people in different countries who look after us.

JG: So, in terms of the band, is it the case that each musician owns his own instruments or is it actually Roy that owns all the instruments? As you know, in the past it would be the bandleader who would own all the instruments.

ROYIE: Well, the individual instruments are the guys' own. But, like, the drum set, the keyboards, the monitors, the two machines, it's Roy's own. They only own, like, the trumpet, the sax, the trombone, the guitar, and the bass.

JG: But not the synthesizer, the amplifiers, none of these things.

ROYIE: The amplifiers are our own, including all the electronic instruments and also the microphones.

JG: But the drum set is also yours.

ROYIE: Yes.

JG: Okay, so, in terms of financial investment for Roy, this is pretty massive.

ROYIE: Yes! A drum set now, a good drum set now is about $16,000 or 17,000 TT. A good keyboard is over $2,500 U.S. So to have a band is very costly and to maintain it is even a bigger cost.

JG: And when you travel now, it's also becoming more and more expensive because you have to pay for all this extra luggage. So it costs more and more money every time, yes?

ROYIE: Yeah. And when you have to buy new stuff, you have to pay duty to come in the country with it. They [the customs officers] go by the weight and sometimes by the price you pay for whatever you are bringing in. That determines what you pay. And uniforms are extra cost. Everything, you see, is an extra cost.

JG: Are you the person in charge of all aspects of management? In addition to booking the airline tickets, getting the visas, and giving the playing schedule to everybody, do you take care of all the costumes that are being made and everything like that?

ROYIE: I take care of the uniforms, yes.

JG: Do you hire tailors to make them for you?

ROYIE: We now buy ready-made things because to go to tailors, they might not get them in time. When you go to a store and purchase something, you have it directly at the musicians' disposal right away. So you don't have to worry and wonder if the designer will bring these things tonight. You have them already. It's less headache.

JG: I remember in Toronto, you could see that the outfits had been made in Trinidad. Because they were all originals and with beautiful cuts. But it is no longer the case that you call on a tailor to do the outfits.

ROYIE: Well, as time goes along, change comes. And you have to change to be with the modern time. The modern-day things now, they are selling nice shirts with prints on them. And you know, the pointy-tipped shoes and the jeans? That's the style. You have to go with the flow. So people will admire you onstage, admire you when you are coming to the audience. You have to have your outlook presentable. As they say, music is sound and sight. If you sound good and you look good, people will admire you. So there were the days where you will go to the tailor; it's no more like that. It's too much fashion, you know. They're saying today, "Today is ultramodern." "Ultramodern" means colors. So you have to blend a lot of colors because colors is what is going to look very nice on the stage with the different lighting and when the lighting hits you. So the more colors you wear, the better.

JG: And you are a stage band, so you really have to move with the flow—sound-wise and look-wise. Over the years, you, and most particularly your father during his long career, have really seen many changes at all levels!

ROYIE: Apart from Joey Lewis [a local bandleader who has been performing for over sixty years], my dad is the only other member of all the bands gone by who walked on Carnival Monday and Tuesday and who is still playing music in Trinidad. He's a walking encyclopedia of Trinidad's culture.

At his age, he's now passing down knowledge. And whatever knowledge you can get from someone like this to advance yourself in a business, it's always welcome. He has knowledge to pass on to us, so that we can advance ourselves.

7 • CIRCULATION
Summarizing a Career

The description of Roy's achievements in public media locally and internationally is not just about living and surviving in a difficult business. It is about success and having become a celebrity.[1] What do the categories of success and celebrity mean for a musician like Roy? In the highly stratified musical environment in Trinidad where most artists are recognized nearly exclusively through competitions, how is his success measured? According to what criteria? What makes his achievements stand out in Trinidad and Tobago and in the Caribbean diasporas?

Accounts of success sometimes flirt with the problem of essentializing the personality or the character of someone who achieves a lot. Just think about the books that list the ten characteristics of the most successful people, as a way to instruct others how to become big achievers themselves. Writing against any essentializing narrative, Roy and I focus instead on the social constituents of success — the kinds of social factors that have enabled Roy to build his reputation and to circulate.

In contrast to the star biography system that emphasizes success as a personal achievement, specifically as triumph over difficulties and adversities, Roy grounds the story of his accomplishments at each step in terms of support, help, friendship, network, opportunities, and serendipity. He grounds it in relation to the great musicians he has learned from and played with, in the past and in the present. In his narration, nothing about achievement is taken for granted. Achievement is not simply attributed to a personal narrative of strength, perseverance, skills, excellence, artistic originality, or any inherent gift. He does not see his success as the outcome of greatness or strictly as the result of personal actions. He presents his achievements as the accumulation of relationships, as the historical synthesis of a work life with people. Even when he is a bandleader, Roy is always first and foremost a bandsman—a musical worker among workers, who musically works with others. He is always in the mix, in relation to and among other players. He thus grounds his accomplishments in the sociality of work.

Reputation and circulation in the music business bear upon one another. In what follows, I address how success for Roy has been defined (and defined differently) through four contrasting social practices of circulation: touring at home and abroad, playing in different spaces, circulating through and thanks to social relations, and passing on knowledge.

PERFORMING AT HOME AND ABROAD

Particularly for island musicians, the importance of touring cannot be overemphasized. Since one show alone can assemble a large portion of the population, island musicians can quickly face a point of saturation. And since most of their income derives from live performances and not from record sales, they have to tour to make a living. However, only a very few musicians attain the level of reputation necessary to be invited to perform outside of their own islands, whether it be regionally or internationally. Bearing this in mind, I address Roy's impressive touring schedule over the years in relation to migration patterns, diasporic organizations, and the institutionalization of artistic hierarchy in Trinidad. I also highlight not only the enduring sociopolitical colonial legacies that still greatly influence where a former colonial British subject can most easily travel to, but also the real material implications of traveling back and forth from an island.

Most musicians and fans who know Roy are aware that he often travels outside Trinidad. Few, however, know exactly where his touring has taken him and the extent to which his travels have been deeply connected to Caribbean migration patterns and diasporic organizations in various parts of the world. Before I examine the story that Roy's touring schedule narrates, I provide a sample of Roy's travel itinerary since the 1960s.

ROY'S TOUR ITINERARY

1961?: Tours with Sel Wheeler to Grenada, Antigua, St. Lucia, Barbados with calypsonians Lord Superior and Lord Brynner.

1968: Travels with Ron Berridge to New York, then returns to Trinidad. In September and October, tours with Sparrow Troubadours to St. Croix, St. Thomas, St. Martin, then up to New York, then to the Bahamas, and the British Virgin Islands.

1969: Tours with Sparrow Troubadours in the Caribbean (Barbados, Aruba, Curaçao). Returns to Trinidad to play during the carnival season. Travels back to New York and New Jersey.

1970–77: Lives in New York (with a brief interruption in 1975).

1979: Travels to Cuba with Black Stalin for Carifesta: "I went to Cuba in '79. We were selected by the government [to go and represent the country]. Black Stalin was the calypso monarch that year. As we had already started out our great friendship that we have, we did the accompaniment for Stalin. I spent ten days among over five thousand Caribbean artists. The whole Caribbean was there."

1986: Tours Sweden (fifty-six shows in forty-two days) with calypsonian Chalkdust. Tours England, performs with Superblue and the United Sisters for the WOMAD Festival at the Hammersmith Palais.

1987: Tours with calypsonians Black Stalin and Denyse Plummer and Twiggy in England, Sweden, Denmark, and Finland for the Helsinki Festival (this was the year of Stalin with "Bun Dem"): *+ USA + France*

> During that same tour, Sonny Blacks, who had been one of our impresarios in England, took Stalin on tour, and so we went to Sweden again. We performed at the same venue, Fasching Jazz Club. We performed also in Finland, sold out, and nobody speaking English! And Stalin and Denyse [Plummer] bring down the house and got numerous encores. We did Denmark and performed at Montmartre, a jazz club where John Coltrane, Miles Davis, Sonny Rollins played. They all played there. We also performed that year at the Jazz Festival in New Orleans with calypsonians David Rudder and Black Stalin. We also did a New York tour with Black Stalin, including Village Gate, S.O.B.'s Manhattan, and Brooklyn. On the same tour, we traveled to Boston and Miami.

1990: Portsmouth Festival, England ("Portsmouth Festival: Sizzling Soca," 1990). Portsmouth Festival followed by concerts in Leeds, Wales, Leicester, and London's Southend. Roy explains:

> My first trip to London with my own band, Roy Cape Kaiso All Stars, was in 1990. It was organized by my good friend, Sonny Blacks. For years Sonny has been the main impresario in propagating our music and our artists in England and Europe. Sonny decided to take us to England. The vocals at that time were Allan Welsh and Kurt Allen. We performed at

the Portsmouth Festival on July twenty-first and twenty-third, and at Southend on July twenty-sixth. We also performed for the Rolling Stones after-tour party in Kensington and continued our tour all over the country.

Two of the high points in the 1990 tour was for the band to be booked at the Rooftop in Kensington, a very exclusive club owned by Virgin Records, and to be asked to play at the Rolling Stones end-of-tour party, which was virtual who's who in the international entertainment industry.

The Kaiso All Stars and Charlie's Roots were the only two bands from T&T to play on the road in the Notting Hill Carnival that particular year [Joseph 1990].

1991: Performs in Toronto for Caribana (Trinidadian-inspired festival), brought to Toronto by Nip Davis.

1992: "Other performances in Toronto, with the help of Jenny Lee [who was in charge of the entertainment company in Trinidad] who brought us with Black Stalin" ("Carnival Bands" 1992).

1993–96: Performs in Barbados for Crop Over (carnival type of festival).

1993: New York playing for fetes, organized by the Trinidad and Tobago diasporas with a mix of people from the various Caribbean diasporas. Performs at Notting Hill Carnival (London).

1994: Performs in Haiti ("Roy Cape on Trip to Haiti" 1995). Contracted by Elsworth James to perform during Caribana; Roy has been going there every year since. Belgium at the Hoogstraten Festival with singer Destra in the band: "For instance, at our second festival in Belgium we managed to attract more than 12,000 people to our performance, all people who were so very different to us and our cultures" (Blood 1994). Frankfurt, Fiesta Caribe, in August.

1995–2007: Franck Wilkinson takes the band to Toronto for Caribana.

1996: Notting Hill, with singers Marvin and Nigel Lewis in the band: "We went to England with Superblue and the United Sisters and Marvin and Nigel Lewis for the WOMAD festival. We also performed at the nightclub Dougies in London and at the Hammersmith Palais also in London."

Holland, for a dance (with Marvin and Nigel Lewis): "Some Trinidadians brought me to Holland. They were working for the United Nations there. And they wanted, well, you know, our people, when they migrate, they want to bring home close to them then."

Belgium, Hoogstraten Festival with Marvin and Nigel: "During that time, with Nigel and Marvin, around '96, we also went to Germany. They wanted to see something, something Caribbean. That was something else. We always tell them that we're accustomed to seeing a really good crowd, but we're accustomed to seeing black hands! But seeing twenty thousand white people? It was fantastic."

Other stops in the same year: Boston Carnival, Labor Day in Brooklyn, Belize, Bahamas, Cayman Islands, Miami Carnival, Montreal, St. Martin, the Bahamas. St. Kitts Six-Day Festival. Roy Cape then "shared the stage with world-renowned Freddie Jackson, Paquito D'Rivera, Andy Narell, to name just a paltry few" (Alexis 1996).

1997: Belgium at the Hoogstraten Festival with singer Kurt Allen in the band.

2000: Belgium at the Hoogstraten Festival with singers Destra and Blaxx in the band.

2006: Tour in Germany for the World Cup Soccer Finals. Played with Black Stalin, Iwer George, Rikki Jai, Maximus Dan, and Kess:

> In 2006 Trinidad made its way to the World Cup Soccer Finals. And we [Roy Cape All Stars] were chosen by the Ministry of Culture to represent Trinidad based on the variety of work that we had to do. So we had to do some of our music, we had to play for Stalin, we had to play for Iwer George, Luta who was the Calypso Monarch. Ricky Jai and Maximus Dan worked with us one night (because Maximus Dan was contracted with Destra).
>
> We had sixteen days and we had eight jobs in six days, so we did more traveling, we saw more places. It was fantastic. Everywhere we worked in Germany, the Germans were saying to us: Trinidad and Tobago and Germany: one! Trinidad and Germany good friends! Everywhere we went in Germany. At one gig, the police association sought to honor us. I still have a button that was given to me by one of the chiefs. When we were walking in the streets, just walking, people knew we were from Trinidad.

2008: Performances in Toronto with manager Godfrey Wickham: "We have been doing a midnight boat ride for Godfrey. We played for Godfrey the last eight years at his boat ride. And we selected Godfrey to be our impresario. So he is now our booking agent when you get to Toronto. Godfrey has proved to us that he can be trusted."

2009: Roy takes over the role of manager and bookings for the band in Toronto. Speaking about the ongoing recession early in the year, Roy adds, "This year, at this time, carnival takes care of itself [i.e., carnival has been financially successful]. Whether it's high or low, carnival takes care of itself. My concern right now is what is going to happen in March. Because inflation and recession is not a Trinidad thing. It's a Grenada, Dominica, St. Lucia, England, France, Germany, America [thing], the whole world [is in recession]. So we don't know what's going to happen next year. What I can predict is that we may do exceptionally [well] because we can play for everybody."

In the 1960s, Roy began to travel—not alone, but as a band member mainly accompanying renowned calypsonians on tour. Until 1986, his tours took him exclusively to the Caribbean region and to New York, where a massive number of West Indians migrated after the new immigration laws in the United States were passed in 1965.[2] The critical mass of new immigrants, principally in New York, quickly translated into new markets for calypsonians and musicians, and more trips for the touring artists between Trinidad and New York. Even though calypsonians had been going there since the 1930s, touring to New York significantly intensified at that time (see Kasinitz 1992; Hill 1993; Scher 2003; and Green and Scher 2007). As a young, upcoming saxophonist playing in well-known bands, Roy thus greatly benefited from the Caribbean populations now living in diaspora in need of social contacts and music from home.

Interestingly, even though Trinidadian calypsonians and musicians were British colonial subjects until 1962, Roy's itinerary as a band member did not include England until 1986. I suspect that this may have been mainly for material reasons: the physical distance between Trinidad and England, and thus the prohibitive cost of travel between the two countries. While a few calypsonians such as the Mighty Sparrow (and their accompanying bands) may have gone to England between the 1960s and the 1980s, most calypso performances in England during that period were by migrant West Indian calypsonians and musicians who had become full-time residents in the mother country.

If the ties between England and its former British subjects did not guarantee musicians living in Trinidad easy access to touring in England, the British colonial legacy continued (and still continues) to be highly evident. As demonstrated by Roy's itinerary from the 1960s until now, Roy never traveled to the Latin American countries right next door, even though, for example, one tip of Trinidad is only seven miles away from Venezuela. Could it be the linguistic difficulties (although Trinidad was a Spanish colony initially, most Trinidadians do not speak Spanish), or the enduring legacy of the trading routes established by Britain that prevented its colonial subjects—in this case, Trinidadians—from developing their own trading contacts? Whatever the case, the lack of opportunities for Roy (and the bands with which he played) to tour in neighboring Latin American countries makes it clear that geographic proximity between countries does not de facto entail the sharing and expansion of music markets. However, colonial (sociopolitical) history does.

According to Chalkdust, Roy's 1986 tour in Sweden was transformative. He connects Roy's recognition in Sweden to Roy's increased consciousness of the work to be done in Trinidad and his commitment to his own country:

CHALKDUST: I think that tour made Roy conscious of his role in Trinidad. Roy was offered a job to play and stay in Sweden. Of course, one of the reasons why he didn't stay was probably because arrangements were not made in terms of salary and housing. But judging from how they treated us during our tour, they would have made Roy a hero in Sweden and given him a home, and given him a good salary to teach in schools. But Roy told them that "my place is in Trinidad and Tobago." That tour made him see who he was. Before that, he was just a simple musician playing in Spektakula. That tour made him see that he had a greater contribution to make to music, and to calypso in particular.

Perhaps seeing the importance given to music abroad in both educational and professional settings, Roy became inspired not only to make the financial conditions better for his own musicians but also to widen the range of his own activities. While his reputation was already well established by then, just a few years after his return Roy began to assume leadership on an expansive scale. This became manifest, as indicated below, not only in relation to where and for whom he performed, but also in the ways he would cultivate the relations he had made abroad in later years.

In 1990, Roy recorded his first album with his own band (see chapter 5). As his touring schedule shows, since then his band has performed calypso and soca in some of the most prestigious festivals and nightclubs in western Europe and at major overseas carnivals in the Caribbean and North America. To give just a brief description of some of the places where Roy and his band performed: WOMAD (World of Music, Arts, and Dance), created in 1982 in England, is an internationally acclaimed festival featuring artists from all over the globe that is recognized for its efforts to create awareness of the potential of multicultural society; the Jazz Festival in New Orleans (officially now dubbed the New Orleans Jazz and Heritage Festival) is one of the most prestigious festival stages in the United States, going back to 1970, and has attracted some of the most reputed artists in the country, the Caribbean, and Latin America; the Hoogstraten Festival (Belgium), with its three different stages each night, has dubbed itself on its website the "Largest Caribbean Festival in the World," and has been a coveted platform for artists from the Caribbean and Latin America.[3] As indicated in the aforementioned list, Roy, either with his whole band or some of its members, has also performed at some of the most recognized nightclubs in Europe, including the Montmartre in Denmark, where John Coltrane, Miles Davis, and Sonny Rollins played and where Dexter Gordon held a long residence; the Fasching jazz club in Stockholm (Sweden), another hot spot for jazz musicians in Europe; and the Rooftop in Kensington (England), the exclusive club owned by Virgin Records.

On the one hand, what accounts for Roy's reputation and the impressive touring schedule and invitations to perform at prestigious places has already been stated: flexibility as a performer and as a bandleader to adapt to different repertoires and different musical styles; discipline to rehearse as long as it takes to produce a great show; consistency over the years to perform at high standards; endurance in the sense of being one of the rare musicians of his generation to be still playing; respect toward his elders and his own musicians, the singers he accompanies, and the media; and reliability to rally performers and audience members in spite of difficult structural or material circumstances.

On the other hand, the personal and collective efforts and financial investments of not only promoters but also of loyal supporters and fans have greatly contributed to providing the conditions of possibility for Roy's band to perform as often, as long, and as widely in the world as he has. As Roy explained, many of the organizations Roy's band played for are Caribbean-led and have attracted mainly audiences of Caribbean descent. Thanks to his reputation at home and in the Caribbean diasporas, he has also been recognized by world music lovers and members of the African diasporas who are themselves world music producers and consumers. There is a snowball effect through all of these social relations. Hence, speaking about his tours, Roy proudly described, "At our second festival in Belgium (in 1994) we managed to attract more than twelve thousand people to our performance, all people who were so very different to us and our cultures," and how at other shows they "attracted 'really good crowd' of mainly white people." As he put it, "We were accustomed to seeing black hands! But seeing twenty thousand white people? It was fantastic!"

Wherever Roy Cape All Stars have circulated, the newspaper commentaries have recognized the quality of the band's performance and simultaneously boosted its reputation. Journalists actively participate in the forging of reputation and circulation. They socially inform and simultaneously direct attention to who matters in the music business. Notice the use of superlatives to boost Roy's reputation and highlight Roy's accomplishments. Only a few years after that tour in Sweden, the band's performance at the Portsmouth Festival earned Roy the reputation of being "the most influential figure for most of the worlds [sic] Soca singers" in the *News Entertainer* in the United Kingdom ("Portsmouth Festival" 1990). In 1994, Roy was referred to as the "Duke Ellington of calypso music" in a local newspaper ("Roy Cape Kaiso All Stars" 1994). In the same year, his band earned the title of Best Playing Band in the Caribana competition in Toronto, Canada (Alexis 1994). The accumulation of these laudatory discourses from newspapers in and of themselves, in addition to the winning of competition titles over the years, have helped ensure both continuous demand and tour contracts for Roy's band. At the same time, his own commitment (agency), as a saxophonist and bandleader from the 1990s onward, in Roy's term, to "service" Trinidad and Tobago and other Caribbean diasporas in the Caribbean region, North America, and Europe, and also to expand calypso and soca markets wherever he plays, have led him to be dubbed the Continental Crusader (Joseph 1990).

The story that follows could thus be seen as highly predictable. The more reputed Roy's band has become, the greater the number of invitations to tour. And the more invitations he has received, the more often Roy Cape All Stars have been asked to serve as the ambassadors—representatives—of Trinidad and Tobago, and at times of the whole Caribbean. One of the most symbolic marks of recognition for Roy and his band members came when they were selected by the West Indian Cricket Board to accompany the Soca Warriors for the World Cup in Germany in 2006. On that occasion, Roy Cape All Stars, as Roy's guitarist Arnold "Sly" Punette put it, "were flying the flag of Trinidad and Tobago and also the Caribbean." As this comment well attests, the choice of Roy's band to perform on such an occasion, not surprisingly, instilled a great sense of accomplishment and work pride.

In Roy's experience, the touring of bands is deeply tied to the distinct ways in which artists and bands are valued in Trinidad. As Roy explained, the hierarchy that the competitions create requires not only creativity and innovation but also the support of audience members and judges. And for touring contracts to be offered, bands depend on the promoters' support in good as well as bad economic times.

RC: If you had hits during carnival, you will get bookings for most of the carnivals around the world. In Trinidad everything [every performance] is depending on the promoters and on how the economics of the country is going. Most shows in Trinidad outside of carnival will be shows that feature the calypsonians. You might have a show in Toronto for Easter. Again, these places have recognized promoters who do this for a living. Everything depends on the economics of the country and whether the promoter can recoup from what he is promoting. And everything depends on how you come out of the carnival season. That is the key for foreign bookings.

And as Roy further explains, without foreign bookings, a band in Trinidad can hardly survive.

RC: At the end of carnival [in Trinidad], hardly anything goes on in terms of big shows until about August. There would be things happening at the

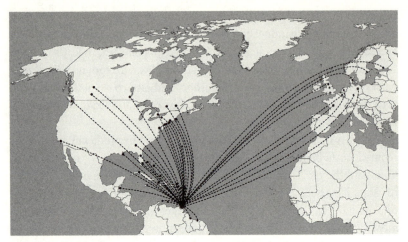

7.1 Roy's touring destinations.

Mas Camp—which is a facility that accommodates the local culture, mainly calypso. Then you have the other bars and clubs that feature the artists from time to time. And you have also other things like jazz in the San Fernando Hills, which would bring in some foreign jazz artists (but we do not play there). But during the year, you would have a serious influence from the reggae artists from Jamaica, e.g., Junior Gong, Jah Cure, and Nas (the hip hop singer) [which means tough competition for local musicians].

It is significant that a band such as Roy Cape All Stars may be able to withstand a year during which none of the band singers has been able to secure a carnival hit and still receive many bookings. Their long-term recognition as one of the premiere bands of the Caribbean of course helps, but the challenge of maintaining the band's reputation is always present, at every carnival, every year, and all the more so during difficult financial times.

On tour, Roy Cape All Stars is rarely viewed solely as a Trinidadian band. Whether it is on a boat ride or at a show at the Harbor Front in Toronto during Caribana, or at a dance in Montreal or Ottawa (Canada), I witnessed how many friends from Guyana, St. Lucia, and Dominica enjoyed hearing what they called "music from home," performed by Roy Cape All Stars. As they live in diaspora, Roy's band brings that elusive feeling of home to them. It is experienced as being from, and representing, home—the Caribbean.[4] Put another way, while the touring of Roy's band is possible due to the quality and reliability of the band, it could not have happened without the many audiences of the Caribbean diasporas that invited the band to perform and financially supported its services—to bring home to them sonically. In spite of the last-minute booking cancellations and the unpredictable hazards of being on the road away from family and the comfort of one's own place, for Roy the success that his band has enjoyed touring has meant earning a living for himself and his musicians. But for him, the reward is not only simply financial, but also social. As he often mentioned to me, he sees the remarkable response his band has received across the Caribbean, and in major cities of North America and Europe, as doing social work—by rallying and assembling people from many different walks of life—as well as creating new bonds and new sources of moral support.

PLAYING IN DIFFERENT SPACES: IN THE TENTS, ON THE ROAD, AND IN THE DANCE HALLS

> The audience needed that transmitter [Roy] to move the music into these different unique spaces.
> **TRINIDADIAN TELEVISION BROADCASTER FRANCESCA HAWKINS, JUNE 2009**

In 1993, when I first heard Roy play at the Spektakula Calypso tent, I saw him sitting along with his horn band members, reading score after score, and accompanying twenty or more calypsonians. Playing the calypsonians' newly composed tunes for the season, Roy and the rest of the horn players had their eyes fixed on the scores. Only from time to time did they glance up at the dance steps and exaggerated gestures of the performers and the packed crowd filling every seat in the venue. The band's dynamics in sound and volume enlivened the show. The punchy lines of the horn section at the end of witty calypso phrases; the solid bass line anchoring the driving calypso rhythms of the drum set; the effective keyboard hook lines complementing the simple yet sweet-ringing harmonic guitar accompaniment: the calypso arrangement for most of the tunes sounded simultaneously familiar and fresh and, judging from the waving of the bodies of some seated audience members, they visibly helped to keep the audience engaged throughout the show.

In 1995, on Carnival Tuesday in Trinidad, I followed on foot with thousands of other revelers, as Roy's band played on a truck moving along the masquerade route traced by the National Carnival Commission. At times sitting down to play his saxophone, at other times standing against the railing of the truck waving a hand at some friends, Roy's face showed the fatigue of many sleepless nights. For at least three weeks preceding Dimanche Gras, Roy had been playing one or two gigs a night. Yet his smile, as he looked at the people on each side of the truck dancing away, was inspiring. You could see love and true happiness. Roy was unquestionably savoring playing for, and being in the full midst of, the moving crowd.

I believe it was in 2001 when I arrived late at the show advertising Roy Cape All Stars at the Atlantis Nightclub at Ontario Place, on the Lakeshore Boulevard in Toronto. When my friend and I entered the dance hall, Destra, then a rising soca star, dressed in a tight black jumpsuit and surrounded by Blaxx and Derrick Seales, was singing "Tremble It," while dancing and demonstrating some highly skilled movements—including "wining" (a local dance term that refers to the gyration of the waist). Judging by the packed room of dancers, with pearls of sweat on their foreheads, it was clear that the band was hot. Everyone in the band, Roy included, was wearing the same outfit: cool-looking long-sleeved shirts hanging over short pants—very much in style for the young crowd, mostly in their early twenties. This time, it was soca songs that predominated in the band's program—fast soca to jump up, and slow ones to allow the dancers to enjoy the closeness of their partners. I was fascinated to see an already not-so-young Roy balance his body from right to left in synchrony with his younger band members moving to the beat. Standing up all night, playing exceedingly fast-tempo soca tunes (a trend of the late 1990s and early 2000s that made everyone, including the best and most experienced dancers, sweat in no time) with only a few slower ones in between, Roy looked radiant and was visibly enjoying himself. This was the same Roy I had seen playing calypso in the typical big band seating arrangement, reading scores to accompany calypsonians, and the same Roy I had seen playing on the road during carnival.

As Trinidadian broadcaster Francesca Hawkins remarked in an interview with me, Roy's playing in these three contrasting spaces continues to be rare in the Trinidadian music industry. Read how she describes Roy's ability to do so, while at the same time producing a discourse that bolsters his reputation.

FRANCESCA HAWKINS: [Playing on] the road, or sitting down [at a calypso tent or competition], or dancing in the dance hall, you know . . . Roy is a connective platform between all of these three special spaces. And each of these spaces is a definitive aspect of our culture. And not everybody can play the audience in the tent, in the dance hall, and on the road. Some could do one, some could do two, but Roy is providing a base for all. If you could make all three of them, you could follow Roy through all these three spaces, right? But not every Trinidadian can handle those three spaces. It's the real culture person that could play a full role as an audience participant in each of these spaces. But here's the man [Roy] and his music that is providing a foundation for whatever cap you could wear.

It was not an easy decision for Roy to move from the calypso tent to the dance hall circuit. After playing for twelve years as the backup band for the calypso shows at Spektakula, Roy had gotten frustrated with the calypso tent conditions, and he knew that to keep the band together he needed to get his musicians better salaries.[5] The money in the dance hall business was better, but the move into that circuit was risky. Roy apparently felt "endless stress, and endless agony" before he made his decision. Apart from taking an economic risk, Roy was wary of damaging social relations that were important to him. After all, it was thanks to Spektakula that Roy had been able to establish his band and to play with everybody in the calypso business. But when he finally did make the decision to leave the calypso tent after the carnival season in 1993, in the words of Hawkins, "he was elated." And, as described above, his decision to perform in dance halls and occasionally to continue accompanying calypsonians proved to be highly rewarding.

Roy's move from the calypso tent to the dance hall circuit opened up two new opportunities. As Brother Resistance indicated to me, Roy could now establish his band, Roy Cape All Stars, as an independent organization, instead of remaining as someone else's band (as was the case at Spektakula). But once again, to do this he needed the support of friends, loyal audiences, and new publics appreciative of his sound production and performance. His first opportunity to explore new musical horizons and audiences came in 1994 from the offer of an old friend, Robert Amar, to become the resident band of his newly created tent, called the Kisskadee Caravan. This is what allowed Roy to begin working with a younger generation of artists. In the Caribbean, where making ends meet often requires not only creativity but skills in many domains, versatility is viewed as a great asset. And for an experienced artist like Brother Resistance, this talent in the music business is particularly admired.

BROTHER RESISTANCE: For Roy and his band, this was a transition, and they handled it extremely well. There were no complaints that the band can't play for younger artists. And Roy's band moved smoothly into that space. And the next step after was, "Roy at the parties." I said to myself, "Roy Cape and the guys of All Stars at the parties?" You know? All right, okay. And then again, it was good. That was a smooth transition, but, you know, to get into the parties is not an easy thing. I've been included in the parties to maintain the status, and I'm telling you, it's not an easy thing.

For Roy's band in particular, composed of musicians ages forty years and older, playing at the parties required the band members to cross generational borders. His band's success indeed depended on being able to connect with the crowd of partygoers who were usually in their late teens and early twenties.⁶ This also involved adopting—as has long been his practice—the latest fashion look. To play at the parties also required a band like Roy's to adopt a new repertoire. While Roy's band still plays at times a few classic calypsos—the music with which it was long associated—it has had to be willing to play, for the most part, the latest hits of the day, that is, the latest hit soca songs of the last carnival. For Roy, to get into the party circuit was in some way like making a new social contract to cater to youth, its distinct aesthetics and ethics. The efforts that Roy and his band members made to renew themselves in combination with the critical acceptance of a new generation of consumers of their music moved Roy to experience a new public and new sources of income for his band.

At the same time, in moving to the dance hall circuit, however, Roy did not try to emulate the other bands already well known in that milieu. Unlike most soca bands, Roy kept the horn section (one trumpet, one trombone, one alto saxophone, and one tenor saxophone) as his distinct signature. (Most soca bands today have replaced the horn section with an electronic keyboard that uses samples to play the horn lines.) Roy's decision to keep his band's sound—to sound like himself—has been the object of much praise locally. Brother Resistance echoes comments made repeatedly by foreign journalists following Roy's performances abroad and the local press, where the theme of circulation typically converges into a theme of pride in local discourse: "He [Roy] didn't compromise. He went in [the dance hall circuit, making it clear that] 'this is the organization, this is what [the instruments] we are playing with, this is our set.' And here's Roy ready to put forward so many of the younger artists, like Destra, Marvin, and Nigel, Kurt Allen, so many. . . . He did forward them, succeeded, and continues to do so to this day."

Roy's initiative to expand the range of his band's musical activities to include playing in the calypso tent, on the road during carnival, and in dance halls (parties), not only during carnival but all year long, has enabled him to be one of the most active dance bands in the Caribbean. With the help of supporters of many kinds, he has kept alive his long-term objectives: (1) to keep his musicians together by giving them opportunities to perform a wide repertoire—musics they like—and providing them with decent salaries; and (2) to continue to act not just as a "Continental Crusader," as a

Trinidadian journalist once put it, but as a crusader *tout court*, by making Trinidadian music better known and developing new markets for it through his own band playing. In addition, his own sense of success has been to see that his entrepreneurial skills and initiatives have paid off.

CIRCULATING THROUGH SOCIAL RELATIONS

As Roy often reminded me, the expression "no man is an island" is especially true for band musicians. This is not just because musicians rarely work as solo performers. In addition to artistic merit, the careers of musicians, and particularly of band musicians, are highly dependent on the connections they are able to establish in the milieus in which they want to play. Thus I think of musicians' circulation not just in terms of physical movements, from point A to point B, or the different spaces in which they play (as in the calypso tent, on the road, and in the dance hall), but also in terms of the social relations they establish with other musicians and with different types of audience members—whether they be listeners, record buyers, dance aficionados, or fans.[7] And these relationships with other musicians and with different types of audiences take different forms: performing with other players, networking among artists, and reaching out through the use of new media technologies.

Border Crossing and Collaborating with Different Artistic Communities

In addition to his distinct sound on the saxophone and his ability to make a horn section blend in, Roy is recognized for his loyalty and his talent for assembling people. As we have seen, Roy's friendship with the other children playing in the orphanage band would last a lifetime and, inadvertently, would provide him with the first opportunities to play professionally. Roy's ability to make friends and his loyalty to them greatly helped him find his way (circulate) among the top musicians of his time.

In the same vein, his efforts to fight the seeming division between musicians and calypsonians have enabled his band to be in great demand by older as well as younger artists. As Chalkdust pointed out to me, Roy's close friendship with calypsonian Black Stalin is well known. What is less known is how much calypsonians, as well as other artists—from Brother Valentino, Nelson, Baron, and Superblue to Ella Andall, Brother Resistance, Maximus Dan, and Shurwayne Winchester, to name only a few—like to work with Roy Cape All Stars. While his professionalism is certainly responsible for the numerous good relations he has established with artists, his focus on creating good social relations has also unquestionably played a great role in his success, and ensured that his band is always in demand.

In the many conversations we have had together about his own musical journey and the music industry in Trinidad, Roy has been careful to avoid the issue of race or ethnicity and how it may have played a role in establishing sociomusical relations. (It should be noted that in Trinidad, the terms "race" and "ethnicity" are often used interchangeably.) In multicultural Trinidad, race has been, and continues to be, a controversial topic, particularly between the two main groups in the island, the Afro-Trinidadians and the East Indians. Today, the latter constitute slightly more than half of the population.[8] So to speak about how race figures in music and in bands can be seen as compromising oneself. But one day, Roy decided to clarify his position on the subject as follows.

RC: Artistically, race plays no part. We work for anyone regardless of color, race, creed, or religion. Music has none of these barriers, as music itself is the antidote to these types of emotions. We are here to embrace each other, not segregate against each other because the Creator would not have meant for us to live in that type of world. We are all God's children and, in God's eyes, all children are his children. Every human being has red blood—regardless of race or color.

Roy stopped speaking, fully aware of how difficult the topic of race truly is in Trinidad and, indeed, everywhere else. After a few long minutes, Roy continued.

RC: You know, Jocelyne, I could talk about race here, but I do not want to go there. This could create some tensions. I don't know how some people could interpret what I say in relation to that. So I want to avoid talking about it.

JG: Roy, I believe musicians hear sounds and become influenced by what they hear; our musical sensibility is in many ways shaped by the environment in which we live—not so much by choice but by being exposed to specific musics, growing up with them. While at times it might be cultivated quite intentionally for all sorts of reasons—political, social, economical, ethnic, and so on—musical sensibility is never completely under one's control. Do you agree?

RC: You will find, Jocelyne, that here in Trinidad calypso and now soca are well established in the general population. I have always known music with a sound from India. But in the past, what we would hear most [in Port of Spain] is Indian music that was more classical sounding. Through the passage of time, people such as Sundar Popo came up with compositions that were the start of chutney soca.⁹ You know, you can do fusion when it is right. So today in Trinidad, we have lots of collaborations going on. Although in the past there was always a love [between Afro-Trinidadians and East Indians], a lot of bridging has been happening—and has happened—in the art form [calypso] and [among] the different races in the country.¹⁰ Today you can't describe Dil E Nadan as an Indian band. No. It is a band of Indian origin that is playing music. Which means that they are not only playing Indian music, but they are playing the whole spectrum. Today, there is a lot of collaboration; but not so, in the past.

Our little space has grown up, and everybody in their own space has excelled, and thus the only thing to do for us now is to get together. This is what we are doing, and have been doing. Rikki Jai is my friend; Adeh Samaroo is my partner. Hitman, Ravi B, from Karma—a young band but one of the top bands in the country. We play often together with the guys in Dil E Nadan. We're all friends. We are walking together.

Through the years, there has been only a small amount of Chinese or Syrian [musicians in bands]. I would say that, at the national level, the performance has been mainly between the people from African and Indian descent. But then, I would go on Charlotte Street to see if one of them—Chinese, Lebanese, Syrians—if any one of them could sponsor us. When I knew [when I was part of] carnival, I knew big shots, because they used to be on trucks and when they moved on the ground, they moved with ropes around their bands.

JG: Okay. That means that even though they have not been often members of music bands or frontliners (singers), people of Chinese, Lebanese, and Syrian descent have always been part of the music scene—or put more accurately, behind the scene.

RC: Yeah, always.¹¹

While this conversation helped me appreciate how much the conditions of possibility for musicians to circulate in different milieus have changed in Trinidad over the past thirty-some years, I was curious to know about Roy's socialization among musicians when he migrated to New York. How did he situate himself as a musician in the metropolis? What musical milieus did he privilege and why?

RC: As an immigrant, the only place you know to go [to] and associate yourself [with] is your own kind. So being in New York, I might have teamed up with Jamaicans or with Ron Berridge [meaning, with Trinidadians]. But you know, the Caribbean diaspora, each of the different islands in it has its own association. So you can't walk in one's man house; you have to find accommodation where you can.

JG: Did you ever play with American musicians?

RC: I never played with American musicians, but you have [steel pan player] Robbie Greenidge, who works with Jimmy Buffett; [percussionist] Michael Tobas, who played with Harry Belafonte; and [bassist] Happy Williams, who played with Roberta Flack and many other top musicians in America. So it is possible.

In music as in any other practice, social relations bear the weight of sociopolitical history and the impact of one's own comfort zone. Even after being heard playing at a show in Trinidad and subsequently asked by Russell Procope of the Duke Ellington orchestra to go and see him in New York for assistance anytime, Roy never went. So could it be that, rather than a lack of opportunities to play with American musicians, Roy has always felt more comfortable in a Caribbean milieu, with its attendant aesthetics and lifestyle?[12] Even if not in close contact socially, however, Roy Cape All Stars has often shared the stage with many non-Caribbean artists. Since the 1990s, Roy's band has been featured next to some of the biggest artists of the Caribbean, North America, and Europe, including Shabba Ranks (Jamaica), Kassav' (Guadeloupe and Martinique), Stevie Wonder, Patti LaBelle (United States), and Sting (England), to name only a few.

Networking and Helping to Make Connections

> I've been dealing with people my whole life. I hung out on the street corners a good part of my life, so I've met people.
> **ROY, JUNE 2008**

For Roy, music making is all about people. Roy is a networker. He believes in the power of collaborative effort, not only because he is a musician who plays in a horn section, but also because he knows intimately how the survival of poverty is often ensured by teamwork—a principle that has long been recognized by people of African descent in the form of sousou. His ability to assemble people could thus be said to come not just from his easygoing personality, but also from hard work, drawing people in, helping others connect, and constantly scouting for new talents. The importance he places on networking has proved to be a major asset in the calypso music business. Roy has often used his own connections to introduce young (and not so young) musicians in need of help to his friends. In that sense, Roy has contributed to the circulation of musicians in Trinidad by finding new musical opportunities for them, enabling some to move from one musical situation to more stimulating ones, and at other times helping others to discover their own talents by asking them to do some work they never dreamed of being able to do before.[13]

To give just a few examples: in 1962 or 1963 while he was in Trinidad, Roy introduced arranger Beverly Griffith to his good friend Rudolf Charles, the inventor of steel pan instruments and the bandleader of the Desperadoes Steel Orchestra. As Roy explained, "He [Beverly Griffith] was the first musical arranger to work for Despers [Desperadoes], and by 1966 they won the triple crown—Panorama, Bomb competition, and People's Choice with 'Melda' of Sparrow." Roy later introduced other arrangers to Rudolf Charles, including Ron Berridge, Scipio Sargeant, Lubert Martin, Clive Bradley, Raff Robertson, and, in 1996, Carlysle "Juiceman" Roberts—arrangers who all became highly recognized figures in Trinidad's music industry.

As you may remember, while in New York in 1972, Roy suggested to the Jamaican bandleader Hugh Hendricks, who used to focus mainly on Jamaican music and with whom Roy was playing at the time, to hire some Trinidadian musicians to record the calypso tracks he wanted to include in his next album.

Back in Trinidad, in 1994, Roy asked Carlysle "Juiceman" Roberts to do arrangements he never dreamed of doing before. Even though Juiceman was still relatively inexperienced as an arranger at that point in his career, Roy recognized not only his musical skills as a keyboard player but also the way he brought original hook lines and powerful rhythmic chord accompaniment to the songs he was accompanying. Juiceman had just started to play in Roy's band when Roy asked him to come with him to Barbados to do the arrangements for the next album that Black Stalin was going to record at Eddy Grant's Blue Wave recording studio, titled *Rebellion*. Roy's offer was so unexpected that, as Juiceman confided to me, "Trust me, I got fever [I was racked by fear]. But that was a beautiful album. And from there, I did the next album for Stalin; I did [calypsonian] Superblue; I worked with Brother Marvin. And Roy set me up with Desperadoes one time too. So I have been doing arrangement since then." As many musicians indicated to me, Roy's influential role and, at times, direct interventions in the hiring of musicians for projects of all kinds (recording, arranging, or playing) has been transformative for many bands and musicians.

Keeping and Developing Contact through New Media Technologies

By circulating in three different spaces (the calypso tent, on the road, and in the dance hall), by playing in a wide range of musical events (private, public, national, regional, and international) year after year for over fifty years, and by having his band singers often rank among the first five positions in competitions, Roy has become a celebrity, a very well-known name in the Caribbean and the Caribbean diasporas. Since I know he likes to keep up with new technologies and to move with the times, I asked him to what extent he uses social media to communicate with his fans, to circulate information about his tours, and to reach out to new audiences.

RC: I have posted on my wall to all my fans and all my friends that I tried to answer all the requests to be their friends. Facebook is so great. You can just type on that laptop and you can get me then. Facebook is a medium where you can meet and greet various types of people from all over the world. It is fantastic. If I go out in the morning, and then come back in the night, I receive twenty messages. And that goes on and on. And I get invitations to turn out to this function on a Friday night or that one on Saturday night. So if people know that Roy is in town, I will get invitations on Facebook to go to different things [events] — not to hire the band. I am not dealing with Facebook in that way.

In every era, we have had a way to inform the public that they have a big jam in Princess Town [a town in Trinidad]. So you know the area and the promoters [you would thus know what is happening]. We also have had small types of billboards and flyers until we moved in modern types. Then you saw massive billboards on the highway for big events. Even the radio, you could look at it as a basic rediffusion. And you know, communities were in charge of communities then [people passed the word around among themselves].

With Facebook, you are building new communication and once you respond, cool! People know that you are responsive to people — which is what our life is all about. People will only want to show appreciation to you, to consider you as a gracious person, because of the kindness that you would have displayed in what you do to make them happy.

Like Stalin says, "I am really a servant of the people." I agree with him, because without them you are nothing. Without the ordinary people, Jocelyne, there's nothing. Ordinary people make up the majority of the population anywhere you go. So there are great expectations for us who have the responsibilities to reassure and to be fair, kind, and loving. So it allows me to develop relationships, and then it multiplies. So then you can run a business on that thing and deal with masses of people. So we have videos of shows we did that reach Facebook and YouTube—and I don't even know how it gets there. It is good. I can put up a promotion, and people from England can see it.

The band got the award of the best soca band for 2010. I saw the whole function commented on Facebook—which was not so visible in the newspapers. But on Facebook, I saw people congratulating us who are not from Trinidad.

As this quote makes clear, Roy views mass communication technologies as an intrinsic part of today's music business. In that sense, Facebook and YouTube for him are only the latest additions to the many other forms of communication that have been used to reach out to publics in Trinidad over the years. Many of these continue to play a vital role in disseminating information about Roy's shows and enable Roy to stay in touch with fans. The big difference with Facebook and YouTube, as he points out, is that these new technologies permit him to reach a massive number of people instantly, across space and borders, and to build new affective and commercial relations.

For Roy, part of his success in the music business has involved having the power to act as an important node in the complex musical network in Trinidad and the Caribbean diasporas. He highly values this particular kind of achievement, especially as life for musicians has become harder with the series of economic recessions in and outside the Caribbean over the past few years, the replacement of musicians by new sound technologies, and the neoliberal policies that have severely cut many of the state subsidies for performing arts in Trinidad as in many other countries where Roy's band has regularly performed. And thanks to new social media, part of his sense of accomplishment has also been to be able to keep in contact with the very people who have been central to his musical journey, his friends and his fans in the Caribbean and beyond.

PASSING ON KNOWLEDGE

> I started my career in the University of Soca. That's what I call Roy Cape, the University of Soca.
> **SINGER DENISE BELFON, JULY 2009**

To hear a singer call Roy "the University of the Local Music"—meaning, from Trinidad and the Caribbean at large—and, again one month later, to hear a reputed soca singer refer to Roy as "the University of Soca" is significant. It indicates how Roy is recognized as a mentor, as someone committed to helping other musicians and singers further their artistic skills. It also signals the informal music education that Roy has provided as an elder. There are not many other Trinidadian (and I suspect, Caribbean) musicians in their late sixties or seventies who are still active in the music business as both musicians and bandleaders in the dance hall circuit, and to my knowledge, there is no one of his generation who is performing with the biggest stars of soca. After accompanying the top calypsonians of the region for years, his experience with younger Trinidadian artists positions him as a sought-after mentor and musical advisor. I think of the way he transmits his own knowledge to generations of musicians and singers as yet another distinct channel for Roy to circulate his musical experience and influence.

Roy's willingness to share his experience with his band musicians and singers has involved not only the passing on of musical skills, work ethics, and an understanding and appreciation of social relations (teamwork, care about one's public, and so on). It has also meant teaching some of them the material aspect of the music business: how to manage their own finances. Like Roy, most of his band members come from very poor families. In Chalkdust's view, Roy would have learned the value of money and of having a stable home at the orphanage. Whether it was at the orphanage or with the help of friends that he developed a good business sense, I believe that Roy knows only too well that a musician's financial problems can have a serious and negative impact on his ability to concentrate and play. While showing genuine care for his musicians by helping them manage their finances, it could be suggested that Roy also works to ensure that their financial peace of mind enables them to fully concentrate on their tasks as band members.

In Roy's philosophy and practice, success in the music business is a total social fact. Young musicians learn from and are judged by others. Personal achievements—whether artistic, material, or in terms of prestige and recognition—thus largely depend on being given a chance by another musician or a promoter, on being offered support by audience members, or on meeting the right people at the right time (serendipity). Success in the music business certainly requires talent. But even what counts as talent, Roy would add, is socially and culturally created, in his own situation, largely by the institutionalization in Trinidad of national and international competitions.

Roy's resilient agency, materialized in his own sense of success over many years, is deeply defined by the ability to find work for himself and for other musicians. His feeling of achievement today has also much to do with being able in this book to pay homage, in as many ways as he could, to the social world that has made it possible for him to perform and thrive.

AFTERWORD
Writing Voices

JOCELYNE GUILBAULT: One of the challenges in this book has been to make clear the distinction between an admiring fan and an inquiring scholar. How does one balance writing that is intrigued and admiring, and writing that is doing work collaboratively and critically? Put another way, how can the accumulation of practices and discourses related to Roy be presented as something more than a rave about Roy, or a tedious fact sheet? What is the positionality of voices, Roy's, mine, and others'?

Music criticism in the form of writing or broadcast hardly exists in the public media in Trinidad. While yearly carnival competitions for artists constitute one form of artistic assessment, the judges of these competitions only make public the results—the points they attributed to each contestant. They do not provide any explanations about their rankings or what, in their view, made one artist win over another. Over the past few years, only in the televised competitions modeled after the *American Idol* show do the judges comment on the candidates' performances and make recommendations on how young aspiring artists could improve their skills. By contrast, while musicians are heard on radio, television, and recordings, in shows, and at parties, they are not part of public discourse. And when the media address the few like Roy Cape, they focus either on the musicians' feats—invitations abroad, tight performances, well-attended shows—or simply provide brief biographies of the artists in question. Too few musicians are mentioned at all to allow for any real comparison in terms of musical skills, sound quality, or arrangements. Hence, those rare musicians who are mentioned are presented as heroes. There is certainly nothing wrong with that. The issue is not whether the writing is critical or uncritical. Even critical writing sometimes serves promotional purposes. The issue is whether music biographies in public media, as well as in academia, address and clarify the musicians' agency and practice.

What distinguishes critical writing from admirational writing per se is the refusal to take agency and practice transparently. It scrutinizes and asks questions (How did Roy do this?), instead of simply describing and praising what Roy did. Foregrounding the how and the why in Roy's biography is what situates my practice as a collaborator and interlocutor. I did not expect Roy to constantly produce critical reflections, commentaries, and queries on his own practices and history. But this is what I could bring to our text, as someone who has worked not only with Roy but in Trinidad and in several other islands, studying Caribbean music history across various musical genres, styles, and practices over the past three decades. I could provide many perspectives that would otherwise not come out in Roy's stories—for example, locating the politics of carnival music within the neoliberal space of Trinidadian nationalism. What differentiates my practice from that of a fan or admirer is that my storytelling does not stop at the media description of Roy's feats or of Roy's narrative. It puts these narratives in critical dialogue with a knowledge of local histories and politics, as well as the economics of Trinidad and other Caribbean and non-Caribbean postcolonial countries. It maps them as part of a tight network, involving the music industries and the ethics and aesthetics of several Caribbean musics and other popular musics. In so doing, I have not tried to hide my admiration for Roy's achievements as a saxophonist and as a bandleader. Rather, putting the media description of Roy's feats and narratives in perspective has helped explain why so many people, including me, have valorized his work.

One other challenge in writing this book has been to gather the documentation necessary to write Roy's biography. Many of the performances Roy described were never recorded. Many of the memorable rehearsals and concerts to which he referred were never captured in photographs. Some of the significant recordings Roy made were impossible to find. How I wish I could have included a CD in this book, one that chronicles in sound everything you've read about, a CD that gives you access to Roy's history of listening and my history of listening to help explain what sounds informed Roy's playing and what I am hearing when I listen to his sound. How I wish I could have included photographs and videos that document, in images, all of the events, situations, and stories that you've read here.[1] I am deeply aware of the burden this lack of documentation has placed on words. Even with the chapter addressing sound and the chapter addressing images, I still feel the gap between the words. Words can summarize, they can evoke, they can detail, they can chronicle. But they can't replace the palpable immediacy of sound and image.

The reality is that this book could not exist as an audio documentary, and it could not exist as a documentary film. More efforts by journalists, academics, fans, and admirers need to be deployed to record in words, images, and sounds the work world, reputation, and circulation of musicians. It is these efforts that will lead the way toward expanding not only the compass of who music biographies include, but also how they look and what they signify.

ROY CAPE: Well, I am not giving you a conclusion here. But I would like to emphasize again the struggles of musicians—not only of Trinidad and Tobago, but all over the world. Here in Trinidad, after fifty-five years, I can say that musicians, in my opinion, have not been seen. Regardless of who composes the songs, you know, you still have to play the music. So in 1969, at the time I was working with the Mighty Sparrow, he became known as the Calypso King of the World. What name should have been found for the musicians? If he was the King of the World, it means that the musicians had to be at the level too.

Through the years, the star musician has been eliminated. At present, there is only Joey Lewis and myself who lead full musical bands. It is important for people to know what is the responsibility of a bandleader in a small country. For an orchestra to be excellent, there has to be total cohesion, total unity. If you have a car and there is one faulty part in the machinery, it may not work; or if it works, it will only work [in a] faulty [way]. This is an example to demonstrate that one undesirable cog can ruin a whole engine. Same thing for an orchestra—in Trinidad and Tobago, in Canada, the United States, everywhere. For an orchestra to be excellent, the bandleader has to know who to hire that will sound good with the band and how to keep everybody happy. You need to work with everybody to create that total unity.

Out of love, musicians here survive at very low means for the quality that they are expected to give at all times. The musician's life is one-off—you do a gig, you get paid, and that's it. No form of royalties whatsoever. This is my story and the story of most other musicians here. We are not complaining, but that is the reality.

A.1 Roy Cape and the chancellor of the University of the West Indies, Sir George Alleyne, bowing to each other, 2011. Courtesy Anthony Moore.

Musicians have been underscored through time, but without musicians there would be no music. We bring love, serenity, and excitement—the essence of complete love for the audiences and the people. There is a saying, "If music is the food of life, play on."[2] That's what I mean: music is vital to humankind. Jocelyne, you wrote that down?

JG: Yes.

RC: Okay. We're good.

NOTES

Introduction

1. In reference to the English-speaking Caribbean: for reggae music, numerous book-length biographies focus on Bob Marley. The other artists who have been the object of in-depth studies include Peter Tosh and Jimmy Cliff. Many other reggae and dance hall singers are referred to in book chapters, but often in reference to something else—to make arguments in relation to national and gender politics, to analyze lyrics, or to examine the workings of the music industries in which these singers circulate. While, to my knowledge, no study of the musicians accompanying these artists yet exists, the musical experiments involved in dub music have attracted scholars and journalists to focus on the music makers. See, for example, the richly detailed studies of Michael Veal (2007) and Christopher Partridge (2010) on dub. In calypso music, small books locally produced focus on a few individual artists. Most calypsonians and soca artists, however, have only been the object of biographies in book chapters or articles. The only publications that exist on instrumentalists in the calypso and soca music scene focus on pan players. See Stuempfle (1995) and Dudley (2001, 2002, 2003, 2008). In spite of the many yearly jazz festivals in many Caribbean islands (Barbados, Trinidad, and St. Lucia, to name only those few), no publications yet exist on Caribbean jazz musicians.
2. One particularly eloquent story that has been told by a musician and bandleader (music director, arranger, and trombone player of James Brown's band) is that of Fred Wesley Jr. (2002) in *Hit Me, Fred*.
3. The expression "public intimacies," which I coined to refer to the cultural work of soca live performances, is here applied to a wide range of musical practices. I use it not only "to speak about the spatial proximity soca [read, music] helps cre-

ate . . . [but also] to address the variety of contacts among people that it makes possible." For an elaboration on the subject, see Guilbault (2010a).
4. Friedson (1990: 151). On the notion of musicians as workers, see Stahl (2013), Packman (2007), Mason (2006), Rodriguez (2006), and Hesmondhalgh (2002).
5. Hardt and Negri (2004: 146). The production to which the authors are referring in this passage is what they call "biopolitical" production because, they argue, "Immaterial production . . . tends to create not the means of social life but social life itself" (146). On "immaterial labor," see also Hardt and Negri (2000) and Lazzarato (1996).
6. These notions of reputation and respectability, first elaborated by Peter J. Wilson's 1973 book *Crab Antics*, have been widely circulated in Caribbean literature. See, for example, Abrahams (1972, 1975). For a critical review of these notions, see Puri (2004).
7. My definition of regimes of circulation here draws on an article titled "Créolité and Francophonie in Music" Line Grenier and I wrote with only a slight revision in the wording. It read, "What appears to be at stake is the emergence of new 'regimes of circulation': that is, particular systems of power/knowledge (Foucault, 1980) viewed as conjunctural linkages of institutions and discourses which allow the regulation of what, who and how circulates, where and why" (Grenier and Guilbault 2006: 230).
8. Miller (2009: 4). For further elaboration of materiality, see Miller (1998, 2005, 2009).
9. Daniel Miller describes two attempts to theorize materiality as follows: "the first, a theory of mere things as artifacts; the second, a theory that claims to entirely transcend the dualism of subjects and objects" (2005: 3). In the latter case, the theory is based on the assumption that "social worlds [are] as much constituted by materiality as the other way around" (Miller 1998: 3). For an elaboration along the same lines, Miller acknowledges the work of Bourdieu (1977), Appadurai (1986), and Miller (1987).
10. My notion of work is inspired by Sylvia Yanagisako's (2002) *Producing Culture and Capital* and Dorinne K. Kondo's (1990) *Crafting Selves*, which address the productive force of sentiment in family firms; Matt Stahl's (2009) "Privilege and Distinction in Production Worlds," which emphasizes the issue of class in the world of creative production; and Dick Blau, Charles Keil, Angeliki Vellou Keil, and Steve Feld's (2002) *Bright Balkan Morning*, which highlights the collective ethical character of musical work. The nexus of labor and business is now being recognized in contemporary music studies; see, for example, Timothy Taylor's (2012) *The Sounds of Capitalism*.
11. In their article "Rethinking Collaboration," Jones and Jenkins question "the logic of White/settler enthusiasm for dialogic collaboration" and "how this desire might be an unwitting imperialist demand—and thereby in danger of strengthening the very impulses it seeks to combat" (2008: 471). The authors

do not reject collaborative work. What they do advocate is a relationship that is based "on learning (about difference) *from* the Other, rather than learning *about* the Other" (471). In Stuart Hall's (1996) own wording, learning should not be despite difference, but through difference.

12. I mention here publications that focus on only one individual. Any biographical project, however, must acknowledge the important work that feminists and postcolonial studies have accomplished by bringing gender, race, and class and diversity of other sorts to the forefront. It has transformed the ways in which history (in the singular) has been told. Works such as Jane Bowers and Judith Tick's (1986) *Women Making Music*, Veit Erlmann's (1991) *African Stars*, Ronald M. Radano's (1993) *New Musical Figurations*, Bernard Lortat-Jacob's (1995) *Sardinian Chronicles*, Jonathan P. J. Stock's (1996) *Musical Creativity in Twentieth-Century China*, Pirkko Moisala and Beverley Diamond's (2000) *Music and Gender*, Maria Teresa Velez's (2000) *Drumming for the Gods*, Regula Qureshi's (2007) *Master Musicians of India*, Nicole T. Rustin and Sherrie Tucker's (2008) *Big Ears*, Helen Rees's (2009) *Lives in Chinese Music*, and *Des vies en musique*, edited by Sara Le Menestrel (2012), have all been inspiring and generative of a new politics of (re)presentation and histories. I want to thank Beverley Diamond, Kay Shelemay, and Bonnie Wade for sharing their insights on the subject.

13. As part of the conversation in the *Writing Culture* moment, Feld formulated this notion in his 1987 article "Dialogic Editing."

14. Raffles (2002: 331). According to N. Scott Momaday, *Wisdom Sits in Places* by Keith Basso (1996) was "the first sustained study of places and place names by an anthropologist" (from the dust jacket of the book). This was followed in the same year by the publication of *Senses of Place*, a collection of ethnographic studies edited by Steven Feld and Keith S. Basso. *Ethnicity, Identity, and Music: The Musical Construction of Place*, edited by Martin Stokes in 1994, was another important landmark in showing how music is involved in place making.

15. Some of the best ethnographies that take on this point include Keith Basso (1996), *Wisdom Sits in Places*, and Kathleen Stewart (1996), *A Space on the Side of the Road*.

16. See James Clifford (1983), "On Ethnographic Authority," and *After Writing Culture*, edited by Allison James, Jenny Hockey, and Andrew Dawson (1997).

17. As Pirkko Moisala writes, "A book focusing on a contemporary composer [read, musician] is a representation of a living person, with real-life consequences. . . . From the researcher's point of view . . . it is important to evaluate the effects and consequences that the research may have on the composer's [musician's] career" (2011: 447–48).

18. I thank Christopher Ballantine for reminding me to stress this important point. For a similar argument, see Moisala (2011).

19. It should be noted that, as a sister island, Tobago also has its own internal government, the House of Assembly, and its own character and culture. Its capital—

Scarborough—is also where Roy Cape plays regularly and where he is equally acclaimed.

20. As Rosa Maria Flavo wrote, "collecting memories and recreating stories" helps "overcome a feeling of uprootedness" (2008: 70).
21. I thank Steven Feld for eliciting these notions of modern and postmodern subjects in reference to our discussion of our respective fieldwork.
22. From the *Collins Cobuild English Language Dictionary* (London, 1987), definition of journey.
23. On the notion of journey, see Le Menestrel (2012). As the editor, Sara Le Menestrel, explains, in this collection "journey [parcours]" is conceived simultaneously as a theoretical framework to address the relation of the individual with the social world, and as a methodological tool to critically address the relations between researcher and interviewees and the production of narratives.
24. On how questions of action are answered by assertions of place, see Feld and Basso (1996).
25. In the introduction to *Jazz Cosmopolitanism in Accra*, Steven Feld writes, "Listening to histories of listening is my way to shift attention to acoustemology, to sound as a way of knowing the world" (2012a: 7). The themes of sound makers (both musicians and speakers) as listeners, of listening biographies, and of listening as habitus have a long history in Feld's writings about Papua New Guinea, from *Sound and Sentiment* (1982, reviewed in the new introduction to the third edition, Feld 2012b) to "Waterfalls of Song" (Feld 1996), as well as in many essays on communication, dialogism, and intervocality throughout the 1980s and 1990s, and his dialogues with Charles Keil (Keil and Feld 1994) and Don Brenneis (Feld 2004). For a theorization of musicians as listeners, see also Negus (1997). For a theorization of sound as mapping space, time, musical trends, and other webs of relationships, see my article "Audible Entanglements: Nation and Diasporas in Trinidad's Calypso Music Scene" (Guilbault 2005).
26. I take this notion of affective labor from Michael Hardt and Antonio Negri, who define it as having to do with the creation and manipulation of affect. As they explain, "What affective labor produces are social networks, forms of community, biopower" (2000: 294). Also see Hardt (1999).
27. On state power, nationalism, and racial politics, see Ryan (1972), Hintzen (1989), and Premdas (2000); on gender politics, see Mohammed and Shepherd (1988) and Reddock (1994); on music and cinema productions, see Rohlehr (1990) and Warner (2000), to name only a few.
28. On visual economy, see her insightful book, *Vision, Race, and Modernity* (Poole 1997).
29. Few studies in ethnomusicology have fully explored the materiality of the visual. Some notable exceptions include Thomas Vennum Jr.'s (1982) *The Ojibwa Dance Drum and Wild Rice and the Ojibway People* (1988), Deborah Wong's (1989–90) "Thai Cassettes and Their Covers"; Beverley Diamond, M. Sam Cronk, and Franziska

von Rosen's (1994) *Visions of Sound*; Hugo Zemp's (1995) *Ecoute le bambou qui pleure*, Bonnie C. Wade's (1998) *Imaging Sound*, Eileen Southern and Josephine Wright's (2000) *Images*, and Dick Blau et al.'s (2002) *Bright Balkan Morning*. I thank Bonnie C. Wade for sharing this information with me.

30. As Tzvetan Todorov succinctly puts it, "The most important feature of the utterance [for Bakhtin] . . . is its *dialogism*, that is, its intertextual dimension" (1984: x). Bakhtin's (1984) concept of dialogism was introduced in his 1929 book, *Problems of Dostoevsky's Poetics*. Bakhtin's (1982) philosophy of language and a detailed exegesis of his notions of heteroglossia, polyphony, and chronotope are more associated with the collection of his essays titled *The Dialogic Imagination*. Several critical volumes are devoted to the exposition of this key idea, including a sustained discussion in *Dialogism* (Holquist 2002).

1. For the Love of Music

1. I am thinking here about Pierre Bourdieu's (1979) *La distinction* and Erik Olin Wright's (1997) *Class Counts* and his article "The Comparative Project on Class Structure and Class Consciousness" (Wright 1989), for example.
2. Early on, when Roy's mother took ill, Bella assumed the role of the mother for her two brothers. To this day, she continues to be the one responsible for assembling everyone in the family.
3. A sousou (also spelled "susu") is a financial system widespread in the Caribbean that is derived from an informal African institution practiced in various ways. It is organized on the principle of saving money. A group of ten people may be formed, each of whom gives $100 weekly to reach $1,000 savings per week (or fortnightly, or monthly). Everyone in the group is then entitled to receive $1,000 (called a "sousou hand") after contributing for ten consecutive weeks (if it is on a weekly basis). In case of an emergency, this money may also be available, with the understanding that that individual must be prepared to continue his or her payments and wait to receive another lump sum until everyone else has received their share. The person who runs the sousou charges a modest fee (called the "box") for collecting the money. The "house" refers to the person who initiates and organizes the sousou. For further information, see Marcy Annisette's (2006) important article, "People and Periods Untouched by Accounting History."
4. Laventille is one of the poorest areas of Port of Spain. It has been historically (and continues to be) viewed as a rough and dangerous place to inhabit and to visit. As the acclaimed calypsonian Shadow once sang, "Poverty Is Hell" (1994). At the same time, it is also known to have produced some of the finest musicians and steelbands in the country.
5. On Trinidad All Stars Steel Pan Orchestra, see Stuempfle (1995: 94–100).
6. The younger members of City Syncopators decided to change the name of the band to Joy Land Syncopators when the captain of the band, Boots, migrated to England.

7. I want to thank Jocelyn Sealy for sharing this information with me on October 26, 2011. She has been the recipient of many awards, including the Hummingbird Gold Medal in 1990—a prestigious state decoration of Trinidad and Tobago.
8. On the formation of brass bands in British colonies and Christian institutions, see Rob Boonzajer Flaes's (2000) important study, *Brass Unbound*.
9. The Police Band directors since independence have included Anthony Prospect, George P. Scott, Roderick Urquhart, Nelson Villafana, and Enrique Moore. Before that, all the music directors were British. Everyone from Trinidad, except Urquhart, was from the Homes (orphanages).
10. In Mexico, young girls learned music at the San Miguel of Bethlen Convent, which from 1740 until its closing in 1821 served also as an asylum (De Couve, Dal Pino, and Frega 2004: 82). During the same period in the Brazilian Colony, "some music schools . . . were strictly private institutions devoted to the upbringing of orphans or abandoned children . . . for whom the State paid an annual contribution" (90). In the United States, the Louisville Methodist Orphans' Home, located in Louisville, Kentucky, and created in 1871, also included music education for the children (Ivey 1918). In Baltimore, the McDonogh School created for poor orphan girls opened in 1872 and also included a music program for the girls (Nurith 1994). In Charleston, the Jenkins orphanage, "one of the longest-operating black orphanages in the country, was founded in 1891" and it became famous for its brass band (Chandler 2009: 65). The important contribution of orphanages to music education cannot be overestimated. After spending over a year (January 1913 to June 1914) at the Colored Waif's Home for Boys in New Orleans, Louis Armstrong, one of the most reputed jazz trumpet players to this day, often recalled how much he learned under the tutelage of Peter Davis, who taught music and formed an orchestra at the Home (Giddins 1988: 65–67).
11. The next paragraph draws on my narrative of Trinidad's colonial history in *Governing Sound* (Guilbault 2007: 24).
12. Over the years since the mid-1990s, official holidays in Trinidad have been created to respect the major celebrations of several religions practiced on the island. In addition to the Christian-related official holidays, these include the Hindu celebration of Diwali, the Muslim celebration of Eid al-Fitr, and the Spiritual Baptist Liberation Shouter Day.
13. The first orphanage in Trinidad was founded in 1857 by the Anglican Church, to care for East Indian children in Tacarigua "near the Orange Grove sugar-cane plantation where many East Indians were working" (Rétout 2001: 45).
14. As Marie Thérèse Rétout, author of *Called to Serve*, writes, "These children needed contact with older ones to develop their speech ability and to socialize as a whole" (2001: 101). Hence the Sisters created family units "by keeping together as long as possible, brothers and sisters within the same house and entrusting the young to the older ones so as to develop caring relationships" (101).

15. From *St. Dominic's Home, 1871–1996*, undated anonymous document in the collection of the St. Dominic's Children's Home. Based on this pamphlet record, in 1967 the institution was the home of 675 children. In 2009, it counted only around 110 children. As Sister Francine explained, today couples have fewer children than in the past and, furthermore, each religious denomination now cares for its own. The Hindus, the Muslims, the members of the Anglican Church, and so on, all have their own children's Homes. It should be noted that the *St. Dominic's Home* pamphlet reports that there were 668 children in 1958 whereas in *Called to Serve*, the number is 656 (Rétout 2001).
16. Sister Francine explained that today, the court can commit children up to eighteen years old.
17. Roy explained, "Miss Rogers, who was a schoolteacher at the orphanage, played piano. She had singing classes. She had friends in Dem Fortunates Steelband from Belmont who gave her the four pans that made up the first entire steelband at the orphanage—the band in which I played the tenor pan."
18. From the pamphlet *St. Dominic's Home, 1871–1996*.
19. Roy specified playing a B-flat clarinet using the simple system of fingering. As time progressed, this fingering was upgraded to the Boehm system. On the simple and Boehm systems, see Hoeprich (2008).
20. The repiano is part of the clarinet section, which included the solo clarinet, the first clarinet, and the repiano clarinet.
21. On Frankie Francis, see Guilbault (2007: 139–44).
22. Prospect, like Roy Cape, spoke unabashedly about growing up in the orphanage. However, many musicians do not want people to know about their past at the orphanage because of the stigma this institution still carries. For that reason, I have omitted the names of several reputed musicians.

2. Working as a Bandsman

1. I draw here on Daniel Miller who, influenced by G. Hegel and many other authors, argues that "our humanity is not prior to what it creates" (2005: 10). Put another way, "social worlds . . . [are] as much constituted by materiality as the other way around" (Miller 1998: 3). This theory about objects and subjects, in Miller's wording, thus "critique[s] definition of humanity as purely social . . . and critique[s] approaches which view material culture as merely the semiotic representation of some bedrock of social relations" (2005: 3). It does not deny human beings' own agency. But in this view, materiality—objects and immaterial infrastructure such as law—has power. It is not simply a sign or a symbol that stands for people. It frames behavior; it creates people's sense of self. Along the same lines, I am suggesting, the material worlds and material cultures in which musicians live become constitutive—albeit in varying degrees—of how these musicians think and perform musically. See Miller (2005).

2. On the notion of memoryscape and a lineage of memory studies going back to the classic treatise of Maurice Halbwachs (1992 [1950]), see Connerton (1989), Boyarin (1994), and Misztal (2003).
3. I owe this insight about how Roy's remembrance of the past comes from a developmental perspective formed over the years to historian Marie Theresa Hernández's (2004: 74) essay "Reconditioning History."
4. See De Leon (1996: 13) for an interview with Roy Cape on the subject.
5. Unlike St. Dominic's Children's Home, St. Mary's Home provided a place to sleep for those who had just left the orphanage. At sixteen years old—the age at which children had to leave the home—and with nowhere to go (not for all, but for many of them), this safe place for the night represented an easier transition to the world outside.
6. This story of how he learned to play among seasoned musicians greatly matters to Roy. In many of the interviews he gave over the years, Roy acknowledges this important period of his life in almost the exact same words. See, for example, De Leon (1996: 13).
7. The microhistory of Roy holding various odd jobs attests to the colonial ordering of racial formations in Trinidad. The shop owners, managers, or friends Roy approached for jobs are either "Portuguese-looking man, white" or East Indians, as the name John Boodoosingh unmistakably suggests. While the whites—whether of Portuguese or other European origins—have historically been more financially privileged, by the 1960s, East Indians were widely acknowledged to own lands and a growing number of businesses. They are also recognized now as having played a major role in the calypso music business. Already in the late 1950s, some of them acted as executive producers for some calypsonians. East Indian businessmen hired calypsonians to sing jingles to advertise their merchandise. Others became involved in the calypso business by renting their sound equipment for calypso shows or by renting trucks for carrying the musical equipment. Some became responsible for most of the media promotion. The race interrelations that brought Portuguese-looking white men, East Indians, and Afro-Trinidadians together through different connections are crucial to an understanding of the multicultural milieu in which Roy lives and the cosmopolitan knowledge and sensibility he has developed as a result. This is something Roy fully acknowledges. On the East Indians' contributions to calypso, see Constance (1991).
8. The importance of networking is vital for musicians to find work. If little has been said in the local or regional media about the central role that orphanages have played in music education in Trinidad and in the other English-speaking islands, even less is known about the profound and lasting impact that musicians from the orphanage have had on each other. Roy speaks of the brotherhood that emerged from growing up together in the orphanage; in other conversations, he refers to the musicians who come from the orphanage as forming,

in his own words, a kind of "lodge," a tightly knit group of musicians who care for each other. It does not matter whether a musician comes from the Belmont or the Tacarigua orphanage. To this day the boys who grew up with Roy at the orphanage continue to be there for him and proudly celebrate his achievements as one of those who made it. And, as I have witnessed many times, he is also there for many of them, as both a friend and a supporter.

9. Women's contributions to the musical life of Trinidad and that of other Caribbean islands have been historically overlooked, and yet the support that scores of women have lent to musicians has enabled many of them to pursue their musical careers. As Roy describes, women provided shelter and food to musicians or helped them find places to stay. In the early 1960s, some of them worked at music venues, collecting money at the entrance doors. (While Roy recounts a negative incident of a woman working at the cash register of a music venue, the point I want to make here is that women have been an integral part of the music scene—as both supporters and workers.) To this day, many West Indian women continue to be involved in the music business. See further Guilbault (2007: 248–49).

10. It should be noted that TELCO had a license agreement with Columbia and was pressing records for this American company.

11. The Ampex model 200 used at TELCO was created in the United States and used for the first time by ABC in 1948. Even though not long after "the line soon expanded into three- and four-track models using ½" tape" ("Ampex," Wikipedia, http://en.wikipedia.org/wiki/Ampex), TELCO continued to use the earlier model up to the early 1960s. Recording studios in Trinidad are not known for having experimented with recording equipment, as was the case in Jamaica during the 1960s. See, for example, Michael Veal's (2007) highly informative book on dub and the musical experiments in Jamaican recording studios during that period.

12. The musical training provided by St. Dominic's Children's School was basic, and concerned mainly, if not exclusively, the playing of selected instruments and the reading of musical notation. While he learned to play clarinet at St. Dominic's, it was only after Roy left the orphanage that he began to play the alto saxophone and to develop his musical skills (transcription and transposition) on his own.

13. Playing "on the road" is a Trinidadian expression that means playing in the streets following a particular path designated by the National Carnival Committee.

14. Roy's description of the bands performing on the road during the late 1950s at carnivals in Trinidad is telling of the profound influence of Britain over its colonies. As Jeffrey Richards (2001: 436) remarks, "Brass-banding was an integral part of the imperial process, 'thunderous proof,' say Trevor Herbert and Margaret Sarkissian [1997], 'of western military and religious superiority.' Every colony had its military bands. Police bands sprang up too—in Canada (1876), Ceylon (1873), South Africa (1897), Barbados (1889) and Rhodesia (1897), for

instance. Bands meant uniforms, order, discipline and regularity, and they acquired a shared Empire-wide repertoire of European romantic classics and British hymns, marches and popular music, such as Gilbert and Sullivan." See Herbert (1991), Flaes (2000), and Newsome (2006). The use of brass bands based on the British military model during Trinidad's carnival also reminds me of the brass bands that perform during the Congo Square festival and funerals in New Orleans. See Michael P. Smith (1994), Raussert (2008), and Sakakeeny (2008, 2011).

15. As Mano Marcelin and Dutchies would explain to Roy, they were responsible for taking mobility to another level, abandoning the box cart. When they used pickup trucks, they would have the rhythm section on the truck while the horn players would still be walking on the road behind the truck. They soon realized that they needed to go still further because the horn players were falling behind. By 1968, they began using big trucks to carry the entire band.

16. On the tangible effects of noise from machines and factories on music making, most particularly on street performances, see Marié Abe's (2010) insightful study of street music in Japan.

17. This strategy of having musicians continue to play during fights to help stop fights and riots has long been acknowledged in Hollywood movies.

18. As Keith Negus (1997) explains, musicians—particularly those involved in popular music—think musically about what they play in relation to both their own personal interests and creative projects and also by imagining the audience's musical tastes. On this subject, see Hennion (1989, 2011).

19. This practice of translating American and British songs into calypso during the 1960s greatly contrasts with the long-held assumption of many cultural activists and academics that so-called globalization would create a "graying-out" of cultures. For debates on the subject, see Wallis and Malm (1984), Feld (2000), Guilbault (2001), and White (2012).

20. The Trinidadian tradition of nonstop among dance bands could be related to what is known in the American jazz scene as a cutting session among jazz players. The difference from Trinidadian nonstop is that in the United States, this cutting session would involve only soloists, and not entire bands. I am reminded here of one scene in a film on Charlie Parker directed by Clint Eastwood (Bird, 1988) in which the young Parker (played by Forest Whitaker) participates in a cutting session (nonstop) with other sax players and how the camera alternates between focusing on the virtuosic performance of the musicians and showing the visible thrill that this session was creating in the audience. On the socialization of jazz players, see Paul Berliner's (1994) *Thinking in Jazz* and Ingrid Monson's (1996) *Saying Something*. This topic is taken up in numerous jazz biographies.

21. Roy mentioned to me that it was quite common for musicians to move from one band to another in a short amount of time during this period. The reasons

for doing so could certainly be monetary, but just as often musicians moved to another band because they preferred the music or because they felt more at ease with, or more respected by, certain musicians over others. See Burns (2006) and Finnegan (1989).

22. To this day, hardly any documentation exists on the contributions of musicians and calypsonians from Chinese or Spanish/Latin American descent in Trinidad. See Rohlehr (1990) for mention of some of these artists and Guilbault (2007) for discussion of calypsonian Crazy (who is of Chinese and Venezuelan Amerindian descent).

23. As Michael Germain (an acoustic bass player who performs jazz, parang, and salsa music, and who was an active musician and music organizer on the University of the West Indies campus in the 1960s) explained in an interview with me, the combo era in Trinidad was deeply influenced by North American groups like the Ventures and the Shadows. Young Trinidadians adopted the combo style format that typically included three guitars, sometimes a keyboard, a drummer, and percussion. Some of these small bands evolved into larger bands with brass sections (e.g., Esquires). Others spawned the format of the new big bands (e.g., Sound Revolution, including lead vocal, synthesizer, guitar, bass, two trumpets, one trombone, one saxophone, drum set, percussion, sound engineer). The combos, modeled after the North American bands and also the Beatles—who were highly influential during that period—began to feature a band singer. The band singer would sing R&B and pop music outside of the carnival season. However, over the years, the bands have become secondary and the singer has become the focal point. In Michael's words, "So it has gone 180 degrees from where it was, where the music and the band was the important thing. It has now become the singer who is the [most] important person in the whole scene" (personal interview, January 2008). To my knowledge, no research has yet been conducted about this highly prolific musical combo era. And yet the number of combos in the 1960s and 1970s was massive. To name just a few: Ambassadors Combo, Javan Wells, Ansel Wyatt, Andre Tanker and the Flamingos, Bert Bailey and the Jets, Casanovas, Dean and the Celebrities, Esquires Combo, Group Solo, Johnny Lee and the Hurricanes, Ken Charles Combo, Life Rockerfellas, Los Muchachos, Silver String Combo, Solid Seven Combo, the Young Ones from Guyana, and Tradewinds Combo.

24. Emory Cook was an audio engineer, inventor, and the founder of the Cook Records label. He was a music enthusiast who recorded music not only in studios but also in the field. Over a quarter of his 140-plus albums feature music from the Caribbean, most particularly, calypsos and steelband music from Trinidad. In 1990, Emory and Martha Cook donated their record company, master tapes, patents, and papers to the Smithsonian Institution.

25. For further information about recording technologies used in different historical eras, see John Eargle's (2003) *Handbook of Recording Engineering*.

26. Here Roy added that "through the years, Ron Berridge had an agreement to transcribe all the musical production done by RCA and the Tropico label owned by Mr. Leslie Samaroo."
27. The list of artists and composers that Roy refers to as having provided the main repertoire performed in dance bands during the 1960s shows how the musical history of Trinidad and Tobago cannot be dissociated from that of the United States. The musical interrelation between the two countries—while being deeply unequal—cannot be overstated. While there is clearly a shared musical sensibility among African diasporic musicians and singers—attested by the great number of African American musicians and singers Roy lists—it is equally clear that the repertoire that was played in Trinidad during that period was not dictated by the issue of race. Trinidadian musicians played the music of the artists who were most listened to and most commercially successful at the time. This meant performing songs by the Beatles, Elvis Presley, and Glen Miller, next to those by Marvin Gaye and Aretha Franklin, to name only a few. Even though in the aftermath of independence, several musicians, including Art de Coteau and Lord Shorty (renamed Ras Shorty I), made a real effort to play "local," many others continued to perform a mixed repertoire of local and international musics. Several studies exploring repertoire selection in relation to the issues of race and the tensions between local and global in various parts of the world come to mind: Guilbault (1993), Erlmann (1999), Born and Hesmondhagh (2000), Radano and Bohlman (2000), Meintjes (2003), Feld (2012a).
28. In 1965, after some dispute between the calypsonians and the management, the Revue was renamed the Caravan. However, it returned to its original name in 1966. I thank Shawn Randoo and Rudolph Ottley for sharing this information with me.
29. Publicity for a dance in the 1960s was done through radio broadcast, newspaper ads, and flyers stuck on telephone poles—and depending on the organizer's budget, using all three media or only one of them. However, equally efficient was what has been termed the folk media, the informal networks (*de bouche à oreille* among workers, family members, and friends) in which news circulated. If a particular musical event such as a nonstop was organized at the last minute, then musicians would often choose to place a few posters at strategic locations in the hope that it would generate a chain reaction among several informal networks, reaching potential audience members in some of the most isolated parts of Trinidad and Tobago. As I experienced in my first few weeks doing fieldwork in St. Lucia in the late 1970s, foreigners just coming to the island would often find out about such musical events only after the fact. The importance of folk media throughout the islands cannot be overstated to this day, even though since the early 1980s in most Caribbean countries private radio stations and TV stations began to emerge and assume a significant role in the broadcast of news media.

30. Roy's mention that "it was easier to get a guitar than a saxophone" addresses a most important challenge for the majority of musicians at the time. In most Caribbean islands, musical instruments were considered luxury items under customs law. This meant that the importation of a musical instrument could entail paying a tax as high as 90 percent, making the cost of the instrument prohibitive. For that reason, many musicians up to the 1980s did not own their instruments. Instead they would depend on the bandleader, who typically owned most of the band's instruments. Not only did this state of affairs give considerable power to the bandleader, it also meant that many musicians could not practice outside the rehearsals organized by the bandleader. Hence, it is not too surprising that the combo formation caught on in the islands like wildfire, as guitars were far more affordable than any wind instrument. Customs laws about the importation of musical instruments were dramatically eased throughout the islands by the mid-1980s.
31. The passing of the new immigration laws in the United States in 1965 encouraged many Trinidadian musicians to migrate. This topic is addressed at length in chapter 7.
32. Roy's acknowledgment that Clive Bradley was a math teacher here not only emphasizes Bradley's exceptional musical talent but also alludes to the issue of class. As a teacher, and therefore someone with higher education, Bradley was not expected to be hanging out in clubs and was harshly criticized for doing so by the principal of Fatima College where he taught. The bad reputation of musicians as drunkards, womanizers, and unreliable people, and the association of a teacher with such people in nightclubs, may have been frowned upon for fear of tarnishing the reputation of the school (personal interview with Clive Bradley, January 1997).
33. Several musicians and artists in their careers made it a point to "play local" in the aftermath of independence. In an interview with me, Clive Bradley told me that in 1976, he was fired by Lord Kitchener for writing a too jazzy kind of arrangement and moving too far away from straight calypso. The famous arranger Art de Coteau, in the 1960s and 1970s, is known to have scolded some of his band members for playing jazz riffs on their instruments to warm up before rehearsals. He insisted that anyone doing an improvisation had to sound Trinidadian, not American—whether it was on stage or in rehearsal. Gordon Rohlehr, one of the most authoritative academic writers on calypso, recounts that before independence, Guyanese calypsonians could participate in the annual Calypso King Competition held in Trinidad during carnival. In the spirit of nation building and with the desire to affirm Trinidad's cultural identity and difference after independence, the Carnival Development Committee, later renamed the National Carnival Commission, created a new regulation stipulating that only local Trinidadian residents singing local compositions could participate in the competition. See Rohlehr's interview with Shalini Puri (Rohlehr 2003: 240–69).

34. Until now, I had not realized the profound influence that films—and the songs they premiered—have exercised on Trinidadian musicians. I should have remembered that in the 1960s, musicians heard music either on the radio, at live music performances, or by listening to LPs. Very few Trinidadians then owned a television set. In this context, films represented an easy access to some of the latest songs on American and English-speaking mainstream media. Hollywood films, that is. In Trinidad, particularly in the 1950s and 1960s, Trinidadians were exposed not only to Hollywood but also to Indian films. The East Indian population of Trinidad at that time was close to 43 percent, and they encouraged many East Indian entrepreneurs to open several cinemas not only in the "south" (the southern part of Trinidad where the largest populations of East Indians live), but also in the capital of Port of Spain, where many Afro-Trinidadians had also had the opportunity to view Indian films since the 1940s. Even though many Afro-Trinidadian musicians may have seen Indian films during the 1950s and 1960s, hardly anyone incorporated these songs in their musical practice. But East Indian musicians did. However, very little has been written on the subject. For a reference to the importance of Bollywood movies in Trinidad, see Manuel (2000a) and Ramnarine (2001).

35. As Roy points out, musicians of dance music, as is the case for deejays today, by necessity, have to be "cosmopolitan" to reach audiences. They have to stay attentive to new trends—locally and internationally—and know a wide repertoire. In the 1960s, they played foreign hits, but also calypsos. Roy insists that, in the 1960s as today, musicians of popular dance music, just like their audience, can be "all" at the same time, to use the wording of Kwame Anthony Appiah, "cosmopolitan—celebrating the variety of human cultures; rooted—loyal to one local society (or a few) that you count as home; liberal—convinced of the value of the individual; and patriotic—celebrating the institutions of the state (or states) within which you live" (1998: 106). In contrast to long-held and widespread assumptions, playing foreign music does not necessarily entail the erasure of one's own identity or loyalty to one's nation-state. As Roy explains, it is in relation to knowing (and playing) other people's music that one can better position and promote one's own musical practice. Put another way, it is through a play of difference that one's own (musical) identity comes to be constituted and recognized (Hall 2007: 270).

36. What I understand Roy to be saying here is not that cover versions—even in the case of today's bands—can actually be the exact replica of original songs, but that in contrast to today's bands, the 1960s arrangers made an explicit attempt—a point of honor—to produce cover versions that sounded different. Naturally there is always some difference at some level, whether in the timbre of the lead singer, the ability of the guitar player, and so on, that makes the cover versions different—even if only to a slight degree—but what Roy posits is much more

than these natural variations. These bands sought to create novelty while performing songs that sounded familiar to the audiences—an aesthetic that was not unique to Trinidadian musicians and their audiences' musical tastes, but also a dominant trend in the United States at the time. My belief is that the Trinidadian dance bands doing cover versions today perform sometimes more like tribute bands. Like tribute bands, they strive to capture as closely as possible the sound of the original bands and songs they are performing, to pay tribute to these bands and songs, but also to benefit financially from the wide appeal and commercial success these bands and songs once enjoyed (or continue to enjoy). While this practice of performing cover versions as close to the originals as possible is widespread among Trinidadian bands, I do not know any local band that is recognized as being a tribute band (that is, as focusing exclusively on re-creating the songs of a single band). On cover versions in the United States during the 1960s, see Gracyk (1996, 2001) and Lacasse (2007). On tribute bands, see Homan (2006). See also Christopher Tonelli's (2011) critical discussion of the difference between tribute bands and those that do pastiche. The crucial work of musical arrangers in Trinidad has been ignored until recently. For seminal work on the subject, see Hill (1993), Dudley (2002, 2003), Guilbault (2007), Helmlinger (2008).

37. To refer to markings on scores as "maps of expression" strikes me as powerfully evocative of the ways pitches and rhythms become inflected with human expression, and of how sounds are given a particular declamatory style—unique to the arranger's musical sensibility and his experience as a Trinidadian.

38. Byron Lee (1935–2008) was a bass player, record producer, and musical entrepreneur. He became internationally famous for his work as the bandleader of Byron Lee and the Dragonaires. For more on this exceptional Jamaican musician, see Leslie (2006) and Veal (2007).

39. "Sa Sa Yea," a song title in French Creole, reminds us of Sparrow's birthplace, Grenada, where French Creole was widely spoken until some twenty years ago. The use of French Creole expressions continues to circulate in Trinidad even among monolingual English speakers. The historical importance of French Creole in Trinidad has been profound. Names of places, birds, and common expressions in French Creole continue to be part of Trinidad's multicultural and multilingual past and present.

40. The Mighty Sparrow is known not only for his exceptional voice but also for his sharp musical ear and creative ideas for song arrangements. He has been known to be very selective about the musicians he chooses to work with. Roy's story about how Sparrow asked him to hear his new composition is thus important. It shows how being recognized by such a musical icon in calypso was significant for him as a musician. The common saying that "the closer you get to a powerful person, the more powerful you yourself become" holds true in the

music business. Conversely, this story also shows how Roy's remarkable musical skills and warm personality have led him to work with one of the most famous—artistically and financially—artists of the English-speaking Caribbean.

41. Road March competitions are based on the number of times a calypso song is heard on Carnival Tuesday (Mardi Gras). As I wrote elsewhere, "This competition is supposed to represent the people's choice. There the judges have little to say; their function is simply to keep a tally of the Road Marches played at various designated spots in the city" (Guilbault 2007: 76).

42. Bandleader and arranger Ed Watson wrote the arrangement for Lord Kitchener's song "Sugar Bum Bum," which became an instant success in 1978 and remained the most commercially successful song of Lord Kitchener's impressive repertoire.

43. The Mighty Sparrow's intense touring schedule reflects his unparalleled stature in calypso ever since 1956, when he won the Calypso King competition. On his exceptional contributions, see Rohlehr (1970, 1975, 1990), Warner (1982), Liverpool (1993), Regis (1999), and Guilbault (2007).

44. Having reached the highest level one can reach in a given place, and with no other prospects in sight, musicians often seek better opportunities elsewhere. This phenomenon is particularly acute in islands where the populations are small and the point of saturation is reached in a short amount of time. The hope of making a better living is in playing music elsewhere. In the 1970s this became a synonym among West Indians for going to the United States, and most specifically to New York (not London, England, which in the late 1940s and 1950s was the favorite destination for West Indians, as Lord Kitchener memorialized with his song, "London Is the Place for Me," and the CD compilation of the same name). However, the protectionist measures against foreign competitors instituted in U.S. law, the history of racism in that country, and the lack of work during weekdays led many musicians to be disillusioned and to turn to other kinds of jobs to make ends meet. On migrating Caribbean musicians, see Hill (1993), Allen and Wilcken (2001), Scher (2003), and Green and Scher (2007).

45. Byron Lee and the Dragonaires used two trumpets, one trombone, one tenor sax, and the normal rhythm section, including guitar, bass, drums, keyboards, and percussion. The band also featured two or three singers.

46. Drummer and percussionist Michael Tobas toured internationally with Harry Belafonte for five years, from 1972 to 1977. As his website indicates, Tobas "also had the privilege of working with such renowned musicians as jazz pianist/composer Randy Weston, saxophonist Warne Marsh, French guitarist Jean-Pierre Jumez, producer/percussionist Ralph McDonald, South African singer Letta Mbulu, Caribbean Nobel Prize laureate Derek Walcott, Brazilian multi-instrumentalist 'Suvica,' and the late Marvin Gaye," to name only a few ("Biography: Michael 'Toby' Tobas," Toby: Steel Drummer/Percussionist, 2004, http://www.tobzmusic.com/bio.htm). The point here is that Roy played with top mu-

sicians, some of whom were able to make a successful career in their adopted country.

47. I was struck when Roy reported having said to Hugh, "Jamaican musicians are not that versed in playing calypso music," and for that reason recommended hiring Trinidadian musicians to play calypso with him. Discourses of authenticity pervade the way musicians discuss not only style and genre but also who the legitimate representatives of a music considered national are. Sometimes this goes in the way of policing; at other times, it is generous sharing; at still other times, it goes in the direction of just looking for one's own—friends and colleagues. As Turino (2000) argues, the national often comes first in thinking about regional interchanges. On this subject, see Gage Averill's (1998) revealing story about the complex relations among Caribbean musicians living in New York.

48. As Percy Hintzen remarks in *West Indian in the West*, even when New York's West Indian diasporas come together for important events such as the Labor Day festival, "Country-specific identities do not disappear but are reflected in patterns of participation at the Carnival festivities that publicize national rather than regional identity" (2001: 43). From this perspective, the recognition of a Trinidadian musician by Jamaican audiences is significant—particularly if one recalls that historically the musicians from these two islands have competed for regional and international recognition.

49. In our many meetings to write this book since 2008, Roy rarely spoke about the hardships that being a full-time musician has entailed for his family—for his wife, his children, and himself. His prolonged absence not only when he left alone to return to New York, but over the years his four to six weeks on the road at a time, as well as his nightlong performances with the band on weekends or for important holidays must have been at times difficult for those left behind and also for him. But Roy did not address these hardships.

3. Listening to Roy Sounding

1. It is in this sense that, as Miller reports, "In his *Phenomenology of Spirit*, Hegel (1977) suggests that there can be no fundamental separation between humanity and materiality" (2005: 8). The objects or material world humans create inform how humans come to think of themselves, perform, and behave. In other words, materiality and humanity are defined through their synergetic relations.
2. For a thorough discussion of the politics of aesthetics, see Rancière (2004, 2010). For critical ethnographies on the subject, see Meintjes (2003), Brinner (2009), Weintraub (2010), and Feld (2012a).
3. As Roy points out, "Choy's band had been one of the leading lights, maybe in the late and middle forties, into the fifties, and when I started to go around, Choy Aming was big and famous in Trinidad. Choy had also an entertainment complex, upstairs [in] the old [Salvatory] building that has been demolished now.

The name of that club was the Penthouse, and there were shows from Monday to Sunday, every week, every month. So you had tourists and different people come into the club, and Choy had good musicians who were able to play not only by music [score sheets], but by memory and by feelings. So someone could have requested to play 'Stardust,' and it could have been played then." It can thus be concluded that for a musician from Choy's band to tell Roy that he would be a very sweet alto player was thus a very big compliment and meaningful recognition in the musical milieu of the time.

4. I thank Steven Feld for sharing as a scholar and as a trombonist his insights about Roy's production of sound and numerous musical references while playing solos on his saxophone.

5. The theme song in that 1952 film was actually called "Where Is Your Heart." The music was composed by George Auric, and the original French lyrics were written by Jacques Larue. The lyrics were later translated into English by William Engvick. See "The Song from Moulin Rouge," Wikipedia, http://en.wikipedia.org/wiki/The_Song_from_Moulin_Rouge.

6. "Lollipops and Roses" is a song written by Tony Velona that became very well known through many cover versions recorded by artists such as Jack Jones (1962), Perry Como (1962), Doris Day (1963), and relatively recently by Natalie Cole (2008). See "Lollipops and Roses (Song)," Wikipedia, http://en.wikipedia.org/wiki/Lollipops_and_Roses_%28song%29.

7. Roy indicated that Leslie Coard could also play drums, guitar, bass, and piano.

8. While it is undoubtedly influenced by Caribbean aesthetics, I also associate Roy's tone and playing with the saxophonists of the 1950s and 1960s, and in particular with those recognized as Charlie Parker's disciples, those who are associated with the late 1950s postbebop era. These sax players are deeply influenced by Parker's harmonic sense and improvising style. They use long phrases over chord changes and have strong roots in the blues. Among them, the saxophonist that first comes to mind is Julian "Cannonball" Adderley—the Adderley in his 1962 bossa nova period, not the Adderley of 1959, in which he played with Miles Davis on the studio album *Kind of Blue*, with a different, more forceful approach.

This connection I make between Adderley and Roy Cape may surprise a few people. As the sobriquet "Cannonball" suggests, Cannonball Adderley was a big man, whereas Roy Cape has a slim body. Journalistic accounts, as well as those of music aficionados, often view the physical stature of a musician as indicative of his sound on the instrument. For example, if you hear a big sound you imagine the sax player as a big man. Yet despite their sharply contrasting physical statures, I want to suggest that Roy and Cannonball share a very similar approach to sound production and, to a large extent, a style of improvisation.

Like Roy, Cannonball produces full-bodied notes and warm tones. For example, in the recording of "Cannonball's Bossa Nova," he lands right in the middle of the note with a clean tone and then wiggles a descending melodic line. Listen to how he moves from one pitch to a higher tone with smooth, light legato. Hear how Adderley demonstrates his talent as a melodist in songs like "O Amor Em Paz (Once I Loved)," or "Corcovado (Quiet Nights)." He uses chord substitution and a modal framework, and he anticipates chord changes to create wonderful long phrases in his improvisation. Similarly, when Roy performs his solo in "Name the Game '79" on the *Black Stalin Live* album, he plays all over the mode, with spiraling, swirling eighth notes and, like Adderley in "Bossa Nova," lands on the particular notes that have value in the rhythmic phrases.

Some Trinidadian musicians, including the renowned trumpet player Errol Ince, associate Roy's sound, however, not with Cannonball Adderley but rather with Paul Desmond. In an interview with me, Errol Ince explained how in the early 1960s Paul Desmond was heard over and over on the radio playing "Take Five" (composed by Paul Desmond and performed by the Dave Brubeck Quartet on the 1959 album *Time Out*). In Ince's words, "I think that he [Roy] has just adopted that sound, even if he got it a bit heavier, but I think that he has a Paul Desmond kind of sound." As we listened together to "Take Five," Ince added, "Not harsh, very soulful, this is how Paul Desmond plays. So when you hear Paul Desmond, you hear Roy Cape in my view. Or when you hear Roy Cape, you hear Paul Desmond. . . . Although he didn't study him, Roy captured everything—the feelings and the approach, you know. . . . Since he never really concentrated on solo in other bands, he never developed to another style and moved on to a Cannonball or Charlie Parker or John Coltrane, and nothing wrong with that. . . . Roy's a very lyrical, lyrical player. He's not a bebop player, but once you know, you could say he [Roy] studied Miles too. . . . Because Miles is very lyrical. He moved on from what he used to do into a more lyrical type in a certain era. So that kind of approach between a Miles 'Kind of Blue' and a Paul Desmond figure, that's Roy definitely" (interview with Errol Ince, June 2012). On these different playing styles, see Sheridan (2000) and Yanaw (2005) on Cannonball Adderley; Gioia (1988) and Brown (2000) on Paul Desmond; and Szwed (2002) and Tirro (2009) on Miles Davis.

9. The description that I just presented of improvisation in a calypso style, I should emphasize, is based on how most local wind players would perform for a local audience in the 1960s and 1970s. The local style of improvisation varies tremendously depending on the instrument and the performing venue. For example, several steel pan players today, such as Boogsie Sharpe, use a virtuosic style of playing in their improvisation over calypso tunes. Many pianists in the 1950s and 1960s, including Otmar De Vuglt (also musical director of the Dutchy Brothers), playing in nightclubs for mostly a listening audience, were also famous for their virtuosic style of playing and improvising.

10. The station was set up in 1943 and broadcast until 1947 (see Nepture 2007).

11. Roy differs from Paul Desmond in one other important way: his improvisational

style. As Steven Feld remarked after listening to Roy's playing, in contrast to Paul Desmond, who was a cerebral improviser who played select notes that demonstrated his deep knowledge of harmony, Roy is a melodist, a romantic balladeer. On Paul Desmond's improvisation style, see Gioia (1988).

12. In consulting several archives of Trinidadian newspapers from the 1960s to the 1980s, I was struck by the frequent visits of African American artists and by the announcement of the much-awaited performances of major African stars. As Paul Gilroy insightfully remarks, these points of contact have been crucial in forging the intercultural and transnational formation of what he calls "the black Atlantic" and "diasporic intimacies" (Gilroy 1993), and the nurturing of "conviviality" in multicultural societies like Trinidad (Gilroy 2005). On how these points of contact have nurtured a shared musical sensibility among African diasporas, see Monson (1999) and Rommen (2009, 2011).

13. *Trinidad Guardian*, February 2, 1967, 5.

14. In the late 1980s, the Carnival Development Committee was renamed the National Carnival Commission. On the work of these agencies, see Guilbault (2007, chapter 2). On the Best Village Competitions, see Craig (1985), Birth (2008), and Guilbault (2010b).

15. On how calypso acquired pride of place in Trinidad and Tobago, see Warner (1982), Rohlehr (1990), Hill (1993), Liverpool (1993), Koningsbruggen (1997), Regis (1999), and Guilbault (2007).

16. I thank both Shawn Randoo and Alvin Daniell for sharing with me this information on recording studios during this period.

17. Roy indicates that before Frankie Francis, Roderick Borde was already writing scores for calypso from the early 1940s. However, through his reputation as an arranger and the sheer number of arrangements he wrote, Francis is recognized today as having greatly helped make written calypso arrangements the rule rather than the exception.

18. This consolidation of a musical hierarchy allegedly occasioned by the new requirements of recording studios well exemplifies what is meant by the assertion repeatedly made over the past thirty-plus years that "materiality has power" and that it is ineluctably in synergetic relations with humans. See Bourdieu (1977), Appadurai (1986), and Miller (1987, 2005).

19. As Brother Resistance further explains, in spite of the fact that LP records were already available in the first half of the 1970s and enabled the recording of songs over sixteen minutes for dance music and deejays in dance clubs (a U.K. 12-inch version of the disco song, "Love to Love You Baby (Come on Over to My Place Version)" on Casablanca CANX 1014 went as long as 16:50 minutes), the new radio formats aiming to boost record sales and to attract larger audiences prevailed. If during the 1970s there were still some recordings of calypso that lasted six or even seven minutes, the trend of producing shorter recordings was set. By the late 1970s and early 1980s, radio policies in Trinidad required artists to pro-

duce songs of no more than three or four minutes maximum. On radio formats and admissible lengths of recordings at different times in the United States, see Keith (2007).
20. The great popularity of the calypso cover versions of famous foreign songs in Trinidad in the 1960s reminds me of the *Cannibalist Manifesto* (*Manifesto Antropófago* in Portuguese) written by the Brazilian poet Oswald de Andrade, published in 1928. Basically, Andrade believed that Brazil's greatest strength rested in its ability to "cannibalize" other cultures by incorporating them, reappropriating them, and reworking them as new creations. This was one of the concepts that characterized the Brazilian Tropicalia movement in the 1960s and 1970s (see Béhague 1980).

4. Leading the Band

1. On Caribbean immigration, see, for example, Kasinitz (1992), Basch, Schiller, and Blanc (1994), Hintzen (2001), Puri (2003), and Scher (2003), to name only a few. On migrants' return, see Thomas-Hope (1986), Pessar (1996), Goulbourne (1999), and Plaza and Henry (2006).
2. Roy Cape: KH Studio was a big modern studio that Mr. Leslie Samaroo had built on Frederick Street. I guess he realized it was in a bad location, so he moved the studio to Sea Lots. JG: How would you compare his studio with those in New York at the time? RC: Mr. Samaroo built that studio to be compatible to the RCA Studio in New York. It was a beautiful room; a lot of nice music came from there.
3. The Revue Calypso Tent is famously associated with Lord Kitchener, who sang there from 1964 until 2000 when he passed away (with the exception of 1965, when he refused to sing because of a contractual dispute).
4. While in New York, Roy listened to Lord Shorty's music and was impressed to learn that Shorty had his own band—the second calypsonian after Sparrow to have his own band. On Lord Shorty (who later dubbed himself Ras Shorty I), see Guilbault (2007: 172–77).
5. On the confinement of calypso to the carnival season as part of the long legacy of the colonial administration and the Catholic Church, see Rohlehr (1990) and Cowley (1996).
6. The abbreviation TnT refers to Trinidad and Tobago.
7. All the dollar figures mentioned here are in Trinidadian dollars.
8. Here I was thinking that the local has never been just local. It has always been infused with the presence (physical or virtual) of many foreign artists from many different locales with varying degrees of transnational recognition and influence.
9. Artist's description found in "Evelyn King (Singer)," Wikipedia, http://en.wikipedia.org/wiki/Evelyn_King_(singer).
10. Juliet Robin is a classically trained musician who plays several instruments, including violin, viola, piano, cuatro, double bass, clarinet, and drums. As a keyboard player, she performed with several soca bands and toured overseas. She

also played in the all-women's jazz band the Jazz Tripple. She continues to perform locally as an instrumentalist and also as a vocalist while earning a business degree at the University of the West Indies in Trinidad.

11. On how the playing of some instruments is highly gendered, see Brunet (2012).
12. During carnival, "bomb" can also refer to the strategic performance of a new arrangement of a classic song that a steelband has been rehearsing in secret and is now playing, to the delight of its supporters. It refers to a performance of a classic that comes as a surprise (and sometimes annoyance) of the other bands since it may undermine their chances of winning that competition. See Stuempfle (1995) and Dudley (2008).
13. Groovy soca refers to a moderate-tempo soca tune, typically adopting the verse-refrain format and featuring love lyrics. It shares the rhythmic foundation of power soca but differs from the latter by foregrounding soft-sounding arrangements. In contrast, power soca, as its name suggests, refers to a fast-tempo (up to 160 beats per minute) tune aiming to raise energy. It is filled with many melodic ideas and call-and-response sections. Its lyrics, punctuated by brass riffs, are replete with injunctions to let go, free up, and enjoy yourself. While some power soca includes sociopolitical commentaries, the majority of the tunes feature lyrics that have one mission: to incite people to move together, dance, and enjoy themselves.
14. Most musicians in the calypso music scene have typically earned their incomes not through record sales but through live performances.
15. On Eddy Grant's successful career, go to his official website, Eddy Grant, http://www.eddygrant.com/site/main.html.
16. Today known as Ann Marie "Twiggy" Parks-Kojo, Twiggy won her first-year Calypso Queen title in 1985 and won again in 2009.
17. On ringbang, see Best (2004).
18. The writing of four beats in common time is done in one measure, whereas writing four beats in cut time requires the arranger to put down two measures. So writing in cut time represents more work for the arranger.
19. In Trinidad, the term "fete" refers to parties organized privately by music sponsors or individuals during carnival or other occasions throughout the year (e.g., Mother's Day, yearly party of a particular workers' association, and so on). These fetes take place either outdoors (in a public park or the enclosed space of a private institution or residence) or indoors (in large or small venues). The number of attendees at a fete can greatly vary, ranging from one hundred to several thousand people.
20. Charlie's Roots was really the first band that decided they were going to play only local music.
21. Initially, I confused the Brass Festival with what was called Brassorama. As Roy explained, Brassorama was a festival held in the 1960s, long before the Brass Festival. In his recollection, "the first Brassorama was set at Queen's Hall. The

Dutchy Brothers won that first festival after competing with bands like Mano Marcelin, Ray Sylvester, Gemini Brass. I believe that Brassorama began when I was with Clarence Curvan [in the early 1960s]. The Dutchy Brothers, who had two horns, trumpet and tenor saxophone, at some later time also included an alto sax. And that was their brass. You would find that Mano [Marcelin] and Ray [Sylvester] probably would have had four trumpets, three trombones, four saxophones—the standard big band. Our band with Clarence Curvan had four trumpets, three trombones, and four saxophones. We were heavily booked, so at that time we did not see the need to be in Brassorama. Shortly after that, [when I was with] Ron Berridge (I am not talking for Ron, but I am talking for me), we did not see the need to play in Brassorama. Ron Berridge had one year in 1965, at the Original Revue, and after the carnival, we went straight on the road. We did a trip to Barbados, and when we came back from there, we did a nonstop with the Dutchy Brothers. We were a crowd puller. So there was no need for us to be in Brassorama. Not to downplay Brassorama, but from the time that Ron Berridge was launched, we were at the top of the game, we were the top of brass orchestra in Trinidad and Tobago."
22. This shopping mall has now been renamed the Falls of Westmall.
23. The Spektakula calypso tent refers to the cast of artists performing, whereas the Spektakula Forum houses the Spektakula calypso tent.
24. Soon after carnival, people in the streets kept asking Roy whether he would sing again next year. Roy considered returning to the stage and even wrote another soca song called "Trinbago" (also called "Sing Your Song") but finally decided to concentrate his efforts on his band.
25. Since this conversation in 2010, more changes of singers have occurred. In December 2011, the singer Olatunji left Roy's band, and was replaced by another male singer, Ricardo Drue. And at the beginning of the 2012 carnival season, Rita was replaced by another female singer, Darnelle Simmons.

5. Remembering with Pictures

1. Poole (1997: 8), quoted in Pinney (2005: 8). As Pinney reports, Poole uses the term "economy" for another reason: "I use the word 'economy' . . . with the intention of capturing this sense of how visual images move across national and cultural boundaries." The problem of not finding many visual images of musicians in the Trinidadian newspaper archives indeed is not simply a problem unique to this newspaper or to Trinidadian culture, but rather a problem that crosses national and cultural boundaries.
2. On recording technologies, see John Eargle's (2003) useful *Handbook of Recording Engineering*.
3. On Caribbean diasporic connections among artists, see Hill (1993), Aparicio and Jáquez (2003), Scher (2003), Green and Scher (2007), and Ramnarine (2007).
4. "Roy Cape: Still Top Brass after 41 Years" (1999: 8).

5. Krister Malm is a highly recognized Swedish ethnomusicologist who has done research on several musical cultures of many countries, including Sweden and different parts of Africa, South Asia, and Latin America. Professor Malm also served as an assistant director of the Trinidad and Tobago Government Folklore Archives between 1969 and 1972. On his impressive career, see "Krister Malm: Biographical Note," http://www.kaiso.se/km.
6. Many bandleaders like Roy have indeed opted to include a female lead singer in their bands, including Byron Lee (of Byron Lee and the Dragonaires), Bobby Quan (of Blue Ventures), Cliff Harris (of Atlantik), Andy Joseph (of Traffik), Joey Ng Wai (of Imaj and Co.), Colin Lucas (of Sound Revolution), Bunji Garlin (of Asylum Band), Machel Montano (Machel Montano HD Band), Carl Jacob (of Shandileer), Robin Imamshah (of Taxi), and Raymond Ramnarine (of Dil E Nadan), to name only a few.

6. Working with Roy

1. Affective labor, Michael Hardt writes, is one face of what he calls "immaterial labor" (1999: 90). It is immaterial "in the sense that its products are intangible: a feeling of ease, well-being, satisfaction, excitement, passion—even a sense of connectedness of community" (96). It has long been recognized that affect plays a foundational role in the entertainment music industry. What has been far less often acknowledged is how a bandleader's affective labor plays a crucial role not only in keeping musicians in a band, but also in making them play to the best of their abilities.
2. On the performativity of words, see Austin (1961) and Butler (1993, 1997).
3. On the nuts and bolts of making documentary and ethnographic films and videos, see Barbash and Taylor (1997).
4. I thank Steven Feld for sharing with me his experience of filmmaking and his knowledge of the vocabulary used in creating documentaries.
5. See John A. Lucy's (1993) classic book *Reflexive Language*, and the well-known sociological study of Erving Goffman (1981), *Forms of Talk*.

7. Circulation

1. I use the term "celebrity" here in terms of social recognition. Sometimes, people imagine celebrity as synonymous with fame and fortune. The sociology of these categories is treated in many studies of stardom, including *Stardom and Celebrity: A Reader*, edited by Sean Redmond and Su Homes (2007).
2. The new immigration laws passed in 1965 abolished the national origins quota system to replace it "with a preference system that focused on immigrants' skills and family relationships with citizens or residents of the U.S." "Immigration and Nationality Act of 1965," Wikipedia, http://en.wikipedia.org/wiki/Immigration_and_Nationality_Act_of_1965. See the informative work of Cordero-Guzman and Grosfoguel (2000). See also Cordero-Guzman, Smith, and Grosfoguel (2001).

3. The description of WOMAD is a paraphrase of material from its website, "Our WOMAD Story," WOMAD, http://womad.org/about/.
4. Many population groups in the Caribbean—East Indians in particular, who represent in Trinidad slightly more than half of the population—could contest this assertion that Roy Cape All Stars represents the Caribbean. After all, Roy's band does not include any East Indian musicians or only very rarely East Indian sounds. However, the affective attachments that sounds create after having been heard by East Indians and Afro-Caribbeans alike sometimes bypass people's differences to emphasize instead a sense of place. This is, I believe, what my friends from different islands living in diaspora—in Canada—mean when they say they hear Roy's band as a band from home.
5. By "calypso tent conditions," I mean little time to rehearse, having to accompany calypsonians of varying musical abilities, playing tunes that you did not choose, and so on.
6. While parties in Trinidad usually assemble crowds who are in their late teens and early twenties, there are always several audience members that are older—at times, much older. To connect parties only with youth is thus problematic. For an in-depth exploration of this issue, see Huq (2006: 1–89).
7. On space as social relations, see Lefebvre (1992) and Massey (2005). For an inspiring publication on the productive force of social relations in music, see Diamond (2007).
8. On the thorny issue of race relations in Trinidad, see Ryan (1972), Hintzen (1989, 1999), Puri (1999), Allahar (2000), Manuel (2000a), and Khan (2004).
9. As the term indicates, chutney soca refers to the mix of chutney (an East Indian musical tradition), and soca (itself the product of mixing calypso rhythms and harmony with chutney-inflected melodies and/or East Indian lyrical themes). Also see Ramnarine (1996, 2001), Manuel (1998, 2000b), and Guilbault (2007).
10. Roy is referring to the fact that in the late 1960s and early 1970s, calypso was combined with Indian rhythms to produce what has become known as soca. Around the same time, calypso was also combined with the vocal delivery of poetry based on Trinidadian speech—a fusion that led to the emergence of yet another musical style, dubbed rapso. The popularity of soca in the late 1970s in its turn contributed to the production of other musical offshoots, chutney soca and ragga soca.
11. On the role of East Indians in the calypso music scene, see Constance (1991) and Reddock (2000).
12. As has been widely acknowledged, race alone cannot be conceived as providing a guarantee for sharing sensibilities and experiences. Colonial histories, socioeconomic conditions, class, and so on all contribute to the production of difference. See Hintzen and Rahier (2003) and Bodenheimer (2010).
13. I am reminded here of Benjamin Brinner's (2009) book *Playing across a Divide*, in which he usefully elaborates the notion of networking. See also Packman (2007).

Afterword

1. It is not for lack of trying. I spent months trying to assemble the images and sounds, but was thwarted both by the nonexistence of material and by copyright issues, which severely limit circulation.
2. Roy here is reminded of Shakespeare's *Twelfth Night* and the lovesick duke's remark, "If music be the food of love, play on."

SELECT DISCOGRAPHY

Roy Cape has made hundreds of recordings. What is included here represents a very select discography of his work with only his own band, sometimes appearing as Roy Cape Kaiso All Stars and at other times as simply Roy Cape All Stars. As is now often the case for many soca recordings, in some recent productions Roy's lead singers record with only Roy's band arranger. Their voices are then accompanied by electronic keyboard and computer-generated sounds. Even in theses cases, however, Roy Cape All Stars is the executive producer and the title appears under this name.

Roy Cape Kaiso All Stars. 1990. *First Time*. Rainbow Wirl.
———. 1995. *Highway to Kaiso*. Ice Records.
———. 1996. "Judgement Day." *Hotter Than July*. CRS Music.
———. 1999. *1999*. RCSLP.
———. 1999. "Dust Dem (Stampede)" featuring Kurt Allen. *Soca Stampede*.
———. 1999. *Ready to Go!* Hot Vinyl.
———. 2000. *Ready Again*. Rituals Music.
———. 2000. "Mudd" featuring Derrick Seales. *Jouvay* RCRP.
———. 2000. "Rags." *Caribbean Party Rhythms 5*. Rituals Music.
———. 2001. *Now and Beyond*. Hot Vinyl.
———. 2001. "Tremble It," featuring Destra. *Soca Anthems 2*. Hot Vinyl.
———. 2001. "Tremble It," "Doh Take It On (A Horn Is a Horn)." *Caribbean Party Rhythms Six*. Rituals Music.
———. 2002. *Still Together*. Hot Vinyl.
———. 2003. "Fun Cyar Done," "De Count," "Friends," "Pan in Paradise," and "Dr. Seales" featuring Derrick Seales, "Stick on It" featuring Esther Dyer, "Stop D War" and "We Jammin" featuring Blaxx. Various: *Band Fever*. Trinidad and Tobago, 2003 Soca Compilation.

———. 2004. "Sugar Shack" and "Carnival Saga." *Glow '04: The Soundtrack.*
———. 2005. "Dust Dem (Stampede)" featuring Kurt Allen. *Pure Soca.*
———. 2005. "It's Not a Crime" featuring Blaxx. *Glow '05: The Soundtrack.*
———. 2005. *Remember Jah*, featuring Esther Dyer, Blaxx, Derrick Seales. Roy Cape Productions.
———. 2005. "Tremble It" featuring Destra Garcia. *Soca Anthems Collection.*
———. 2006. *Carnival Feeling.* Roy Cape Productions.
———. 2006. "Carnival Feeling" featuring Rita Jones. *Soca Gold 10th Anniversary.* VP Records.
———. 2006. "Name the Game" featuring Black Stalin. *Live! Collector's Edition.*
———. 2007. *Dutty.* Roy Cape Productions. SJP.
———. 2008. *Better Than Ever: Masters of Soca.* Executive producers: Roy Cape and Carlysle "Juiceman" Roberts.
———. 2008. "Breathless" featuring Blaxx. *Soca Gold.* VP Records.
———. 2009. "Tusty" featuring Blaxx. *Soca Gold.* VP Records.
———. 2010. "Huntin'" featuring Blaxx. *Soca Gold.* VP Records.
———. 2011. "Tanty Woi" featuring Blaxx. *Best of the Best Soca Hits and Grooves 11.* VP Records.
———. 2012. "Inna Band" featuring Blaxx. *Soca Gold.* VP Records.
———. 2013. *Spread Yuh Hands an Leh Go.* Compilation of Roy Cape All Stars hits featuring Blaxx. Crosby Distribution.

REFERENCES

Abe, Marié. 2010. "Resonances of Chindon-ya: Sound, Space, and Social Difference in Contemporary Japan." PhD diss., University of California, Berkeley.

Abrahams, Roger. 1972. "Christmas and Carnival on Saint Vincent." *Western Folklore* 31(4): 275–89.

———. 1975. "Negotiating Respect: Patterns of Presentation among Black Women." *Journal of American Folklore* 88(347): 58–80.

Alexis, Anthony. 1994. "Caribana Glory: Roy Cape Cops 'Best Playing Band' Title." *Sunday Punch*, August 7.

———. 1996. "Soca Cape of Good Hope: RC and Kaiso All Stars Enjoying Cash-Register Success in a Big Way." *Sunday Punch*.

Allahar, Anton. 2000. "Popular Culture and Racialisation of Political Consciousness in Trinidad." In *Identity, Ethnicity and Culture in the Caribbean*, edited by Ralph R. Premdas, 246–81. St. Augustine, Trinidad: School of Continuing Studies, University of the West Indies.

Allen, Ray, and Lois Wilcken, eds. 2001. *Island Sounds in the Global City: Caribbean Popular Music and Identity in New York*. Champaign: University of Illinois Press.

Anderson, Tim J. 2006. *Making Easy Listening: Material Culture and Postwar American Recording*. Minneapolis: University of Minnesota Press.

Andrade, Oswald de. 1928. "Manifesto Antropófago." *Revista de Antropofagia* 1(1).

Annisette, Marcy. 2006. "People and Periods Untouched by Accounting History: An Ancient Yoruba Practice." *Accounting History* 11(4): 399–417.

Aparicio, Frances R., and Cándida F. Jáquez. 2003. *Transnationalism and Cultural Hybridity in Latin/o America*. New York: Palgrave Macmillan.

Appadurai, Arjun, ed. 1986. *The Social Life of Things: Commodities in Cultural Perspective*. Cambridge: Cambridge University Press.

———. 1996. *Modernity at Large: Cultural Dimensions of Globalization*. Minneapolis: University of Minnesota Press.

Appiah, Kwame Anthony. 1998. "Cosmopolitan Patriots." In *Cosmopolitics*, edited by Pheng Cheah and Bruce Robbins, 91–114. Minneapolis: University of Minnesota Press.

Austin, J. L. 1961. *Philosophical Papers*. Oxford: Oxford University Press.

Averill, Gage. 1998. "Moving the Big Apple: Tabou Combo's Diasporic Dreams." In *Island Sounds in the Global City: Caribbean Popular Music and Identity in New York*, edited by Ray Allen and Lois Wilcken, 138–61. New York: New York Folklore Society and Institute for Studies in American Music.

Bakhtin, Mikhail M. 1982. *The Dialogic Imagination: Four Essays by M. M. Bakhtin*, edited by Michael Holquist and Caryl Emerson and translated by Vadim Liapunov and Kenneth Brostrom. Austin: University of Texas Press.

———. 1984 [1929]. *Problems of Dostoevsky's Poetics*, translated by Caryl Emerson. Minneapolis: University of Minnesota Press.

Barbash, Ilisa, and Lucien Taylor. 1997. *Cross-Cultural Filmmaking: A Handbook for Making Documentary and Ethnographic Films and Videos*. Berkeley: University of California Press.

Basch, Linda, Nina Glick Schiller, and Cristina Szanton Blanc. 1994. *Nations Unbound: Transnational Projects, Postcolonial Predicaments and Deterritorialized Nation-States*. New York: Gordon and Breach.

Basso, Keith. 1996. *Wisdom Sits in Places: Landscape and Language among the Western Apache*. Albuquerque: University of New Mexico Press.

Becker, Howard. 2008. *Art Worlds: 25th Anniversary Edition, Updated and Expanded*. Berkeley: University of California Press.

Béhague, Gerard. 1980. "Brazilian Musical Values of the 1960s and 1970s: Popular Urban Music from Bossa Nova to Tropicalia." *Journal of Popular Culture* 14(3): 437–52.

Bennett, Andy, and Richard A. Peterson, eds. 2004. *Music Scenes: Local, Translocal, and Virtual*. Nashville, TN: Vanderbilt University Press.

Berliner, Paul. 1994. *Thinking in Jazz: The Infinite Art of Improvisation*. Chicago: University of Chicago Press.

Best, Curwen. 2004. *Culture @ the Cutting Edge: Tracking Caribbean Popular Music*. Mona, Jamaica: University of the West Indies Press.

Birth, Kevin K. 2008. *Bacchanalian Sentiments: Musical Experiences and Political Counterpoints in Trinidad*. Durham, NC: Duke University Press.

Björnberg, Alf. 2009. "Learning to Listen to Perfect Sound: Hi-Fi Culture and Changes in Modes of Listening, 1950–80." In *The Ashgate Research Companion to Popular Musicology*, edited by Derek B. Scott, 105–29. Burlington, VT: Ashgate.

Blau, Dick, Charles Keil, Angeliki Vellou Keil, and Steven Feld. 2002. *Bright Balkan Morning: Romani Lives and the Power of Music in Greek Macedonia*. Middletown, CT: Wesleyan University Press.

Blood, Peter Ray. 1994. "Soca's Cape of Good Hope." *Sunday Guardian*, November 27, 41.

Bodenheimer, Rebecca. 2010. "Localizing Hybridity: The Politics of Place in Contemporary Cuban Rumba Performance." PhD diss., University of California, Berkeley.

Born, Georgina, and David Hesmondhagh, eds. 2000. *Western Music and Its Others: Difference, Representation, and Appropriation in Music*. Berkeley: University of California Press.

Bourdieu, Pierre. 1977. *Outline of a Theory of Practice*. Cambridge: Cambridge University Press.

———. 1979. *La distinction: Critique sociale du jugement*. Paris: Editions de Minuit.

Bowers, Jane, and Judith Tick, eds. 1986. *Women Making Music: The Western Art Tradition, 1150–1950*. Urbana: University of Illinois Press.

Boyarin, Jonathan. 1994. *Remapping Memory: The Politics of TimeSpace*. Minneapolis: University of Minnesota Press.

Brinner, Benjamin. 2009. *Playing across a Divide: Israeli-Palestinian Musical Encounters*. New York: Oxford University Press.

Brothers, Thomas, ed. 1999. *Louis Armstrong in His Own Words: Selected Writings*. New York: Oxford University Press.

Brown, L. B. 2000. "'Feeling My Way': Jazz Improvisation and Its Vicissitudes, a Plea for Imperfection." *Journal of Aesthetics and Art Criticism* 58(2): 113–23.

Brunet, Carla. 2012. "Carnaval, Samba Schools and the Negotiation of Gendered Femininities in São Paolo, Brazil." PhD diss., University of California, Berkeley.

Burns, Mick. 2006. *Keeping the Beat on the Street*. Baton Rouge: Louisiana State University Press.

Butler, Judith. 1993. *Bodies That Matter: On the Discursive Limits of "Sex."* New York: Routledge.

———. 1997. "Sovereign Performatives." In *Excitable Speech: A Politics of the Performative*, 71–102. New York: Routledge.

"Carnival Bands: The Cape That Covers Kaiso." 1992. *Sunday Guardian*, February 16.

"Carnival Dance Diary." 1967. *Trinidad Guardian*, February 2, 5.

Chandler, Karen. 2009. "Jazzforum: Jazz and Its South Carolina Roots: A Jazz History and Education Model of the Charleston Jazz Initiative." *JAZZed: Practical Ideas and Techniques for Jazz Educators*, 63–65.

Charles, Ray, and David Ritz. 1978. *Brother Ray: Ray Charles' Own Story*. New York: Dial.

Clifford, James. 1983. "On Ethnographic Authority." *Representations* 2: 118–46.

Clifford, James, and George E. Marcus, eds. 1986. *Writing Culture: The Poetics and Politics of Ethnography*. Berkeley: University of California Press.

Connerton, Paul. 1989. *How Societies Remember*. Cambridge: Cambridge University Press.

Constance, Zeno Obi. 1991. *Tassa, Chutney and Soca: The East Indian Contribution to the Calypso*. Trinidad: Author.

Cordero-Guzmán, Héctor R., and Ramón Grosfoguel. 2000. *The Demographic and Socio-economic Characteristics of Post-1965 Immigrants to New York City: A Comparative Analysis by National Origin.* Oxford: Blackwell.

Cordero-Guzmán, Héctor R., Robert C. Smith, and Ramón Grosfoguel. 2001. *Migration, Transnationalization, and Race in a Changing New York.* Philadelphia: Temple University Press.

Cowley, John. 1996. *Carnival, Canboulay and Calypso: Traditions in the Making.* Cambridge: Cambridge University Press.

Craig, Susan. 1985. "Political Patronage and Community Resistance: Village Councils in Trinidad." In *Rural Development in the Caribbean*, edited by P. I. Gomes, 173–93. New York: St. Martin's.

Cross, Richard. 2012. "Vivaldi's Girls: Music Therapy in 18th Century Venice." Accessed May 16. http://www.users.cloud9.net/~recross/why-not/Vivaldi.html.

Dance, Stanley. 1970. *The World of Duke Ellington.* New York: C. Scribner's Sons.

Danielsen, Anne, ed. 2010. *Musical Rhythm in the Age of Digital Reproduction.* Burlington, VT: Ashgate.

Danielson, Virginia. 1997. *The Voice of Egypt: Umm Kulthum, Arabic Song, and Egyptian Society in the Twentieth Century.* Chicago: University of Chicago Press.

De Couve, Alicia C., Claudia Dal Pino, and Ana Lucía Frega. 2004. "An Approach to the History of Music Education in Latin America Part II: Music Education 16th–18th Centuries." *Journal of Historical Research in Music Education* 25(2): 79–95.

De Leon, Sherry Ann. 1996. "Roy Cape: The Sweetest Sax in Soca Music." [Trinidad] *Daily Challenge* 25(121): 12.

Diamond, Beverley. 2007. "The Music of Modern Indigeneity: From Identity to Alliance Studies." *European Meetings in Ethnomusicology* 12: 169–90.

Diamond, Beverley, M. Sam Cronk, and Franziska von Rosen. 1994. *Visions of Sound: Musical Instruments of First Nations Communities in Northeastern America.* Waterloo, ON: Wilfrid Laurier University Press.

Dudley, Shannon Kingdon. 2001. "Ray Holman and the Changing Role of the Steelband, 1957–72." *Latin American Music Review* 22(2): 183–98.

———. 2002. "The Steelband's 'Own Tune': Nationalism, Festivity and Musical Strategies in Trinidad's Panorama Competition." *Black Music Research Journal* 22(1): 13–36.

———. 2003. "Creativity and Constraint in Trinidad Carnival Competitions." *World of Music* 45(1): 11–34.

———. 2008. *Music from behind the Bridge: Steelband Spirit and the Politics of Festivity in Trinidad and Tobago.* Berkeley: University of California Press.

Eargle, John. 2003. *Handbook of Recording Engineering.* Boston: Kluwer Academic.

Erlmann, Veit. 1991. *African Stars: Studies in Black South African Performance.* Chicago: University of Chicago Press.

———. 1996. *Nightsong: Performance, Power, and Practice in South Africa.* Chicago: University of Chicago Press.

———. 1999. *Music, Modernity, and the Global Imagination: South Africa and the West.* New York: Oxford University Press.

Faris, James. 2005. "Navajo and Photography." In *Photography's Other Histories*, edited by Christopher Pinney and Nicolas Peterson, 85–99. Durham, NC: Duke University Press.

Feld, Steven. 1987. "Dialogic Editing: Interpreting How Kaluli Read *Sound and Sentiment.*" *Cultural Anthropology* 2(2): 190–210.

———. 1996. "Waterfalls of Song: An Acoustemology of Place Resounding in Bosavi, Papua New Guinea." In *Senses of Place*, edited by Steven Feld and Keith Basso, 91–135. Santa Fe, NM: School of American Research Press.

———. 2000. "A Sweet Lullaby for World Music." *Public Culture* 12(1): 145–71.

———. 2004. "Doing Anthropology in Sound (A Conversation with Don Brenneis)." *American Ethnologist* 31(4): 461–74.

———. 2007. "Gazing through Transparency." In *Exposures: A White Woman in West Africa, Virginia Ryan.* Santa Fe, NM: VoxLox.

———. 2012a. *Jazz Cosmopolitanism in Accra: Five Musical Years in Ghana.* Durham, NC: Duke University Press.

———. 2012b. *Sound and Sentiment: Birds, Weeping, Poetics, and Song in Kaluli Expression*, 3rd ed. Durham, NC: Duke University Press.

Feld, Steven, and Keith H. Basso, eds. 1996. *Senses of Place.* Santa Fe, NM: School of American Research Press.

Finnegan, Ruth. 1989. *The Hidden Musicians: Music-Making in an English Town.* Cambridge: Cambridge University Press.

Flaes, Rob Boonzajer. 2000. *Brass Unbound: Secret Children of the Colonial Brass Band.* Amsterdam: Royal Tropical Institute.

Flavo, Rosa Maria. 2008. "Postfasione." In *Multiple Entries: Africa e Oltre 2001–2008*, edited by Virginia Ryan. Spoleto, Italy: Galleria Civica d'Arte Moderna.

Foucault, Michel. 1980 [1972]. "The Eye of Power." In *Power/Knowledge: Selected Interviews and Other Writings 1972–1977*, edited by Colin Gordon. New York: Pantheon.

Franklin, Aretha, and David Ritz. 1999. *Aretha: From These Roots.* New York: Villard.

Friedson, Eliot. 1990. "Labors of Love: A Prospectus." In *The Nature of Work: Sociological Perspectives*, edited by Kai Erikson and Steven Peter Vallas, 149–61. New Haven, CT: Yale University Press.

Frisbie, Charlotte, ed. 2001. *Tall Woman: The Life Story of Rose Mitchell, a Navajo Woman, c. 1874–1977.* Albuquerque: University of New Mexico Press.

Giddins, Gary. 1988. *Satchmo.* New York: Doubleday.

Gilroy, Paul. 1993. *The Black Atlantic: Modernity and Double Consciousness.* Cambridge, MA: Harvard University Press.

———. 2005. *Postcolonial Melancholia.* New York: Columbia University Press.

Gioia, Ted. 1988. *The Imperfect Art: Reflections on Jazz and Modern Culture.* New York: Oxford University Press.

Goffman, Erving. 1981. *Forms of Talk*. Philadelphia: University of Pennsylvania Press.

Goulbourne, Harry. 1999. "Exodus? Some Social and Policy Implications of Return Migration from the UK to the Commonwealth Caribbean in the 1990s." *Policy Studies* 20(3): 157–72.

Gracyk, Theodore. 1996. "Record Consciousness." In *Rhythm and Noise: An Aesthetics of Rock*. Durham, NC: Duke University Press.

———. 2001. "Texts and Intertextuality." In *I Wanna Be Me: Rock Music and the Politics of Identity*. Philadelphia: Temple University Press.

Green, Garth, and Philip W. Scher, eds. 2007. *Trinidad Carnival: The Cultural Politics of a Transnational Festival*. Bloomington: Indiana University Press.

Grenier, Line, and Jocelyne Guilbault. 2006. "Créolité and Francophonie in Music: Socio-musical Positioning Where It Matters." *Cultural Studies* 11(2): 207–34.

Guilbault, Jocelyne. 1993. "On Redefining the Local through World Music." *World of Music* 35(2): 33–47.

———. 2001. "World Music." In *The Cambridge Companion to Pop and Rock*, edited by Simon Frith and Will Straw, 176–92. Cambridge: Cambridge University Press.

———. 2004. "On Redefining the Nation through Party Music." In *Culture in Action: Carnival in Trinidad and Tobago*, edited by Milla Riggio, 228–38. New York: Routledge.

———. 2005. "Audible Entanglements: Nation and Diasporas in Trinidad's Calypso Music Scenes." *Small Axe* 17: 40–63.

———. 2007. *Governing Sound: The Cultural Politics of Trinidad's Carnival Musics*. Chicago: University of Chicago Press.

———. 2010a. "Music, Politics, and Pleasure: Live Soca in Trinidad." *Small Axe: Journal of Criticism* 31: 16–29.

———. 2010b. "The Question of Multiculturalism in the Arts in the Postcolonial State of Trinidad and Tobago." *Music and Politics* 5(1), http://www.music.ucsb.edu/projects/musicandpolitics/past.html.

Guralnick, Peter. 1999. *Careless Love: The Unmaking of Elvis Presley*. Boston: Little, Brown.

Halbwachs, Maurice. 1992 [1950]. *On Collective Memory*. Chicago: University of Chicago Press.

Hall, Stuart. 1996. "New Ethnicities." In *Critical Dialogues in Cultural Studies*, edited by David Morley and Kuan-Hsing Chen, 441–49. New York: Routledge.

———. 2007. "Epilogue: Through the Prism of an Intellectual Life." In *Culture, Politics, Race, and Diaspora: The Thought of Stuart Hall*, edited by Brian Meeks, 269–91. Kingston, Jamaica: Ian Randle.

Hardt, Michael. 1999. "Affective Labor." *Boundary* 2(26): 89–100.

Hardt, Michael, and Antonio Negri. 2000. *Empire*. Cambridge, MA: Harvard University Press.

———. 2004. *Multitude: War and Democracy in the Age of Empire*. New York: Penguin.

Hasse, John Edward. 1993. *Beyond Category: The Life and Genius of Duke Ellington*. New York: Simon and Schuster.

"Hats Off to Roy Cape." 1998. *Sunday Guardian*, January 7.

Hegel, G. 1977. *Phenomenology of Spirit*. Oxford: Oxford University Press.

Helmlinger, Aurélie. 2008. "Les steelbands de Trinidad et Tobago: Ethnomusicologie cognitive d'une mémoire d'orchestre." *Intellectica* 1(48): 81–101.

Hennion, Antoine. 1989. "An Intermediary between Production and Consumption: The Producer of Popular Music." *Science, Technology and Human Values* 14(4): 400–24.

———. 2011. "The Production of Success: An Anti-musicology of the Pop Song." In *Creative Industries*, edited by B. Moeran and A. Alacovska, 159–93. London: Berg.

Herbert, Trevor, ed. 1991. *Bands: The Brass Band Movements in the 19th and 20th Centuries*. Milton Keynes, U.K.: Open University Press.

Herbert, Trevor, and Margaret Sarkissian. 1997. "Victorian Bands and Their Dissemination in the Colonies." *Popular Music* 16(2): 165–79.

Hernández, Marie Theresa. 2004. "Reconditioning History: Adapting Knowledge from the Past into the Present." In *Experiments in Rethinking History*, edited by Alun Munslow and Robert Rosenstone, 56–76. New York: Routledge.

Hesmondhalgh, David. 2002. *The Cultural Industries*. London: Sage.

Hill, Donald. 1993. *Calypso Calaloo: Early Carnival Music in Trinidad*. Miami: University of Florida Press.

Hintzen, Percy C. 1989. *The Costs of Regime Survival: Racial Mobilization, Elite Domination and Control of the State in Guyana and Trinidad*. Cambridge: Cambridge University Press.

———. 1999. "The Caribbean: Race and Creole Ethnicity." In *The Blackwell Companion to Racial and Ethnic Studies*, edited by David Theo Goldberg and John Solomos, 475–94. Oxford: Blackwell.

———. 2001. *West Indian in the West: Self-Representations in an Immigrant Community*. New York: New York University Press.

Hintzen, Percy C., and Jean Muteba Rahier. 2003. *Problematizing Blackness: Self-Ethnographies by Black Immigrants to the United States*. New York: Routledge.

Hoeprich, Eric. 2008. *The Clarinet*. New Haven, CT: Yale University Press.

Holquist, Michael. 2002. *Dialogism: Bakhtin and His World*, 2nd ed. New York: Routledge.

Homan, Shane, ed. 2006. *Access All Eras: Tribute Bands and Global Pop Culture*. Maidenhead, U.K.: Open University Press.

Huq, Rupa. 2006. *Beyond Subculture: Pop, Youth and Identity in a Postcolonial World*. London: Routledge.

Ivey, Thomas Neal. 1918. *Southern Methodist Handbook*. Nashville, TN: Publishing House of the Methodist Episcopal Church.

James, Allison, Jenny Hockey, and Andrew Dawson. 1997. *After Writing Culture: Epistemology and Praxis in Contemporary Anthropology.* New York: Routledge.

Jones, Alison, with Kuni Jenkins. 2008. "Rethinking Collaboration: Working the Indigene-Colonizer Hyphen." In *Handbook of Critical and Indigenous Methodologies,* edited by Norman K. Denzin, Yvonna S. Lincoln, and Linda Tuhiwai Smith, 471–86. London: Sage.

Joseph, Terry. 1990. "Roy Cape . . . Continental Crusader." *Trinidad Guardian,* September 7.

———. 1996. "Kaiso All Stars Shows Superiority." *Express,* September 25.

Kasinitz, Philip. 1992. *Caribbean New York: Black Immigrants and the Politics of Race.* Ithaca, NY: Cornell University Press.

Keightley, Keir. 1996. "'Turn It Down!' She Shrieked: Gender, Domestic Space, and High Fidelity, 1948–1959." *Popular Music* 15(2): 149–77.

———. 2003. "Low Television, High Fidelity: Taste and the Gendering of Home Entertainment Technologies." *Journal of Broadcasting and Electronic Media* 47(2): 236–59.

Keil, Charles, and Steven Feld. 1994. *Music Grooves: Essays and Dialogues.* Chicago: University of Chicago Press.

Keith, Michael C. 2007. *The Radio Station: Broadcast, Satellite and Internet.* Oxford: Focal Press.

Kelley, Robin D. G. 2009. *Thelonious Monk: The Life and Times of an American Original.* New York: Free Press.

Khan, Aisha. 2004. *Callaloo Nation: Metaphors of Race and Religious Identity among South Asians in Trinidad.* Durham, NC: Duke University Press.

Kondo, Dorinne K. 1990. *Crafting Selves: Power, Gender, and Discourses of Identity in a Japanese Workplace.* Chicago: University of Chicago Press.

Koningsbruggen, Peter van. 1997. *Trinidad Carnival: A Quest for National Identity.* London: Macmillan.

Kratz, Corinne, A. 2012. "Ceremonies, Sitting Rooms, and Albums: How Okiek Displayed Photographs in the 1990s." In *Photography in Africa: Ethnographic Perspectives,* edited by Richard Vokes, 242–65. Rochester, NY: James Currey.

Lacasse, Serge. 2007. "Intertextuality and Hypertextuality in Recorded Popular Music." In *Critical Essays in Popular Musicology,* edited by Allan F. Moore, 147–84. Burlington, VT: Ashgate.

Langness, L. L., and Gelya Frank. 1981. *Lives: An Anthropological Approach to Biography.* Novato, CA: Chandler and Sharp.

Lassiter, Luke Eric. 2005. *The Chicago Guide to Collaborative Ethnography.* Chicago: University of Chicago Press.

Latour, Bruno. 2005. *Reassembling the Social: An Introduction to Actor-Network Theory.* New York: Oxford University Press.

Lawler, Vanett. 1945. "Music Education in Fourteen Latin-American Republics." *Music Educators Journal* 31(4): 20–23, 30.

Lazzarato, Maurizio. 1996. "Immaterial Labour." In *Radical Thought in Italy: A Potential Politics*, edited by Paolo Virno and Michael Hardt, 133–50. Minneapolis: University of Minnesota Press.

Lee, Benjamin, and Edward LiPuma. 2002. "Cultures of Circulation: The Imaginations of Modernity." *Public Culture* 14(1): 191–213.

Lefebvre, Henri. 1992. *The Production of Space*. Oxford: Blackwell.

Le Menestrel, Sara, ed. 2012. *Des vies en musique: Parcours d'artistes, mobilités, transformations*. Paris: Herman.

Leslie, Colin O. 2006. "Caribbean Dragon: Blazing a Trail of Unity with Caribbean Sounds." Paper presented at the African-Caribbean World View: The Making of Caribbean Society—conference in honor of Barry Chevannes, University of the West Indies, Mona Campus, Jamaica, January 19–21.

Leu, Lorraine. 2000. "'Raise Yuh Hand, Jump Up, and Get on Bad!': New Developments in Soca Music in Trinidad." *Latin American Music Review* 21(1): 45–58.

Lipsitz, George. 2010. *Midnight at the Barrelhouse: The Johnny Otis Story*. Minneapolis: University of Minnesota Press.

Liverpool, Hollis Urban Lester. 1993. "Rituals of Power and Rebellion: The Carnival Tradition in Trinidad and Tobago." PhD diss., University of Michigan.

Lortat-Jacob, Bernard. 1995. *Sardinian Chronicles*. Chicago: University of Chicago Press.

Lucy, John A., ed. 1993. *Reflexive Language: Reported Speech and Metapragmatics*. Cambridge: Cambridge University Press.

Lyndersay, Mark. 1998. "Bring the Rhythm Down." *Trinidad Express*, February 18, 9.

Maharaj, Sateesh. 2004. "Driven by the Music." *Trinidad Express*, September 5.

Manuel, Peter. 1998. "Chutney and Indo-Trinidadian Cultural Identity." *Popular Music* 17(1): 21–44.

———. 2000a. *East Indian Music in the West Indies: Tan-Singing, Chutney, and the Making of Indo-Caribbean Culture*. Philadelphia: Temple University Press.

———. 2000b. "Ethnic Identity, National Identity, and Music in Indo-Trinidadian Culture." In *Music and the Racial Imagination*, edited by Ronald Radano and Philip V. Bohlman, 318–45. Chicago: University of Chicago Press.

Marcus, George E., and Michael M. J. Fischer. 1986. *Anthropology as Cultural Critique: An Experimental Moment in the Human Sciences*. Chicago: University of Chicago Press.

Mason, Kaley Reid. 2006. "Socio-musical Mobility and Identity in Kerala, South India: Modern Entanglements of Ritual Service, Labouring Musicians, and Global Artistry." PhD diss., University of Alberta, Canada.

Massey, Doreen B. 2005. *For Space*. London: Sage.

Meditz, Sandra W., and Dennis M. Hanratty. 1987. "Trinidad and Tobago: Economy." In *Caribbean Islands: A Country Study*. Washington, DC: GPO for the Library of Congress, http://countrystudies.us/caribbean-islands/45.htm.

Meintjes, Louise. 2003. *Sound of Africa: Making Music Zulu in a South African Studio.* Durham, NC: Duke University Press.

Miller, Daniel. 1987. *Material Culture and Mass Consumption.* Oxford: Blackwell.

———, ed. 1998. *Material Cultures: Why Some Things Matter.* Chicago: University of Chicago Press.

———, ed. 2005. *Materiality.* Durham, NC: Duke University Press.

———, ed. 2009. *Anthropology and the Individual: A Material Culture Perspective.* Oxford: Berg.

Milner, Greg. 2010. *Perfecting Sound Forever: An Aural History of Recorded Music.* New York: Faber and Faber.

Misztal, Barbara. 2003. *Theories of Social Remembering.* Berkshire, U.K.: Open University Press.

Mohammed, Patricia. 2009. *Imaging the Caribbean: Culture and Visual Translation.* Oxford: Macmillan.

Mohammed, Patricia, and Catherine Shepherd, eds. 1988. *Gender in Caribbean Development.* St. Augustine, Trinidad: University of the West Indies.

Moisala, Pirkko. 2011. "Reflections on an Ethnomusicological Study of a Contemporary Western Art Music Composer." *Ethnomusicology Forum* 20(3): 443–51.

Moisala, Pirkko, and Beverley Diamond. 2000. *Music and Gender.* Chicago: University of Illinois Press.

Monson, Ingrid T. 1996. *Saying Something: Jazz Improvisation and Interaction.* Chicago: University of Chicago Press.

———. 1999. "Riffs, Repetition, and Theories of Globalization." *Ethnomusicology* 43(1): 31–65.

Muller, Carol Ann, and Sathima Bea Benjamin. 2011. *Musical Echoes: South African Women Thinking in Jazz.* Durham, NC: Duke University Press.

Myers, Fred R., ed. 2002. *The Empire of Things: Regimes of Value and Material Culture.* Santa Fe, NM: School of American Research Press.

Negus, Keith. 1997. *Popular Music in Theory: An Introduction.* Middletown, CT: Wesleyan University Press.

Nepture, Harvey R. 2007. *Caliban and the Yankees: Trinidad and the United States Occupation.* Chapel Hill: University of North Carolina Press.

Neville, Art, Aaron Neville, Cyril Neville, David Neville, and David Ritz. 2000. *The Brothers Neville: An Autobiography.* Boston: Little, Brown.

Newsome, Roy. 2006. *The Modern Brass Band.* Burlington, VT: Ashgate.

Nurith, Zmora. 1994. *Orphanages Reconsidered: Child Care Institutions in Progressive Era Baltimore.* Philadelphia: Temple University Press.

Oakdale, Suzanne. 2005. *I Foresee My Life: The Ritual Performance of Autobiography in an Amazonian Community.* Lincoln: University of Nebraska Press.

Packman, Jeff Loren. 2007. "'We Work Hard at Entertainment': Performance and Professionalism in the Popular Music Scenes of Salvador da Bahia, Brazil." PhD diss., University of California, Berkeley.

Partridge, Christopher. 2010. *Dub in Babylon: Understanding the Evolution and Significance of Dub Reggae in Jamaica and Britain from King Tubby to Post-punk*. London: Equinox.

Pessar, Patricia R. 1996. "New Approaches to Caribbean Emigration and Return." *Center for Migration Studies* 13(4): 1–11.

Pinney, Christopher. 2005. "Introduction: 'How the Other Half . . .'" In *Photography's Other Histories*, edited by Christopher Pinney and Nicolas Peterson, 1–16. Durham, NC: Duke University Press.

Plaza, Dwaine E., and Frances Henry, eds. 2006. *Returning to the Source: The Final Stage of the Caribbean Migration Circuit*. Mona, Jamaica: University of the West Indies Press.

Poole, Deborah. 1997. *Vision, Race, and Modernity: A Visual Economy of the Andean Image World*. Princeton, NJ: Princeton University Press.

"Portsmouth Festival: Sizzling Soca." 1990. *News Entertainer*, July 16.

Potter, Robert B., Dennis Conway, and Joan Phillips. 2005. *The Experience of Return Migration: Caribbean Perspectives*. Burlington, VT: Ashgate.

Premdas, Ralph R., ed. 2000. *Identity, Ethnicity, and Culture in the Caribbean*. St. Augustine, Trinidad: University of the West Indies, School of Continuing Studies.

Puri, Shalini. 1999. "Canonized Hybridities, Resistant Hybridities: Chutney Soca, Carnival, and the Politics of Nationalism." In *Caribbean Romances: The Politics of Regional Representation*, edited by B. J. Edmondson, 12–38. Charlottesville: University Press of Virginia.

———, ed. 2003. *Marginal Migrations: The Circulation of Cultures within the Caribbean*. Oxford: Macmillan Caribbean.

———. 2004. *The Caribbean Postcolonial: Social Equality, Post-nationalism, and Cultural Hybridity*. New York: Palgrave Macmillan.

Qureshi, Regula Burckhardt. 2007. *Master Musicians of India: Hereditary Sarangi Players Speak*. New York: Routledge.

Radano, Ronald Michael. 1993. *New Musical Figurations: Anthony Braxton's Cultural Critique*. Chicago: University of Chicago Press.

Radano, Ronald Michael, and Philip V. Bohlman, eds. 2000. *Music and the Racial Imagination*. Chicago: University of Chicago Press.

Raffles, Hugh. 2002. "Intimate Knowledge." *International Social Science Journal* 54(173): 325–35.

Ramnarine, Tina K. 1996. "'Indian' Music in the Diaspora: Case Studies of 'Chutney' in Trinidad and in London." *British Journal of Ethnomusicology* 5: 133–53.

———. 2001. *Creating Their Own Space: The Development of an Indian–Caribbean Musical Tradition*. Mona, Jamaica: University of the West Indies Press.

———. 2007. *Beautiful Cosmos: Performance and Belonging in the Caribbean Diaspora*. London: Pluto.

Rancière, Jacques. 2004. *Politics of Aesthetics*. New York: Continuum.

———. 2010. *Dissensus: On Politics and Aesthetics*, edited and translated by Steven Corcoran. London: Continuum International.

Raussert, Wilfrid. 2008. "Hollers, Blue Notes, and Brass Sounds." *Louisiana Culture from the Colonial Era to Katrina*, edited by John Lowe, 255–83. Baton Rouge: Louisiana State University Press.

Reddock, Rhoda. 1994. *Women, Labour and Politics in Trinidad and Tobago*. London: Zed.

———. 2000. "Jahaji Bhai: The Emergence of a Dougla Poetics in Contemporary Trinidad and Tobago." In *Identity, Ethnicity, and Culture in the Caribbean*, ed. Ralph R. Premdas, 185–210. St. Augustine, Trinidad: University of the West Indies, School of Continuing Studies.

Redmond, Sean, and Su Homes, eds. 2007. *Stardom and Celebrity: A Reader*. Thousand Oaks, CA: Sage.

Rees, Helen, ed. 2009. *Lives in Chinese Music*. Urbana: University of Illinois Press.

Regis, Louis. 1999. *The Political Calypso: True Opposition in Trinidad and Tobago 1962–1987*. Mona, Jamaica: University of the West Indies Press.

Rétout, Marie Thérèse. 2001. *Called to Serve*. Laventille, Trinidad: Scrip-J Printers.

Richards, Jeffrey. 2001. *Imperialism and Music: Britain 1876–1953*. New York: Manchester University Press.

Rodriguez, Russell C. 2006. "Cultural Production, Legitimation, and the Politics of Aesthetics: Mariachi Transmission, Practice, and Performance in the United States." PhD diss., University of California, Santa Cruz.

Rohlehr, Gordon. 1970. "Sparrow and the Language of Calypso." *Savacou* 1(2): 87–99.

———. 1975. "Sparrow as Poet." In *David Frost Introduces Trinidad and Tobago*, edited by Michael Anthony and Andrew Carr, 84–98. London: André Deutsch.

———. 1990. *Calypso and Society in Pre-independence Trinidad*. Port of Spain, Trinidad: Author.

———. 1998. "'We Getting the Kaiso That We Deserve': Calypso and the World Music Market." *Drama Review* 42(3): 82–95.

———. 2004. "'This Thing Called a Nation': An Interview with Gordon Rohlehr." In *Marginal Migrations*, edited by Shalini Puri, 240–69. Oxford: Macmillan Education.

Rommen, Timothy. 2009. "'Come Back Home': Regional Travels, Global Encounters, and Local Nostalgias in Bahamian Popular Musics." *Latin American Music Review* 30(2): 159–83.

———. 2011. *Funky Nassau: Roots, Routes, and Representation in Bahamian Popular Music*. Berkeley: University of California Press.

"Roy Cape Kaiso All Stars: A Top Class Band." 1994. [Trinidad] *Newsday*, January 8.

"Roy Cape on Trip to Haiti: Why Complain about Food When Haitians Go Hungry?" 1995. *Weekend Heat*, January 14.

"Roy Cape: Still Top Brass after 41 Years." 1999. *Sunday Guardian*, January 10.

Rustin, Nichole T., and Sherrie Tucker. 2008. *Big Ears: Listening for Gender in Jazz Studies*. Durham, NC: Duke University Press.

Ryan, Selwyn. 1972. *Race and Nationalism in Trinidad and Tobago: A Study of Decolonisation in a Multicultural Society*. Toronto: University of Toronto Press.

Sakakeeny, Matt. 2008. "Instruments of Power: New Orleans Brass Bands and the Politics of Performance." PhD diss., Columbia University.

———. 2011. "New Orleans Music as a Circulatory System." *Black Music Research Journal* 31(2): 291–325.

Scher, Philip W. 2003. *Carnival and the Formation of a Caribbean Transnation*. Gainesville: University Press of Florida.

Shakespeare, William. 1901. *Twelfth Night, or, What You Will: A Comedy in Five Acts*. London: Hacon and Ricketts.

Sheridan, Chris. 2000. *Dis Here: A Bio-discography of Julian "Cannonball" Adderley*. Westport, CT: Greenwood.

Smith, Michael P. 1994. "Behind the Lines: The Black Mardi Gras Indians and the New Orleans Second Line. *Black Music Research Journal* 14(1): 43–73.

Southern, Eileen, and Josephine Wright. 2000. *Images: Iconography of Music in African-American Culture (1770s–1920s)*. New York: Norton.

Stahl, Matt. 2009. "Privilege and Distinction in Production Worlds." In *Production Studies: Cultural Studies of Media Industries*, edited by Vicki Mayer, Miranda J. Banks, and John T. Caldwell, 54–68. New York: Routledge.

———. 2013. *Unfree Masters: Recording Artists and the Politics of Work*. Durham, NC: Duke University Press.

Stewart, Kathleen. 1996. *A Space on the Side of the Road: Cultural Poetics in an "Other" America*. Princeton, NJ: Princeton University Press.

Stock, Jonathan P. J. 1996. *Musical Creativity in Twentieth-Century China: Abing, His Music, and Its Changing Meanings*. Rochester, NY: University of Rochester Press.

Stokes, Martin, ed. 1994. *Ethnicity, Identity, and Music: The Musical Construction of Place*. Oxford: Berg.

Stuempfle, Stephen. 1995. *Steelband Movement: The Forging of a National Art in Trinidad and Tobago*. Mona, Jamaica: University of the West Indies Press.

Szwed, John. 2002. *So What: The Life of Miles Davis*. London: Heinemann.

Taylor, Timothy. 2012. *The Sounds of Capitalism: Advertising, Music, and the Conquest of Culture*. Chicago: University of Chicago Press.

Teachout, Terry. 2009. *Pops: A Life of Louis Armstrong*. Boston: Houghton Mifflin Harcourt.

Thomas-Hope, Elizabeth M. 1986. "Transients and Settlers: Varieties of Caribbean Migrants and the Socio-economic Implication of Their Return." *International Migration* 24(3): 559–72.

Tiedge, Faun Tanenbaum. 1993. "The Partbook Collection from the Ospedale della Pieta and the Sacred Music of Giovanni Porta." PhD diss., New York University.

Tirro, Franck. 2009. *The Birth of the Cool of Miles Davis and His Associates*. Hillsdale, NY: Pendragon.

Todorov, Tzvetan. 1984. *Mikhail Bakhtin: The Dialogical Principle*, translated by Wlad Godzich. Minneapolis: University of Minnesota Press.

Tonelli, Christopher J. 2011. "Musical Pastiche, Embodiment, and Intersubjectivity: Listening in the Second Degree." PhD diss., University of California, San Diego.

Trujillo, Gregory. 1996. "Roy Cape's Band Is the Crowd Mover." [Trinidad] *Newsday*, February 3.

Tucker, Mark. 1991. *Ellington: The Early Years*. Urbana: University of Illinois Press.

———, ed. 1993. *The Duke Ellington Reader*. New York: Oxford University Press.

Turino, Thomas. 2000. *Nationalists, Cosmopolitans, and Popular Music in Zimbabwe*. Chicago: University of Chicago Press.

Vander, Judith. 1988. *Songprints: The Musical Experience of Five Shoshone Women*. Urbana: University of Illinois Press.

Veal, Michael. 2007. *Dub: Soundscapes and Shattered Songs in Reggae*. Chicago: University of Chicago Press.

Velez, Maria Teresa. 2000. *Drumming for the Gods: The Life and Times of Felipe García Villamil, Santero, Palero, and Abakuá*. Philadelphia: Temple University Press.

Vennum, Thomas, Jr. 1982. *The Ojibwa Dance Drum: Its History and Construction*. Washington, DC: Smithsonian Institution Press.

———. 1988. *Wild Rice and the Ojibway People*. St. Paul: Minnesota Historical Society Press.

Vidal, André-Jean, and Gilles Delacroix. 2011. "Emile Antile, le roi de la biguine." In *Franceantilles*, December 7. http://www.guadeloupe.franceantilles.fr/actualite/culture-et-patrimoine/musique-emile-antile-le-roi-de-la-biguine-12-07-2011-130972.php.

Wade, Bonnie C. 1998. *Imaging Sound: An Ethnomusicological Study of Music, Art, and Culture in Mughal India*. Chicago: University of Chicago Press.

Wallis, Roger, and Krister Malm. 1984. *Big Sounds from Small Peoples*. London: Constable.

Warner, Keith Q. 1982. *Kaiso! The Trinidad Calypso: A Study of the Calypso as Oral Literature*. Washington, DC: Three Continents Press.

———. 2000. *On Location: Cinema and Film in the Anglophone Caribbean*. Warwick University Caribbean Studies series. London: Macmillan Caribbean.

Watt, Eva Tulene, with Keith Basso. 2004. *Don't Let the Sun Step over You: A White Mountain Apache Family Life (1869–1975)*. Tucson: University of Arizona Press.

Weintraub, Andrew N. 2010. *Dangdut Stories: A Social and Musical History of Indonesia's Most Popular Music*. New York: Oxford University Press.

Wesley, Fred, Jr. 2002. *Hit Me, Fred: Recollections of a Sideman*. Durham, NC: Duke University Press.

Weston, Randy (composer), and Willard Jenkins (arranger). 2010. *African Rhythms: The Autobiography of Randy Weston*. Durham, NC: Duke University Press.

White, Bob W., ed. 2012. *Music and Globalization: Critical Encounters*. Bloomington: Indiana University Press.

Wilson, Peter J. 1973. *Crab Antics: The Social Anthropology of English-Speaking Negro Societies of the Caribbean*. New Haven, CT: Yale University Press.

Winter, Jack. 1982. "The Cannonball Adderley Rendez-vous: Coda Interview." *Coda Magazine*, no. 186. http://www.cannonball-adderley.com/article/coda.htm.

Wong, Deborah. 1989–90. "Thai Cassettes and Their Covers: Two Case Histories." *Asian Music* 21(1): 78–104.

Wright, Erik Olin. 1989. "The Comparative Project on Class Structure and Class Consciousness: An Overview." *Acta Sociologica* 32: 3–22.

———. 1997. *Class Counts: Comparative Studies in Class Analysis*. Cambridge: Cambridge University Press.

Yanagisako, Sylvia Junko. 2002. *Producing Culture and Capital: Family Firms in Italy*. Princeton, NJ: Princeton University Press.

Yanaw, Scott. 2005. *Jazz: A Regional Exploration*. Westport, CT: Greenwood.

Zemp, Hugo. 1995. *Écoute le bambou qui pleure: Récits de quatre musiciens mélanésiens ('Aré'aré, Iles Salomon)*. Paris: Gallimard.

ABOUT THE COMPANION CD

Roy Cape: A Calypso and Soca Anthology

A companion CD produced by Alvin Daniell, Major and Minor Productions, Ltd. (http://www.majorandminoronline.com)

1. Selwyn Wheeler Orchestra, "The Ugly Duckling," c. 1961.
2. Selwyn Wheeler Orchestra, cover version of "Mocking Bird," c. 1961.
3. Clarence Curvan Orchestra, cover version of "Moulin Rouge," c. 1963.
4. Ron Berridge Orchestra, cover version of "Lollipop and Roses," c. 1964.
5. Ron Berridge Orchestra, cover version of "My Favorite Things," c. 1966.
6. Sparrow's Troubadours, cover version of "Sa Sa Yea," 1969.
7. Sparrow's Troubadours, cover version of "Bongo," 1969.
8. Black Stalin, "Kaiso Gone Dread," with music by Earl Rodney and Friends, 1978.
9. Roy Cape Kaiso All Stars, "Watch Out My Children," 1990.
10. Nigel Lewis, "War Party," with Roy Cape All Stars, 1995.
11. Superblue, "Barbara," with Roy Cape All Stars, 1997.
12. Roy Cape All Stars featuring Destra, "Tremble It," 2000.
13. Black Stalin and Roy Cape, "Leroy, Roy," with Roy Cape All Stars, 2002.
14. Roy Cape All Stars featuring Blaxx, "Carnival Question," 2002.
15. Blaxx, "Breathless," 2008.

INDEX

Adderley, Julian (Cannonball), sound of, 84, 250n8
aesthetics (musical): and biguine, 85; of Caribbean popular music, 86; and ethics, 220; politics of, 249n2; of the present, 86; theoretical perspectives on the politics of, 249n2; and time, 91; of togetherness, 80. *See also* calypso; sound
affective labor: as care, 184; notion of (Hardt and Negri), 19, 236n26. *See also* immaterial labor
agency: accounts of, 10; and art worlds, 6; and biographies, 230; and conjuncture, 101, 228; human and material, 6, 23, 239n1; in many senses, 14; and memory, 18; and the musician's body, 82; and Roy, 15; and transparency, 230. *See also* materiality; Miller, Daniel
Aggarrat, Frank, sound engineer, 104
Aird, Neville, saxophonist, 59
Alexander, Joseph, tenor saxophonist, 45–46, 142–43; and brothers John and Joshua, 142
Allen, Kurt, Roy's singer, 124; and "Stampede," 129
Amar, Robert, and the Kisskadee Caravan, 119–20, 219

Aming, Choy, and his band and entertainment complex, 249n3
Anderson, Tim J., 93
Antile, Emile, and biguine's aesthetics, 85
Appiah, Kwame Anthony, and notion of cosmopolitanism, 246
awards (musical), and controversies, 179–80

Bakhtin, Mikhail M., on dialogism, 237n30. *See also* dialogic editing; dialogic writing
bandleader: as agent of change, 105–6; and keeping lead singers, 130–31; and the management of relations, 100, 174; and rehearsal, 110, 112–14; Roy's philosophy as, 170–71, 231; and scouting musicians, 108–9; work world of, 3. *See also* Cape, Roy; musicians; rehearsal
bandsmen: and gender, 140; as wage laborers, 42; working consciousness of, 43. *See also* musicians
Basso, Keith, 8
Becker, Howard, on art worlds, 6
Belfon, Denise ("Soca Queen"), 129, 227
Benjamin, Sathima Bea, 8

Berridge, Ron(ald): arranger, 1; band of, 57–61; as band member, 54; names of players, 74, 139; new Ron Berridge orchestra in New York, 69–71; recordings for Lord Kitchener and the Mighty Sparrow, 96; repertoire with, 63–64
biography: versus admirational writing, 230; and musicians, 4; and representation, 235n17; research perspectives on, 7–11, 235n12; theorization of, 7–11
Björnberg, Alf, 93
Black Stalin (Leroy Calliste): as coauthor of "Jam Mih, Mr. Cape," 125, 128; as 1995 Calypso Monarch, 162; reputation of, 12; Roy and, 105–6, 154–56, 165; short biography of, 190; and *To the Caribbean Man*, 103–4
Blaxx (Dexter Stewart), Roy's singer, 129, 172
Blues Busters, 72. *See also* James, Phillip
bomb (musical), Trinidadian notion of, 254n12
Bonnelle, Peter, trumpet player, 59
Borde, Roderick, and the writing of scores, 40, 252n17
Boynes, Anthony (Bassie), bass player and dancer, 153–54, 186
Bradley, Clive: arranger, 1; as arranger for Clarence Curvan and the Mighty Sparrow, 61, 66; as arranger of Desperadoes, 146–47; as bandleader and arranger of Songs Incorporated, 61; as teacher, 146, 245n32
brass bands: and orphanage, 34–37; research perspectives on, 241n14; and schools, 29. *See also* Police Band
Brass Festival, 120–21
Brassorama, in contrast to Brass Festival, 254n21
Brother Resistance (Lutalo Masimba): and his contributions, 191; on recording technologies and radio formats, 252n19; about Roy in the dance hall, 219–20

Brothers, Thomas, 8
Brother Valentino (Emrold Phillip), as calypsonian with Roy, 105–6
Bryan, Fitz Vaughn, band of, 54, 143
BUCKS (the Biggest Universal Calypso King Show), 113–14. *See also* Munroe, William
Byron Lee: his band formation, 248n45; short biography, 247n38

calypso: and colonial administration, 253n5; and discourses of authenticity, 249n47; and East Indians, 257n11; and gender, 170; and improvisation, 251n9; melodies and style of, 85; and performing conditions, 148; and posture onstage, 153; research perspectives on, 252n15; and tent conditions, 257n5
Calypso Rose, as Calypso Monarch, 129
Campbell, Lloyd, as Blues Busters' singer, 72
Cape, Roy: affective labor of, 201–3; as band member, 46–73; as bandleader, 104–24, 129–31; in contrasting spaces, 217–21; improvisation style of, 84–85, 251n11; instrumental tone of, 78–86, 97, 250n8; and making connections, 224–27; and musical training in orphanage, 37–41; and pan, 27–28; on race and ethnicity in music, 222–24; and recording, 114–18; singing moment of, 124–28; testimonies about, 192–206; on tour, 208–16; work ethics of, 193–98. *See also* bandleader; musicians; rehearsal; Roy Cape (Kaiso) All Stars
Cathedral CYO band, names of players in, 74
Chalkdust (Hollis Liverpool): as calypsonian, 158–60, 190–91; and Roy in Sweden, 81, 212
Charles, Rudolf: the Desperadoes Steel Orchestra, 225; and Roy, 146
Charlie's Roots: as accompanying band

for Soca Monarch competitions, 122; and local music, 254n20
chutney soca: notion of, 257n9; and Sundar Popo, 223
circulation: as an asset, 101; four social practices of, 208; and material worlds and social relations, 43; new political economy of, 93; notion of, 21; and photographs, 20; regimes of, 6, 17, 22, 234n7; and its reification through praise, 184; and reputation, 22; and Roy's career, 207–28; and the work world of musicians, 3
Clifford, James, 11
Coltrane, John, musical approach of, 85–86
combos: and economics, 245n30; in Trinidad, 56, 243n23
Cook, Emory: Cook Recording of, 56; short biography, 243n24
cover versions: in the aftermath of independence, 64; and Cannibalist Manifesto, 253n20; and "Take Five," 60–61; theoretical perspectives on, 246n36. See also independence
cultural politics: and hairstyle, 143–44, 148–50, 158; and journalistic discourse, 148–49; and representation in Trinidad, 181, 222–24, 257n4
Curvan, Clarence: band of, 54–57; names of players, 74, 138; repertoire, 56–57

Dance, Stanley, 183
Danielson, Anne, 93
Danielson, Virginia, 8
Davidson, Fillmore (Boots), pannist, 27
de Coteau, Art(hur): arranger, 1; and calypsonians, 203; and conception of a musician, 195; in Frankie Francis Studio Band, 74; and the Kingdom of the Wizards calypso tent, 103; and local music, 244n27, 245n33; and Roy, 64; and salary, 193
De Freitas, Harold (Vasso), saxophonist, 141–42

De Leon, Sherry Ann, 41
Desmond, Paul: playing style of, 250n9, 251n11; sound of, 81, 87
De Vuglt, Otmar, pianist, 251n9
dialogic editing, notion of (Feld), 10–11, 22, 235n13
dialogic writing: A side and B side of the record in, 44; conversations in, 100; difference between fan and scholar in, 229–30; and negotiated knowledge, 11; research perspective on, 234n11
Diaz, Cyril, saxophonist, 83
Dil E Nadan, chutney soca band, 223
documentary: editing plan of, 21; research perspectives on, 256n3
Dubois, Kerwin, soca artist and composer, 172
Duncan, Sel, band of, 54
Dutchy Brothers, band of, 51, 56, 60
Dyer, Ester, Roy's singer, 130, 168–69

Earl Rodney and Friends, names of players, 103
Erlmann, Veit, 7

Faris, James, and visual representations, 135. See also Poole, Deborah
Feld, Steven: on dialogic editing, 10; on reading photographs, 136; on storytelling, 8–9
fete: Trinidadian definition of, 254n19; and youth, 257n6
film: and influence on Trinidadian musicians, 63, 246n34
Fischer, Michael M. J., 11
Francis, Frankie: arranger, 1; band on the road on carnival day, 50; and calypso tent, 52; musician, 40, 51; names of players in his Studio band and his Calypso Tent orchestra, 74; repertoire with, 52–53; and Roy, 48–49, 64; and Roy's band at Spektakula, 146–47; saxophonist, 51; and scores, 92, 252n17; and TELCO recording studio, 49–50
Frank, Gelya, 8

INDEX 281

Franklin, Conrad, promoter for tours in Japan, 121
Friedson, Eliot, labor of love concept, 4
Frisbie, Charlotte, 8

Garcia, Destra, Roy's singer, 129–30, 168
gender: and calypso, 170; feminist and postcolonial studies, 235n12; and Girl Pat Steel Orchestra, 27; and instruments, 254n11; and musicians, 108–10; and musicians' work and networks, 7; and music in orphanage, 36–37; and Police Band, 110; and representation, 181; and reputation and respectability, 5; research perspectives on, 236n27; and Roy Cape (Kaiso) All Stars, 108–10; and soca, 170, 256n6; women's contributions to musical life, 241n9
Gilroy, Paul, and diasporic intimacies, 252n12
Girl Pat Steel Orchestra, and gender, 27
Goddard, Pehlam, arranger, 1
Grant, Eddy: and Ice label and the Blue Wave Recording Studio, 115–16; ringbang show of, 117; and Roy's band, 148
Green, Garth, 212
Griffith, Beverly, arranger, 52, 54, 225
Guralnick, Peter, 7
Gypsy (Winston Peters), as calypsonian and politician, 165

Hall, Stuart, and difference, 234n11, 246n35
Hanratty, Dennis M., 94
Hardt, Michael, and Antonio Negri, notion of immaterial labor by, 5–6, 234n5. *See also* affective labor; immaterial labor
Harris, Cliff, and the Brass Festival, 120–21
Hawkins, Francesca, 217–19
Henderson, Carl (Beaver), and TnT Rainbow band, 104

Hendricks, Hugh: and the Buccaneers, 71; and his singers, 72
Hill, Donald, 212
Hinds, Alison, soca singer, 129
Hintzen, Percy, and West Indian diasporas, 249n48. *See also* migration; race
Hitman (Neeshan Prabhoo), soca and chutney soca artist, 223
Hodges, Johnny, sound of, 79, 91

immaterial labor: and bandleader, 100; notion of (Hardt and Negri), 5–6, 234n5, 256n1; and production of music, 18. *See also* affective labor
Ince, Errol: about Roy's tone, 250n8; trumpet player, 40
Independence (Trinidad and Tobago), and repertoire, 53, 62–63, 95–96, 245n33
Inniss, Bertram, arranger and bandleader for the Mighty Sparrow, and Ron Berridge, 64
island-based musicians, challenges of, 118

Jacob, David (Jakey), 186
James, Elsworth, promoter in Toronto, Canada, 121
James, Phillip, as Blues Busters' singer, 72, 145
"Jam Mih, Mr. Cape" (song), and Roy as coauthor and singer, 125–28, 174–76
Jardine, Stephen, 187
Jenkins, Willard, 8
Jones, Quincy, musical approach of, 85–86
Jones, Rita, Roy's singer, 130–31
journey, notion of, 14, 17–18, 236n23

Kasinitz, Philip, 212
Keightley, Keir, 93
Kelley, Robin D. G., 7
knowledge: local, 10; relational, 11; sensuousness of, 18
Kratz, Corinne, on potentials of photographs, 20, 137

labor of love, concept of, 4, 23, 78
Langness, L. L., 8
Lassiter, Luke Eric, 11
Latapy, Russell, football player, 176–77
Latour, Bruno, on art worlds, 6
Layne, Kenneth, 83
lead singers: and gender, 170; in soca bands, 122–23; as stars, 3. *See also* calypso; soca
Lee, Byron, Jamaican band of, 65
Lewis, Curtis, 187
Lewis, Joey: band of, 56; song "Joey Saga" of, 63
Lewis, Marvin and Nigel, Roy's singers, 120, 124, 168
Lewis, Nigel, and "Moving to the Right," 124
Lindsay, Michael (Lion), 187
Lipsitz, George, 8
listening: history of, 19; theoretical perspectives on, 236n25. *See also* sound
Liverpool, Hollis (Chalkdust). *See* Chalkdust
"Lollipops and Roses" (Berridge's band), Roy's solo in, 79
Lord Kitchener: and Clive Bradley, 245n33; and migration, 248n44; and the Revue calypso tent, 253n3; with Ron Berridge's band, 59–60, 62; and "Sugar Bum, Bum," 248n42; and the telethon, 160
Lord Shorty (Garfield Blackman, later renamed Ras Shorty I), calypsonian and soca artist, 104, 253n4
Lovelace, Earl, novelist, 183

Malm, Krister: concert tour organizer in Sweden, 158; ethnomusicologist, 256n5
Marcelin, Mano, 51
Marcelle, Garvin, 188
Marcus, George E., 11
Martineau, Claude, 46; and Franck with Spektakula calypso tent, 105
materiality: and musical sensibility and work ethic, 43; and musicians' labor, 6; notion of, 234n9; and power, 252n8; of sound production, 42, 80; theoretical perspectives on, 234n9; of the visual, 236n29, 239n1. *See also* Miller, Daniel
McIntosh, Frankie, arranger, 1, 117–18
media (social): Roy's use of, 226–27; in Trinidad, 244n29
Meditz, Sandra W., 94
memoryscape, 43; theoretical perspectives on, 240n2
Mighty Sparrow, the: band of, 65–69; in concert, 107; and musical skills, 247n40; as performer, 68–69, 140–42; research perspectives on his contributions, 248n43; with Ron Berridge's band, 60, 62
migration: and Caribbean musicians, 248n44; and the law, 245n31, 256n2; migrants' (musicians') return, 97–98, 101–2; narratives of, 24, 69–73; research perspectives on, 253n1. *See also* awards; Hintzen, Percy
Miller, Daniel: on material worlds, 6, 249n1; on objects and subjects, 239n1. *See also* agency; materiality
Milner, Greg, 93
Mitchell, Clyde (Mitch), 188
modern subject, notion of, 15
Montano, Machel, soca artist, 177–78
Moore, Enrique, director of Trinidad and Tobago Police Band, 29
"Moulin Rouge" (Curvan's band), Roy's solo lead part in, 79
Muller, Carol Ann, 8
Munroe, William: and the Kingdom of the Wizards calypso tent, 102–3, 105–6; and Socathon at the Spectrum, 120
musicians: and calypsonians, 154–57; as cosmopolitans, 63, 246n35; in diasporas, 69–73, 145–46, 255n3; and gender, 108–10; instrumental voice of, 78; in Jamaica and Trinidad, 233n1; as listeners, 77, 242n18; multicultural interaction of, 140, 160, 253n8; notion of, 44; from orphanage, 41;

musicians (continued)
  and performing in the streets, 131–34; revenue on performance basis for, 99, 231; the scouting of, 108–10; as workers, 91, 234n4. See also bandleader; bandsmen; work

Naipaul, V. S., novelist, 183
"Name the Game" (Black Stalin's song), Roy's 1979 solo in, 80
Negri, Antonio. See Hardt, Michael
networks (social): and orphanage, 240n8; and research perspectives on, 257n13; and social media, 152, 226–27; of supporters, 162
nonstop: and cutting sessions in American jazz, 242n20; with large bands and combos, 60–61; Trinidadian notion of, 59

Oakdale, Suzanne, 8
Olatunji (Yearwood), Roy's singer, 131, 170
orphanage: and brotherhood, 240n8; as Children's Home, 31–32; concerts and music festivals with children from, 35; and the court, 26; and French missionaries, 30; and long-term friendship, 140; and musical education of brass musicians, 24, 39, 150, 241n12; musical repertoire at, 39–40; music and gender, 36–37; music as discipline in, 34; in the New World, 238n10; and the Police Band, 29, 40
Oxley, Neville, trombone player, 59, 143–44

Parker, Charlie, technical prowess and style of, 84, 250n8
Parker, Maceo, sound of, 87
Parks-Kojo, Ann Marie (Twiggy), Roy's singer, 116, 254n14
party music, performance of, 134
Paul, Leston: arranger, 1; in Roy's band, 109
Penguin (Sedley Joseph), calypsonian and president of the calypsonians' organization, 165
Phillip, Lambert, 188–89
Pinney, Christopher, and photographs, 135–36
place (and time): and memoryscape, 43, 100; names of, 18; research perspectives on, 235n14
pleasure, force of, 6, 150–52
Police Band: and experience (Lion), 192; and female players, 110; and performance (Garvin), 198; Trinidadian directors of, 238n9. See also orphanage
Poole, Deborah, on visual economies, 20, 135, 255n1
postmodern subject, notion of, 15
praise, notion of, 184
Prospect, Anthony: first Trinidadian director of Trinidad and Tobago Police Band, 40; and the orphanage, 239n22
public intimacies, notion of, 4, 233n3
Punette, Arnold (Sly), 189

race: and musical repertoire, 244n27; politics of, 222–24, 240n7; research perspectives on, 236n27, 257n8, 257n12; and selective representation of musicians, 243n22. See also Cape, Roy
Raffles, Hugh, on local knowledge, 10–11
rapso, notion of, 257n10. See also Brother Resistance
Rastafarian. See cultural politics
Ravi B (Ravi Bissambhar), chutney soca artist from Karma band, 223
recording: money out of, 115; studios in the early 1960s, 137–39, 241n11; technologies, 25, 252n19, 255n2
reflexive writing, 11
rehearsal (musical): and authority, 158; and performance, 163–65; and socializing, 172
reputation: notion of, 5–6; in Roy's definition, 206–7, 213–14
respectability, notion of, 5–6

Rikki Jai, calypso, soca, and chutney soca artist, 223

Ritz, David, 8

Rivers, Vincent, as accompanying band for Soca Monarch competitions, 122

Roach, Felix: names of players, 74; pianist, 61

Road March, definition of, 248n41

Roberts, Carlysle (Juiceman), 189–90, 225

Robin, Juliet: and her musical experience, 253n10; as member of Roy Cape (Kaiso) All Stars, 109; and women in bands, 110

Rodney, Earl: arranger, 1; arranger in Sparrow's band, 65–66, 68, 145; arranger of calypso songs for Hugh Hendricks's band, 72; arranger of *To the Caribbean Man*, 103–4; bass player and pan arranger, 65; and Earl Rodney and Friends, 103

Roy Cape (Kaiso) All Stars (the band): and the band's name, 107; and gender, 108–10; names of lead singers in, 125; names of musicians in, 111, 152–53; *1990 First Time*, 165–66; playing on the road, 131–34; repertoire of, 114–15; reputation of, 192. *See also* bandsmen; Cape, Roy; musicians; rehearsal

Royie (Roy C. Cape, son of Roy Cape), manager of Roy Cape (Kaiso) All Stars, 186, 203–6

Ruiz, Fortunia: member of Roy Cape (Kaiso) All Stars, 111; musician, 152; Roy's relationship with, 72, 145; trumpet player and bandleader of Sparrow's band, 66, 145

Samaroo, Adeh, chutney soca artist, 223

Samaroo, Leslie: and KH Studio, 253n2; and Lord Kitchener, 59; and the Original Revue Calypso tent, 57; and RCA franchise in Trinidad and Tobago, 56

Sargeant, Scipio, guitarist, 59

"Sa Sa Yea" (Sparrow's band), Roy's understanding of aesthetic togetherness, 80

Scher, Philip W., 212

Seales, Derrick, Roy's singer, 124

Sealy, Jocelyn, 28–29, 238n7

Sharpe, Boogsie, pan player, 251n9

Singing Sandra, Calypso Monarch, 129

Sister Paul, 191

soca: arrangements in Roy's band, 110–12; definition of, 105, 257n10; and gender, 170, 256n6; groovy and power (soca) styles in, 113, 254n13; posture onstage, 153; Roy's accompaniment for competitions of, 121–22. *See also* lead singers

solo (improvisation): five reasons for the demise of, 91–97; research perspectives on, 250n8; since the 1960s, 156

sound: constitution of, 3–4, 77, 79; and fashion, 138–40, 166–68; as history of listening, 19, 86–90; as index of modernity, 139; materiality of, 80–83; as part of a circulatory history, 77; of Roy, 78–86, 97; signature, 79

Sounds Incorporated (Clive Bradley): as band, 61; names of players, 74

sousou: as mutual aid society, 25, 237n3

space: as sites of distinct practices, 217; and social relations, 221, 257n7

Sparrow's Troubadours: albums of, 68; definition of, 65; names of players, 74. *See also* Mighty Sparrow, the

Spektakula Promotions (Munroe), and Roy's band, 107–8

star, notion of, 3; in contrast to celebrity, 256n1

"Stay Giving Praises" (Black Stalin), Roy's solo in, 83–84

storytelling: as ethical project, 16–17; and ethnographic commitment, 22; experiment in, 7, 10; and performativity, 256n2; and speech registers, 185, 256n5. *See also* biography

Straker, Granville: and calypso recording in Brooklyn and owner of Straker's

INDEX   **285**

Straker, Granville (*continued*)
Calypso Record Store, 69, 71; and the Caribbean Strikers, 71
Superblue (Austin Lyons), as Road March winner, 162

Telfer, Junior, 12, 162
testimonies, use of, 21; in documentary, 184–85
Tobas, Michael, percussionist, 71, 248n46
Trini Jacobs, Roy's singer, 131, 170

Vander, Judith, 8
visual economy (Poole), 149–50, 180–82

Washington, Grover, musical approach of, 85–86

Watkins, Watty, band of, 55–56
Watson, Ed: arranger for Lord Kitchener, 248n42; arranger for the Mighty Sparrow, 66, 68; leader of dance band, 118
Watt, Eva Tulene, 8
Weston, Randy, 8
Wheeler, Selwyn: and the "Mocking Bird," 95; names of players in, 74; tour with, 46–48; trombonist, 46
Wise, Errol, drummer, 121
work: and ethics, 15; research perspectives on, 234n10. *See also* affective labor; bandleader; bandsmen; Cape, Roy; immaterial labor; musicians

Yorke, Dwight, football player, 176–77